AFFECTIVE STATES

Studies in Social Analysis
General Editor: Martin Holbraad
University College London

Focusing on analysis as a meeting ground of the empirical and the conceptual, this series provides a platform for exploring anthropological approaches to social analysis while seeking to open new avenues of communication between anthropology and the humanities, as well as other social sciences.

AFFECTIVE STATES
Entanglements, Suspensions, Suspicions

Edited by

Mateusz Laszczkowski and Madeleine Reeves

berghahn
NEW YORK · OXFORD
www.berghahnbooks.com

First published in 2018 by

Berghahn Books

www.berghahnbooks.com

© 2018 Berghahn Books

Originally published as a special issue of *Social Analysis*, volume 59, issue 4.

Library of Congress Cataloging-in-Publication Data

Names: Laszczkowski, Mateusz, editor. | Reeves, Madeleine, editor.
Title: Affective states : entanglements, suspensions, suspicions / edited by
    Mateusz Laszczkowski and Madeleine Reeves.
Description: New York : Berghahn Books, 2017. | Series: Studies in social
    analysis ; 5 | Includes bibliographical references.
Identifiers: LCCN 2017022655 (print) | LCCN 2017051498 (ebook) |
    ISBN 9781785337192 (ebook) | ISBN 9781785337178 (hardback : alk
    paper) | ISBN 9781785337185 (paperback. : alk. paper)
Subjects: LCSH: Political anthropology--Case studies. | State, The--Case studies.
    | Affect (Psychology)--Political aspects--Case studies.
Classification: LCC GN492.6 (ebook) | LCC GN492.6 .A44 2017 (print) |
    DDC 306.2--dc23
LC record available at https://lccn.loc.gov/2017022655

British Library Cataloguing in Publication Data

A catalogue record for this book is available from the British Library.

For Ania, with love and longing.

— *Mateusz*

For Aitkul and Adil, with gratitude.

— *Madeleine*

CONTENTS

ACKNOWLEDGMENTS

This book began life as a conference panel for the 2011 meetings of the American Anthropological Association in Montreal entitled "Between Thrill and Disillusion: Ethnography and the Affective Life of the State." We are grateful to our fellow conference panelists—Nayanika Mathur, Mariya Ivancheva, Hannah Knox, and Michelle Obeid—for their questions, comments, and feedback on the early drafts of our papers presented there. Many of these same participants took part in a follow-up workshop at the University of Manchester in May 2012 entitled "Affective States: Exploring Emotion in Political Life." We are grateful to the students and colleagues from Manchester and beyond who shared their research and their insightful commentary during the two days of workshop discussion. In particular, we would like to thank Sarah Green, Damian O'Doherty, Jenny Peachey, Aliaa Remtilla, Chris McLean, Gillian Evans, Jackie Stacey, Atreyee Sen, Jon Mair, and Adi Kuntsman for their penetrating comments and questions.

Yael Navaro provided the workshop keynote address, and the influence of her work on the intersections of affect and political life can be seen on many of the pages of this book. The Manchester workshop was generously sponsored by the School of Social Sciences of the University of Manchester and the ESRC Centre for Research on Socio-Cultural Change. We would like to thank both of these centers for their intellectual and financial support throughout the life of this project, and in particular Susan Hogan and Bussie Awosanya for their logistical assistance in organizing the workshop.

This book was originally published as a special issue of *Social Analysis* in 2015. We are grateful to the anonymous peer reviewers for their comments and to the then editors of the journal, Bjørn Enge Bertelsen and Knut Mikjel Rio, for their guidance and feedback. We would also like to thank Vivian Berghahn, Nora Haukali, and Kristyn Sanito for their editorial assistance. David Montgomery generously shared his photograph of the Kyrgyz bard Sagynbek Mombekov and the crowds on Ala-Too Square, Bishkek, taken the day after President Akaev was overthrown by a popular uprising in March 2005. The image beautifully captures not just a moment of affective intensity, but one of affective *indeterminacy*, when—after a day of political drama and a night of urban looting—hope and anticipation mingled with, and morphed into, boredom, cynicism, and disillusion, circulating between bodies and things. Mombekov sings to the crowd a song that narratavized the events of the preceding day—a story of political corruption and mythic justice entitled "Sold, sold sold!" But the response is not straightforward: not everyone is looking at, or listening to, the bard. It is precisely this indeterminacy of affect and its political salience that we seek to capture in this book.

Above all, we are grateful to our contributors, who have responded with patience throughout the various stages of this project. The intensity of exchange and feedback among them has made this a truly collaborative undertaking, and we thank them all for pushing us to articulate more precisely our understanding of the intersection of affect and political life.

Mateusz Laszczkowski
Madeleine Reeves

INTRODUCTION
Affect and the Anthropology of the State

Mateusz Laszczkowski and Madeleine Reeves

In his novel *The Satanic Verses*, Salman Rushdie ([1988] 2006: 454) describes a police raid on a nightclub, the epicenter of a riot in a migrant-populated London neighborhood: "A helicopter hovers over the nightclub, urinating light in long golden streams … The machine of state bearing down upon its enemies … The noise of rotor blades drowns the noise of the crowd … A man lit by a sun-gun speaks rapidly into a microphone. Behind him there is a disorderment of shadows … The reporter speaks gravely: petrolbombs plasticbullets policeinjuries watercannon looting." At a time when anthropologists are highlighting the narrativized nature of 'the state' and the role of imagination in its emergence and maintenance (Aretxaga 2000; Hansen and Stepputat 2001; Navaro-Yashin 2002; Taussig 1997), it seems appropriate to introduce a project exploring new ways to understand the state ethnographically with a fictional scene—all the more so, a scene written by an author whose own biography became one of the central narratives shaping contemporary public imaginaries of the political.

References for this section begin on page 11.

The helicopter in the quoted passage embodies many of the attributes of the state as depicted in recent anthropological writing (Aretxaga 2003; Hansen and Stepputat 2005; Harvey 2005; Linke 2006; Navaro-Yashin 2012; Scott 1998; Spencer 2007). It is abstract and remote, yet simultaneously tangible and concrete. It is empowered through technology, yet seemingly possessed of an autonomous organicity, able to affect its subjects in ways at once denigrating and elevating. It is capable of prodigal displays of violence. It is inimical, awe-inspiring, and irresistible. It overpowers the senses and turns human lives on the ground into a confusing, insubstantial tangle dependent on the state's force for sense and substance. And all the same, 'the state,' like the helicopter, remains just a construct, a man-made machine that could be chased away or even shot down, as numerous other scenes from popular fiction and newsreels remind us. Despite that, the state captivates and excites. Numbing and deafening, it also provokes speech that is 'rapid' and 'grave'. In Rushdie's episode, the reporter trying to capture the agitation of the state in action spurts out a violent frenzy of portmanteaus: "petrolbombs plasticbullets policeinjuries watercannon." Scholars' attempts to describe the state's workings have produced a similarly frantic language of hybrid neologisms: nation-state state-system state-idea governmentality power/knowledge state-effect state-fetishism (Abrams [1977] 1988; Foucault 1980, 1991; Mitchell 1999; Taussig 1992).

The chapters in this book address the affective charge that 'the state'—the signifier, the fiction, the fantasy, the social fact—evokes and that so often leaves analysis resorting to neologisms. Although commonly treated in scholarship as a 'fantasy' and an object of deconstruction, the state remains one of the most powerful institutions for enacting and organizing difference in the contemporary world (Trouillot 2001) and as such continues to elicit powerful emotions: hope, fear, desire, hatred, pride (Aretxaga 2003). With the present chapters, we highlight that affects are not just epiphenomenal to the political, "a smokescreen of rule … a ruse masking the dispassionate calculations that preoccupy states" (Stoler 2004: 6). Rather, we argue that the affective is "the substance of politics" (ibid.), a complex, dynamic, and resilient reality that structures both opportunities and challenges for political actors and is constitutive of the acting subjects themselves. We use the expression 'affective states' (borrowed from Ann Stoler) to cover a range of affects, feelings, and emotions for and about 'the state' and its agents, and explore how those contribute to the state's emergence, transformation, endurance, or erosion.

Recent political anthropology has foregrounded the multiplicity of modalities—now banal, now exceptional—through which the state materializes in daily life (Chalfin 2010; Das and Poole 2004b; Ferguson and Gupta 2002; Gupta 2012; Jeffrey 2013; Krohn-Hansen and Nustad 2005; Navaro-Yashin 2002). There has been a flourishing of scholarship attentive to the ways in which the state is reproduced in the enactments of state officials and citizens alike, from form filling and letter writing to laying roads, attending court sessions, or searching for the documents needed to certify a birth or death (Beyer 2014; Cabot 2012; Dunn 2008; Friedman 2011; Hull 2012; Knox and Harvey 2011; Mathur 2012) to acts of terror involved in policing, surveillance, crossing and controlling borders, or resolving conflicts (Aretxaga 2005; Jeganathan 2004; O'Neill 2012; Reeves 2014; Sluka 2000). Scholars have drawn attention to 'sovereign' violence (Agamben 1998) as the core of state power, sometimes hidden beyond layers of rationalized government practice (Graeber 2012) and at other times spectacularly exposed (Kapferer 1988; Mbembe 2001; Spencer 2007). Recognizing that the secret of modern state power lies precisely in the interpenetration of reason and violence (Taussig 1992), ethnographers have begun to highlight how state bureaucracy operates through the production and circulation of fear, hope, and suspicion as much as through practices of classification and inscription (Navaro-Yashin 2007; Nuijten 2004). This multi-directional approach has enabled anthropologists to embrace the empirical diversity of the 'social lives' of the state (Ssorin-Chaikov 2003).

However, in the proliferation of ethnographic studies of bureaucratic practice, ideological production, or organized violence, the emotional or affective intensities elicited by the state often risk being obscured. Affect and emotion, when brought into an analysis of the political, are often reduced to an instrumental mechanism of governmental power or are treated as epiphenomenal to the real business of rule. The current study builds on recent concerns to explore the state as the object of emotional investment—a site of fear, paranoia, or mutual suspicion (Aretxaga 2000; Thiranagama and Kelly 2010), of desire for political recognition and political participation (Hasty 2005), or perhaps just of hope for order and a 'normal' life (Greenberg 2011; Jansen 2014; Laszczkowski 2014; Reeves 2011)—by considering how emotion is implicated in a variety of everyday and exceptional encounters between citizens, state agents, and the dispersed material traces of state power. We contend that affects and emotions are much more than epiphenomena of the political: through their "embodied agency" (Linke 2006: 207), affects and emotions are crucial in structuring political fields, imaginaries, subjects, and objects. How, we ask, does the state become 'real' through the mobilization or suspension of affect? What is the role of affect in sustaining the state as (putatively) sovereign, as a source of authority, seemingly over and above its population? How are affects entangled in the coupling of reason and violence at the heart of state power? And how do emotions come to be invested in particular sites, people, material infrastructure, projects, documents, and legal enactments?

The seven chapters in this book bring ethnographic specificity to these questions by focusing on particular sites and spaces of affective engagement: Uzbek-language online political discourse (Kendzior); land rights administration in post-apartheid South Africa (Beyers); migrants' encounters with the Russian migration bureaucracy (Reeves) and Eritrean refugees' experience of the transnational powers of the regimes they flee (Bozzini); citizens' appeals to the post-war Salvadoran state at the time of elections (Montoya); the negotiation of legal and technical uncertainty surrounding the building of new infrastructures in rural Peru (Pinker and Harvey); and domestic space in rural China (Steinmüller). Linking all of the chapters is a concern to understand how these practices, whether routine or exceptional, are affectively charged: how petitioning a land claim, negotiating the route of a new railway, or just getting one's right to temporary residence acknowledged is charged with feeling, and how this exchange of feeling is itself integral to the 'state effect' (Mitchell 1999).

Specifying the 'Affect' in 'Affective States'

To try to get at this affective working of the state, the chapters in this collection engage a range of theoretical approaches to affect, feeling, and emotion. They offer a critical reading, through the lenses of ethnography, of the recent 'affective turn' in cultural theory (Clough and Halley 2007; Gregg and Seigworth 2010), along with the earlier anthropological scholarship on emotion (Lutz and Abu-Lughod 1990; Lutz and White 1986). Ours is an exploratory project rather than a prescriptive one, however; the chapters are united less by a single set of theoretical debts than by a common concern to understand the ways in which sensitivity to affect, feeling, or emotion might enliven the ethnography of the political. The project is guided by the contention that while the affective dimensions of state practice have often been noted in recent scholarship—for instance, Gupta (2012: 113) has recently argued that "affect needs to be seen as one of the constitutive conditions of state formation"—they have not yet received sufficient ethnographic attention.

Two sets of reasons can be identified for this scholarly gap. The first, we suggest, has to do with the disparate nature of the theoretical field. Affect, feeling, and emotion have been widely invoked in scholarly literature in ways that are sometimes contradictory and not necessarily easily conducive to ethnographic inquiry. Within cultural studies and allied fields, the body of literature that has recently come to be loosely designated as 'affect theory' encompasses a variety of approaches, diverse in theoretical orientation and methodological commitment. In much of the literature on the entanglements of the political and the affective (e.g., Ahmed 2004; Stoler 2004), the terms 'affect', 'emotion', and 'feeling' are often used interchangeably, without specifying what differences of meaning are implied. So far in this introduction, we too have frequently concatenated those terms in a similarly imprecise manner. However, there are subtle variations in usage that deserve elaboration. For some authors, 'affect' designates a category of subjective feeling. For others, especially in the intellectual tradition deriving from Spinoza via Gilles Deleuze and Félix Guattari (1987) and Brian Massumi (1995), 'affect' evokes a presubjective intensity that is the living current of social formation (see Mazzarella 2010; in this book, see also Pinker and Harvey). This approach places conceptual emphasis on intensity and emergence that is rather different from earlier anthropological scholarship, which focused on the cultural constructedness of emotions and the role of language in establishing fixed, culturally specific categories of feeling (Lutz and Abu-Lughod 1990; Lutz and White 1986). While emotion describes the subjective experiences of an individual, affect is an intersubjective (or, as some say, presubjective) intensity. In Nigel Thrift's (2008: 221) words: "[E]motions are everyday understandings of affects ... constructed by cultures ... with their own distinctive vocabulary."

There are also significant variations in how authors conceive of the transmission of affect. While some authors argue that material objects, documents, buildings, and public and intimate places can be considered autonomous agents and sources of affect (Brennan 2004), for others this represents an error of attribution: affects may be elicited by particular socio-legal formations, but can be transmitted only by the feeling (human) subject (see, e.g., Jansen 2009). Massumi (1995: 96) notes that affect engages the synesthetic system, so in this sense affect is bodily, sensory. It connects human subjectivity with the material environment (Navaro-Yashin 2012; Thrift 2008). Moreover, affect exceeds and 'escapes' the individual body. Emotion, in this reading, is a form of blockage or capture of affect—as well as an expression of the fact that there is always some surplus that is not captured. William Mazzarella (2010: 292) sums up much of this theorizing when he emphasizes that affect implies something corporeal, tactile, sensory, and involuntary, and (unlike emotion) "is not always already semiotically mediated."

Further disagreement emerges when we turn to the political implications of affect. Some authors have explicitly contrasted the realm of 'affect' as distinct from the realm of state practice. Deleuze and Guattari (1987) construe affect as an original, visceral intensity, animating pre-cultural forms of sociality: multiplicities such as 'schools' (as in a school of fish), 'bands', 'herds', 'populations', and 'packs'. They juxtapose these to "organizations such as the institution of the family and the State apparatus" (ibid.: 242) and accordingly they contrast "pack affects [to] family feelings and State intelligibilities" (ibid.: 246). As anthropologists, we are as suspicious of the implicit romanticization of 'non-state' or 'non-institutional' forms of sociality as we are of a vision of the state as a coherent subject of intelligibility (cf. Scott 1998). We appreciate, however, the impulse to seek the non-rational, visceral, vibrant core of the social. The chapters in the present collection explore the possibility that the state is not necessarily a disenchanted and rational apparatus of containment and regulation, but might rather be one of those "dark assemblages, which stir what is deepest within us" (Deleuze and Guattari 1987: 242). The spaces, documents, laws, and material objects through which the state is encountered in everyday life are not merely artifacts of contemporary bureaucracy. They are, like the helicopter in Rushdie's *Satanic Verses*, constitutive of the political as a field that is capable of eliciting intense feeling.

Part of the analytic purchase we find in introducing affect to political analysis is that it helps highlight the domain of feeling that comes before or beyond its narration as emotion. That domain, we contend, is a space of productive encounters between subjectivity, language, aesthetics, and the materiality of state-like practice, a space infused with the often violent intensities and ruptures of routine through which 'the state' acquires viscerally felt features. But the language that scholars associated with recent 'affect theory' use—a language of 'dark assemblages' and 'non-linear complexity'—points in turn to the second challenge of exploring 'affective states' ethnographically: the empirical difficulty of capturing the quality of a 'pre-subjective intensity' or, still more, the way that intensity might be animated or shaped by particular material-political formations (Pelkmans 2013). In the Spinozan-Deleuzean perspective, affect is considered non-discursive and non-representational. As Guattari (1996: 158) puts it with characteristic ellipsis, affect is "hazy, atmospheric, and nevertheless perfectly apprehensible." In this line of reasoning, grasping affect ethnographically is akin to "chasing tiny firefly intensities that flicker faintly in the night, registering those resonances that vibrate, subtle to seismic, under the flat wash of broad daylight, dramatizing (indeed, for the unconvinced, *over*-dramatizing) what so often passes beneath mention" (Gregg and Seigworth 2010: 4).

'Chasing tiny fireflies' might not sound like an invitation to sustained ethnographic inquiry. We confront this challenge by drawing on the capacity of detailed ethnographic description to trace capillary movements and exchanges and to register the difference often made by the seemingly insignificant, contingent, or ephemeral. Ethnography helps to highlight the complexities involved in the generation of affects and to explain the force of affective intensities in generating social dynamics. It does so without reducing the effects of those intensities to the play of 'objective' structures or 'subjective impressions'. We suggest that attempting to register affective resonances ethnographically promises to open up horizons of the political beyond objectivism, semiosis, and the world of bounded subjects. This is what we understand Kathleen Stewart (2007: 3) to be gesturing toward when she writes that affects are "more directly compelling than ideologies, as well as more fractious, multiplicitous, and unpredictable than symbolic meanings."

Recognizing the heuristic potential of affect, as well as the difficulties it poses for description and analysis, several anthropologists have sought ways to flesh out the workings of affect ethnographically by locating the (not exclusively human) bodies that affects animate, mapping the milieus they shape, and identifying the various media through which affects circulate (Kuntsman 2009; Kuntsman and Stein 2015; Navaro-Yashin 2012; Richard and Rudnyckyj 2009; Schwenkel 2013; Winegar 2012). In her study of 'affective geography' in northern Cyprus, for instance, Navaro-Yashin (2012: 159) argues that affect "is produced neither by materialities nor by the inner world alone; it is produced through their interaction … within the contingencies and historicity of those specific interactions between spatial materialities and human beings that change through time." Navaro-Yashin underscores the linguistic (or discursive) mediation of affects, arguing that while spaces and things 'discharge' affects upon people, people qualify affects through discourse and politicize them. The politicization of the affects of particular spaces—that is, the act of tying these intensities to political symbols and discourses—is an important way that the state acquires a tangible, affective, and spatial reality. The chapters collected in this book pick up the exploratory effort initiated in that literature. They examine the political resonances of diverse 'affective states' distributed across the conceptual spectrum spanning from 'affect' to 'emotion'. Some of the authors are concerned more with the political uses of emotions relatively fixed in a cultural idiom (e.g., Steinmüller), while others explore the wavering productivity of affective flows (e.g., Pinker and Harvey, Reeves). We follow Mazzarella's contention that processes of social formation, including state-like political processes, involve both the energy of affective currents and cultural efforts at fixing affect.

Mapping 'Affective States'

The various approaches to affect, we suggest, can usefully be brought into conversation with anthropological attempts to understand the force of the political beyond rationality and governmentality and, specifically, to understand the state's enduring hold in shaping subjectivities and social relations. The present volume, while inspired by the burgeoning anthropological literature on the state, seeks to advance this conversation in three distinct ways. First, as our contributors document ethnographically, the 'state effect' (Mitchell 1999) emerges and is reproduced not only through the routine operations of bureaucratic practice, infrastructural development, or the application of coercive force, but also through the affective engagements of ordinary citizens and non-citizens in relation to state agents and state-like activities: their feelings, their emotions, their embodied responses as they navigate state bureaucracy or anticipate state violence. Affect should be considered not merely as an epiphenomenon of political life—an outcome of state practice or a consequence of particular techniques of governance—but as constitutive of the political itself.

One dimension of this is to take seriously the state as a locus of affective investment, to recognize hope 'for' the state as well as 'against' it (Jansen 2014; cf. Spencer 2007: 141–142). In the current book, Montoya and Beyers both demonstrate how in specific political circumstances—here, those of post-war El Salvador and post-apartheid South Africa—there can be a short-lived, partial, but viscerally powerful sense of anticipation that the state, as a locus of redistributive power, might be able to wrong past injustices. Hope, however, is just one of the many affective registers that animate 'the state'. Kendzior's and Bozzini's chapters both demonstrate, for example, how cynicism and paranoia can replace hope with menace, turning the state into a 'boogeyman', as Kendzior puts it, and colonizing personal relationships through fear.

Second, the chapters that follow collectively demonstrate that any consideration of the role of affect in political life needs to be attentive to history and, more specifically, to the historical specificity of particular state forms and modes of governance. One important critique of 'affect theory' in its Deleuzian key is that by foregrounding questions of emergence and sudden rupture in its rejection of linear temporality and its antipathy to analyses of structure—that "place where nothing ever happens, that explanatory heaven in which all eventual permutations are prefigured in a self-consistent set of invariant generative rules" (Massumi 1995: 87)—affect theory displaces questions of history and forecloses (indeed, in some readings, explicitly rejects) the possibility of critique. In his review of the 'affective turn', for instance, Stef Jansen (2016) criticizes precisely this dehistoricizing move: "The 'affective turn' calls on us to 'perform' affect and to refrain from hermeneutic attempts to historicise it: the autonomy of affect, its theorists say, places it beyond interpretation." This is true of certain accounts of affect and certain experiments in narrative form in certain theoretical traditions, to be sure. But we contend that an attentiveness to the visceral, pre-linguistic, unsettled moments of intensity (to 'affect', as we are defining it here) does not necessarily entail a displacement of considerations of history or of power and inequality.

What emerges forcefully from the chapters in this book is the way that the salience of particular moments of subjective feeling—the sense of expectation and indignation that characterized FMLN supporters in El Salvador (Montoya), the anxiety of Eritrean refugees in Switzerland hiding from the Eritrean secret service (Bozzini), the crippling circulation of suspicion and fear between on- and off-line worlds among the Uzbek opposition-in-exile (Kendzior), or the longing and betrayal that overwhelm the forms filled out by South African land claimants (Beyers)—stems from specific histories of subjectification and particular experiences of rule, whether colonial, authoritarian, apartheid, or clientelist. Likewise, the languages used to render legible those affects and to forge relations with the state—the intimacy of 'My Old Man Mao' for farmers in rural Bashan (Steinmüller), or the addressing of a Russian border guard as 'little brother' to undermine his claim to stately authority (Reeves)—need to be understood in the context of such situated histories of rule. Attending to the 'affect' in 'affective states,' in our reading, may require attentiveness to states of feeling that are experientially fleeting and elusive. However, this does not mean that they are not historically constituted, nor does it preclude the recognition that certain kinds of feelings (fear, hope, abandonment, nostalgia) are found with particular regularity or intensity in specific social formations.

Indeed, it is precisely an attentiveness to such historical layerings and regularities that enables a properly ethnographic elucidation of affect, acknowledging the relational dynamics entailed in any attempt to interpret another person's experience. Recognizing the 'autonomy' of affect in the sense that it is taken up, for instance, in the chapter by Pinker and Harvey does not entail a depoliticization of the concept, nor does it foreclose the possibility of intersubjective understanding. As Pinker and Harvey express it: "Instead of attempting to demonstrate how the study of affective practices may be made to comply with empiricist demands … we argue that the turn to affect is helpful precisely in offering a renewed emphasis on what has always been characteristic of ethnographic work: that its 'findings' are crafted out of fields of doubt and indeterminacy."

The question of indeterminacy brings us to the final contribution that we wish to highlight concerning the relationship between ambivalence, governance, and what we might gloss as the 'distributed state'. Much critical literature on the state in a Foucauldian tradition has drawn attention to the increasing governmentalization of society, whether this is articulated in the grand schemes for human improvement critiqued by James Scott (1998) or the tendency for ever-proliferating domains of life to become objects of technical expertise, data management, and state or para-state governance. This literature has been immensely generative, theoretically and empirically, in illuminating the ever-brachiating capillaries of power, but it also tends toward the rearticulation of boundaries between 'state' and 'society', 'power' and 'resistance'. A focus on the role of affect in political life, we suggest, provides a way, ethnographically, for moving beyond this dichotomization. Attending ethnographically to the possibility that it is precisely the ambivalence or indeterminacy of affect that may be socially generative (Mazzarella 2010) gives specificity to what Michael Taussig (1992: 113) calls the "powerful insubstantiality" of the state (see also Laszczkowski 2015).

For example, in this collection, Pinker and Harvey describe a meeting between local government officials and representatives of a railway company in Peru during which subtle and complex negotiations took place regarding the precise routing of a planned railway. In the conversations, the state constantly appeared and disappeared from the conceptual horizon, fleetingly invoked and represented by different actors. In the end, it was the state's "virtual presence" as an organizing signifier but not a stable, coherent, or locatable entity that allowed for a resolution of the conundrum at hand. Kendzior explores another aspect of the state's insubstantiality that produces powerful affects. For Uzbek dissidents, the secret police are all the more maddeningly threatening for appearing simultaneously present and absent. Here, insubstantiality, technologically amplified by the Internet, means that the state's threatening security force "inhibits whatever space [the citizens] inhabit—physical, psychic, and virtual" (Kendzior, this book).

There are two aspects to this ambivalence that we want to emphasize. On the one hand, such an approach illuminates how the state may be the object of conflicting attachments—the 'mixed feelings' of Bashan farmers toward a state that is both intimate and distant (Steinmüller), or the simultaneous hope and disillusion felt toward the state that can rapidly follow electoral change (Montoya). On the other hand, attentiveness to the circulation of affect provides an insight into the intrinsic indeterminacy of the state form itself. The existential condition of "living from the nerves" that Reeves (this book) identifies among undocumented and "fictively hyper-documented" Central Asian migrants in Moscow, for instance, is generated precisely from the 'nervousness' (Taussig 1992) of the Russian state—now powerful and threatening, now a laughing-stock or not there at all—whether one might be fearing it or needing it. Officially promoted narratives of deportation shape an imagining of a righteous Russian state that has no mercy for 'illegal aliens'. Yet stories of corruption, often firsthand, add up to a different picture: a state that causes anxiety to be sure, but also a state that deserves contempt.

What emerges from such accounts is a story not of governance through control but of the proliferation of spaces of indeterminacy and their effects (cf. Dunn and Cons 2013). Bozzini analyzes how, among Eritrean refugees in Switzerland, fears of treason, surveillance, and violence give rise to a spectral image of the threatening state that reaches far beyond the geographic boundaries of Eritrea and into the capillaries of individuals' relationships with their kin, friends, and acquaintances. Where, in such a situation, does the 'state of Eritrea' begin and end? In Montoya's chapter, narratives of mass violence that occurred in the past but may reoccur any moment produce juxtaposed but oddly compatible fantasies of the Salvadoran state as a source of anxiety and as the object of hope for redress. In Beyers's account, applicants to a land restitution program in post-apartheid South Africa narrativize the trauma of dispossession and displacement they suffered at the hands of the state in the past, hoping to elicit an affective response from the renewed state in the present. But that new state, epitomized by offices, forms, and bureaucrats, often remains irresponsive, failing to acquire the holism of a feeling Leviathan. Attending to affect, in other words, provides insights into how the state interchangeably materializes and disappears—contingently yet consequentially—in everyday interactions. In this manner, it becomes possible to think of the 'spectral state' as a visceral reality that has to be navigated in daily life and not simply as a fiction that warrants deconstruction.

Conclusion

As Navaro-Yashin (2009: 15) has argued: "Ethnography works against the grain of paradigm-setting." The chapters here seek to bring ethnographic specificity to debates about the sources, transmission, and specificities of affect that have often been cast in quite abstract and generalizing terms. Their aim is less to 'set a paradigm' than to integrate an influential, if diffuse, debate about affect with growing concerns to consider the anthropology of the state in ways that go beyond deconstruction and critique. The contributors to this book explore a range of affectively charged bureaucratic, technocratic practices, including planning a railroad (Pinker and Harvey), holding an election (Montoya), documenting legal residence (Reeves), filling out claims forms (Beyers), and imposing fines (Bozzini), just as they show the affects that are at stake in remaking the sacred space of a home (Steinmüller) or criticizing state security services (Kendzior). Collectively, they demonstrate that the state needs to be understood not as a seemingly bounded entity—one that is set apart both from individuals and from 'society'. Rather, it should be understood as thriving in embodied, affective resonances within and between persons and things. Without exploring these embodied affects, it is hard to grasp, for instance, why exactly the policeman's cry, "Hey, you there!" should make citizens who have every reason to believe that they have done nothing wrong turn around, as in Althusser's ([1971] 2006: 105) famous example of the spectacular efficacy of "Ideological State Apparatuses." We contend that without affective states in view, it is difficult to comprehend how and why it is that the state "should so powerfully shape … political and moral imagination" (Spencer 2007: 99). If wars are waged and lives are—it often seems—willfully wasted to create or preserve states, and if so much of the ordinary experience of so many people the world over is organized under that signifier, we need to look for something visceral and emotional to begin to understand the 'magic of the state' (Taussig 1997). These chapters signal a sustained attempt to give that affective charge some ethnographic specificity.

Mateusz Laszczkowski is an Assistant Professor at the Institute of Ethnology and Cultural Anthropology at the University of Warsaw, where he teaches Political Anthropology, with a focus on place, space, material infrastructures, and affect. He has previously worked at the Max Planck Institute for Social Anthropology in Halle and is the author of *'City of the Future': Built Space, Modernity and Urban Change in Astana* (2016).

Madeleine Reeves is a Senior Lecturer in Social Anthropology at the University of Manchester and Editor of the journal *Central Asian Survey*. Her interests lie in the anthropology of politics and place, with a particular focus on Russia and Central Asia. She is the co-editor of *Ethnographies of the State in Central Asia: Performing Politics* (2014, with Johan Rasanayagam and Judith Beyer) and author of *Border Work: Spatial Lives of the State in Rural Central Asia* (2014). Her current research focuses on labor migration and the politics of im/mobility between Central Asia and Russia.

References

Abrams, Philip. (1977) 1988. "Notes on the Difficulty of Studying the State (1977)." *Journal of Historical Sociology* 1 (1): 58–89.

Agamben, Giorgio. 1998. *Homo Sacer: Sovereign Power and Bare Life*. Stanford, CA: Stanford University Press.

Ahmed, Sara. 2004. *The Cultural Politics of Emotion*. New York: Routledge.

Althusser, Louis. (1971) 2006. "Ideology and Ideological State Apparatuses (Notes Toward an Investigation)." In *Lenin and Philosophy and Other Essays*, trans. Ben Brewster, 85–126. New York: Monthly Review Press.

Aretxaga, Begoña. 2000. "A Fictional Reality: Paramilitary Death Squads and the Construction of State Terror in Spain." In Sluka 2000, 46–69.

Aretxaga, Begoña. 2003. "Maddening States." *Annual Review of Anthropology* 32: 393–410.

Aretxaga, Begoña. 2005. *States of Terror: Begoña Aretxaga's Essays*. Ed. Joseba Zulaika. Reno, NV: Center for Basque Studies.

Beyer, Judith. 2014. "'There is this law …': Performing the State in the Kyrgyz Courts of Elders." In Reeves et al. 2014, 99–122.

Brennan, Teresa. 2004. *The Transmission of Affect*. Ithaca, NY: Cornell University Press.

Cabot, Heath. 2012. "The Governance of Things: Documenting Legal Limbo in Greek Asylum Procedure." *Political and Legal Anthropology Review* 35 (1): 11–29.

Chalfin, Brenda. 2010. *Neoliberal Frontiers: An Ethnography of Sovereignty in West Africa*. Chicago: University of Chicago Press.

Clough, Patricia, and Jean Halley, eds. 2007. *The Affective Turn: Theorizing the Social*. Durham, NC: Duke University Press.

Das, Veena, and Deborah Poole, eds. 2004a. *Anthropology in the Margins of the State*. Santa Fe, NM: School of American Research Press.

Das, Veena, and Deborah Poole. 2004b. "State and Its Margins: Comparative Ethnographies." In Das and Poole 2004a, 3–33.

Deleuze, Gilles, and Félix Guattari. 1987. *A Thousand Plateaus: Capitalism and Schizophrenia.* Trans. and foreword by Brian Massumi. Minneapolis: University of Minnesota Press.

Dunn, Elizabeth C. 2008. "Postsocialist Spores: Disease, Bodies, and the State in the Republic of Georgia." *American Ethnologist* 35 (2): 243–258.

Dunn, Elizabeth C., and Jason Cons. 2013. "Aleatory Sovereignty and the Rule of Sensitive Spaces." *Antipode* 46 (1): 92–109.

Ferguson, James, and Akhil Gupta. 2002. "Spatializing States: Toward an Ethnography of Neoliberal Governmentality." *American Ethnologist* 29 (4): 981–1002.

Foucault, Michel. 1980. *Power/Knowledge: Selected Interviews and Other Writings, 1972–1977.* Ed. Colin Gordon; trans. Colin Gordon, Leo Marshall, John Mepham, and Kate Soper. New York: Pantheon.

Foucault, Michel. 1991. "Governmentality." In *The Foucault Effect: Studies in Governmentality*, ed. Graham Burchell, Colin Gordon, and Peter Miller, 87–104. Chicago: University of Chicago Press.

Friedman, John T. 2011. *Imagining the Post-Apartheid State: An Ethnographic Account of Namibia.* New York: Berghahn Books.

Graeber, David. 2012. "Dead Zones of the Imagination: On Violence, Bureaucracy, and Interpretive Labor." *HAU: Journal of Ethnographic Theory* 2 (2): 105–128.

Greenberg, Jessica. 2011. "On the Road to Normal: Negotiating Agency and State Sovereignty in Post-Socialist Serbia." *American Anthropologist* 113 (1): 88–100.

Gregg, Melissa, and Gregory J. Seigworth. 2010. *The Affect Theory Reader.* Durham, NC: Duke University Press.

Guattari, Félix. 1996. "Ritornellos and Existential Affects." Trans. Juliana Schiesari and Geroges Van Den Abbeele. Gupta, Akhil. 2012. *Red Tape: Bureaucracy, Structural Violence, and Poverty in India.* Durham, NC: Duke University Press.

Hansen, Thomas Blom, and Finn Stepputat, eds. 2001. *States of Imagination: Ethnographic Explorations of the Postcolonial State.* Durham, NC: Duke University Press.

Hansen, Thomas Blom, and Finn Stepputat. 2005. "Introduction." In *Sovereign Bodies: Citizens, Migrants, and States in the Postcolonial World*, ed. Thomas Blom Hansen and Finn Stepputat, 1–38. Princeton, NJ: Princeton University Press.

Harvey, Penny. 2005. "The Materiality of State-Effects: An Ethnography of a Road in the Peruvian Andes." In Krohn-Hansen and Nustad 2005, 123–141.

Hasty, Jennifer. 2005. "The Pleasures of Corruption: Desire and Discipline in Ghanaian Political Culture." *Cultural Anthropology* 20 (2): 271–301.

Hull, Matthew. 2012. *Government of Paper: The Materiality of Bureaucracy in Urban Pakistan.* Berkeley: University of California Press.

Jansen, Stef. 2009. "After the Red Passport: Towards and Anthropology of the Everyday Geopolitics of Entrapment in Europe's 'Immediate Outside.'" *Journal of the Royal Anthropological Institute* 15 (4): 815–832.

Jansen, Stef. 2014. "Hope For/Against the State: Gridding in a Besieged Sarajevo Suburb." *Ethnos* 79 (2): 238–260.

Jansen, Stef. 2016. "Ethnography and the Choices Posed by the 'AffectiveTurn.'" In *Sensitive Objects: Affect and Material Culture*, ed. Jonas Frykman and Maja Povrzanović Frykman, 55–78. Lund: Nordic Academic Press.

Jeffrey, Alex. 2013. *The Improvised State: Sovereignty, Performance and Agency in Dayton Bosnia.* West Sussex: Wiley-Blackwell.

Jeganathan, Pradeep. 2004. "Checkpoint: Anthropology, Identity, and the State." In Das and Poole 2004a, 67–80.

Kapferer, Bruce. 1988. *Legends of People, Myths of State: Violence, Intolerance, and Political Culture in Sri Lanka and Australia.* Washington, DC: Smithsonian Institution Press.

Knox, Hannah, and Penny Harvey. 2011. "Anticipating Harm: Regulation and Irregularity in a Road Construction Project in the Peruvian Andes." *Theory, Culture & Society* 28 (6): 142–163.

Krohn-Hansen, Christian, and Knut G. Nustad, eds. 2005. *State Formation: Anthropological Perspectives*. London: Pluto Press.

Kuntsman, Adi. 2009. *Figurations of Violence and Belonging: Queerness, Migranthood and Nationalism in Cyberspace and Beyond*. Bern: Peter Lang.

Kuntsman, Adi, and Rebecca L. Stein. 2015. *Digital Militarism: Israel's Occupation in the Social Media Age*. Stanford, CA: Stanford University Press.

Laszczkowski, Mateusz. 2014. "State Building(s): Built Forms, Materiality and the State in Astana." In Reeves et al. 2014, 149–172.

Laszczkowski, Mateusz. 2015. "'Demo-Version of a City': Buildings, Affects, and the State in Astana." *Journal of the Royal Anthropological Institute* 22 (1): 148–165.

Linke, Uli. 2006. "Contact Zones: Rethinking the Sensual Life of the State." *Anthropological Theory* 6 (2): 205–225.

Lutz, Catherine, and Lila Abu-Lughod, eds. 1990. *Language and the Politics of Emotion*. Cambridge: Cambridge University Press.

Lutz, Catherine, and Geoffrey M. White. 1986. "The Anthropology of Emotions." *Annual Review of Anthropology* 15: 405–436.

Massumi, Brian. 1995. "The Autonomy of Affect." *Cultural Critique* 31: 83–109.

Mathur, Nayanika. 2012. "Transparent-Making Documents and the Crisis of Implementation: A Rural Employment Law and Development Bureaucracy in India." *Political and Legal Anthropology Review* 35 (2): 167–182.

Mazzarella, William. 2010. "Affect: What Is It Good For?" In *Enchantments of Modernity: Empire, Nation, Globalization*, ed. Saurabh Dube, 291–309. London: Routledge.

Mbembe, Achille. 2001. *On the Postcolony*. Berkeley: University of California Press.

Mitchell, Timothy. 1999. "Society, Economy, and the State Effect." In *State/Culture: State-Formation after the Cultural Turn*, ed. George Steinmetz, 76–97. Ithaca, NY: Cornell University Press.

Navaro-Yashin, Yael. 2002. *Faces of the State: Secularism and Public Life in Turkey*. Princeton, NJ: Princeton University Press.

Navaro-Yashin, Yael. 2007. "Make-Believe Papers, Legal Forms and the Counterfeit: Affective Interactions between Documents and People in Britain and Cyprus." *Anthropological Theory* 7 (1): 79–98.

Navaro-Yashin, Yael. 2009. "Affective Spaces, Melancholic Objects: Ruination and the Production of Anthropological Knowledge." *Journal of the Royal Anthropological Institute* 15 (1): 1–18.

Navaro-Yashin, Yael. 2012. *The Make-Believe Space: Affective Geography in a Postwar Polity*. Durham, NC: Duke University Press.

Nuijten, Monique. 2004. "Between Fear and Fantasy: Governmentality and the Working of Power in Mexico." *Critique of Anthropology* 24 (2): 209–230.

O'Neill, Bruce. 2012. "Of Camps, Gulags and Extraordinary Renditions: Infrastructural Violence in Romania." *Ethnography* 13 (4): 466–486.

Pelkmans, Mathijs. 2013. "The Affect Effect." *Anthropology of This Century*, issue 7, May. http://aotcpress.com/articles/affect-effect/.

Reeves, Madeleine. 2011. "Fixing the Border: On the Affective Life of the State in Southern Kyrgyzstan." *Environment and Planning D: Society and Space* 29 (5): 905–923.

Reeves, Madeleine. 2014. *Border Work: Spatial Lives of the State in Rural Central Asia*. Ithaca, NY: Cornell University Press.

Reeves, Madeleine, Johan Rasanayagam, and Judith Beyer, eds. 2014. *Ethnographies of the State in Central Asia: Performing Politics*. Bloomington: Indiana University Press.

Richard, Analiese, and Daromir Rudnyckyj. 2009. "Economies of Affect." *Journal of the Royal Anthropological Institute* (n.s.) 15: 57–77.

Rushdie, Salman. (1988) 2006. *The Satanic Verses*. London: Random House.

Schwenkel, Christina. 2013. "Post/Socialist Affect: Ruination and Reconstruction of the Nation in Urban Vietnam." *Cultural Anthropology* 28 (2): 252–277.

Scott, James. 1998. *Seeing Like a State: How Certain Schemes to Improve the Human Condition Have Failed*. New Haven, CT: Yale University Press.

Sluka, Jeffrey, ed. 2000. *Death Squad: The Anthropology of State Terror*. Philadelphia: University of Pennsylvania Press.

Spencer, Jonathan. 2007. *Anthropology, Politics, and the State: Democracy and Violence in South Asia*. Cambridge: Cambridge University Press.

Ssorin-Chaikov, Nikolai. 2003. *The Social Life of the State in Subarctic Siberia*. Stanford, CA: Stanford University Press.

Stewart, Kathleen. 2007. *Ordinary Affects*. Durham, NC: Duke University Press.

Stoler, Ann L. 2004. "Affective States." In *A Companion to the Anthropology of Politics*, ed. David Nugent and Joan Vincent, 4–29. Oxford: Blackwell.

Taussig, Michael. 1992. *The Nervous System*. New York: Routledge

Taussig, Michael. 1997. *The Magic of the State*. New York: Routledge.

Thiranagama, Sharika, and Tobias Kelly. 2010. "Introduction: Specters of Treason." In *Traitors: Suspicion, Intimacy, and the Ethics of State-Building*, ed. Sharika Thiranagama and Tobias Kelly, 1–23. Philadelphia: University of Pennsylvania Press.

Thrift, Nigel. 2008. *Non-Representational Theory: Space, Politics, Affect*. London: Routledge.

Trouillot, Michel-Rolph. 2001. "The Anthropology of the State in the Age of Globalization: Close Encounters of the Deceptive Kind." *Current Anthropology* 42 (1): 125–138.

Winegar, Jessica. 2012. "The Privilege of Revolution: Gender, Class, Space, and Affect in Egypt." *American Ethnologist* 39 (1): 67–70.

Chapter 1

NEGOTIATING UNCERTAINTY
Neo-liberal Statecraft in Contemporary Peru

Annabel Pinker and Penny Harvey

The turn to 'affect' in anthropology embraces a range of possible avenues for empirical research, particularly with respect to the interest in exploring how to address ethnographic insights into embodied or sensory engagement, emotion, and feeling in ways that do not reinstate mind-body dichotomies or return us to individualized, internal, or psychological states of being. The question of how affect should be differentiated from the categories of feeling and emotion supports attempts to focus on the intersubjective (Richard and Rudnyckyj 2009) or that which exceeds established meanings (Massumi 2002), as opposed to recognizable, conventional, narratable subjective experience. The affect concept thus appears to respond to the current analytical commitment to foregrounding the uncertain effects of relational practice and to balancing intentionality, reason, and belief with non-discursive or non-representational understandings of embodied practice. But the term is used in many different ways, its roots being

References for this chapter begin on page 30.

diversely grounded in experimental psychology, psychoanalysis, philosophy, and critical theory (Berlant 2011; Connolly 2002; Massumi 2002; Thrift 2008). With regard to political practice and state power, the dominant trend has perhaps been to extend Foucault's interest in subject formation to how 'states' come to appear as autonomous agents and to the development of feelings, such as fear, hope, and desire, for or about 'the state'.

Our interest in the analytical possibilities of affect goes in a somewhat different direction. We started with the political, that is, with relations of contestation and negotiation and with an ethnographic interest in the multiplicity, ambiguity, and distributed locus of the state in contemporary Peru. Here, as in other places, 'the state' is frequently invoked as a coherent and singular locus of power that variously bears down on or ignores local people, thus provoking emotional responses that range from disgust, despair, or desire to disinterest. However, both 'the state' and 'affect' are problematic starting points with respect to located fields of practice that are amenable to ethnographic study. We chose instead to explore regulatory practice as a site of creativity and experimentation. We were not looking at how people avoid regulation; rather, we were more interested in how regulatory ambiguity, inherent in a multiple and distributed state, becomes a site of opportunity. More specifically, we looked at how legal and technical norms emerged in relation to a newly created instance of the state, the regional government.

Throughout the twentieth century, projects of state formation in Peru have been enacted in response to the challenge of how to build a modern, national economy from the entrenched social, cultural, and geographical differences that mark the contours of this polity. Children are still taught at school to think in terms of three clearly demarcated ecological regions: the modern urban coastal deserts, the largely rural indigenous/peasant Andean highlands, and the more isolated and sparsely populated Amazonian lowlands. Children are also taught that Peru is a rich nation despite the poverty in which so many of its citizens live. Indeed, the poorest regions are rich in minerals and in oil. The Cusco region in which we have been working is also rich in tourism. It is among the world's most favored destinations, the national industry centering on the UNESCO World Heritage Site of Machu Picchu, a fifteenth-century Inka settlement high in the Andes Mountains that escaped detection by invading Spanish forces.

Over the past two decades—subsequent to a prolonged civil war in which tens of thousands of people died, state institutions were weakened, and political parties all but disappeared—successive Peruvian governments have embraced neo-liberal economic policies, most notably ensuring favorable conditions for foreign capital investment and macro-economic growth. These policies are supported by lending institutions, such as the World Bank, which have also promoted a radical program of political decentralization. Our study of regional government is firmly located in this somewhat contradictory state space where the needs of macro-economic growth at the national level sit alongside a new commitment to regional autonomy. The regional governments, newly formed in 2004, intrigued us, as they are overtly experimental—new instances of the state where the possibilities of what state power might be, and what it might become in and through these spaces, are self-evidently in question. Much of this questioning arises from the fact that decentralization is highly partial: the regional state has only limited fiscal autonomy and no legislative or juridical power. And yet the regions have a moral power associated with their specific territoriality and the wealth generated from local resources, which is of particular significance in relation to mining, water, and tourism.

Our decision to focus on the regulatory force of legal and technical norms reflects the fact that one of the things that regional governments can do is administer public works. They can manage the funds assigned to them to develop their regions in ways that best meet the needs of local people. It is through the management of projects and the facilitation of local ownership of such projects that the regional government acquires material, cultural, and political legitimacy. In managing public works, the regional state works through the deployment of technical expertise. However, the conditions for managing such projects are set externally—not simply by the national government, but also by international regulations and normative procedures that are part and parcel of the financial and legal arrangements to which the central state is committed as part of its strategy to attract foreign investment. In short, we have been particularly interested in tracking how political creativity and skill rests in large part on the capacity to engage the possibilities inherent in the regulatory apparatus of the state.

Our project contributes to a growing body of scholarly work that has sought to unsettle conceptualizations of the state as a singular, rational, and stable entity. Anthropologists have drawn attention to the difficulty of distinguishing 'the state' among "an excess of statehood practices" (Aretxaga 2005: 258), suggesting with Foucault that the complex and overlapping forms of government that have emerged with neo-liberal configurations of power have rendered the duality of state and non-state inadequate as an analytical tool (Rose 1999; Rose and Miller 1992). We have taken up the possibilities that ethnographic methods afford to approach the state as a configuration of dispersed and flexible practices, while continuing to recognize the power of state imaginaries. In this way, we have attended to the uses of documents (Kelly 2006; Poole 2004; Riles 2006; Tarlo 2001), infrastructures (Collier 2011; Harvey 2005; Lampland and Star 2009), and the troubling margins between signifier and signified, legibility and illegibility, the real and the magical in those spaces where state power gathers force (Das 2004; Poole 2004; Taussig 1992, 1997; Tsing 2004). These approaches to the state emphasize ambivalence and uncertainty, arguing that state power is reproduced through practices that are less than coherent or fully rationalized, emerging rather as shifting, illegible, decentered, contingent, or capricious. It is here that we return to affect and recent interest in a political anthropology that sets out to explore the force of uncertainty and ambiguity in the constitution of political life (see, e.g., Berlant 2011; Navaro-Yashin 2007, 2012; Nuijten 2003; Richard and Rudnyckyj 2009).

In this regard, we have found William Mazzarella's approach to affect particularly useful. Mazzarella's (2010: 299) suggestion that "any social project that is not imposed through force alone must be affective in order to be effective" speaks very directly to our research concerns. His study of the affective explores the relationship between 'intensity' and 'qualification'. By 'intensity' he is referring to corporeal or visceral sensation that is indeterminate, as yet unformed—a force that moves without intention or explicit articulation. 'Qualification', by contrast, is the field of representation, the particular force of meaning, of determinacy, of articulation. Yet rather than identifying affect with one side of this binary, in terms of 'intensity' as opposed to 'qualification', he argues that it is in the tension between them—between virtuality and actualization in more Deleuzian terms—that power is manifest as the capacity to move, "to harness our attention, our engagement, and our desire" (ibid.: 299). In the ethnographic case that we present here, we aim to show how this relation plays out in practice. More specifically, we seek to show how this charged movement between intensity and qualification allows us to approach the regulatory and the technical as sites in and through which the modern state is at once consolidated and undone.

The ethnographic task of tracking the implicit is complex. Fieldwork takes a long time because it takes a while to know about the many things that are left unsaid, either because they are too obvious or because they are as yet unformulated. One of the most common criticisms of studying affect ethnographically refers to the difficulty, if not impossibility, of empirically tracking and interpreting the movement of affects through the gestures, facial expressions, mood shifts, glances, and host of other micro-exchanges that animate them. A gesture or a tone of voice might imply a particular disposition or mood—or perhaps not. Yet such variability is only an accentuation of the uncertainties that permeate most ethnographic work. Our concern here is not to defend the empirical validity of studying affect, for this could imply that empiricism should be seen as anthropology's highest aim. Rather, we argue that a focus on affect troubles anthropological claims to empiricism by calling attention anew to the intrinsically relational, and by extension uncertain, quality of the ethnographic method. This defining attribute of ethnography continually vexes any attempt to finally disentangle what we think we know about others from the worlds we inhabit ourselves (see also the introduction to this book). In focusing squarely on the gestures, involuntary flinches, moods, and other fleshy micro-phenomena that have always figured more or less explicitly in ethnographic work but have tended to go unnamed, affect returns us to this question of how we purport to 'know' what others know, and what counts as anthropological knowledge. Instead of attempting to demonstrate how the study of affective practices may be made to comply with empiricist demands, then, we argue that the turn to affect is helpful precisely in offering a renewed emphasis on what has always been characteristic of ethnographic work: that its 'findings' are crafted out of fields of doubt and indeterminacy.

In what follows, we have tried to address these issues by setting out what we learned about the framing of one particular public works project. We then move to discuss how this framing was no guarantor of meaning; on the contrary, it provided the grounds for experimentation, anxiety, and possibility. We elaborate two examples that problematize any stable dichotomization between emotion and affect, qualification and intensity. Rather, we show how the state appears in a space that teeters between determinacy and indeterminacy, between the stable certainties promised by regulatory frameworks and the doubts generated through their ambiguities and overlaps. Engaging Andrew Barry's (2002: 270) point that an action is political to the extent that it opens up the possibility of disagreement, we use these examples to show that the state does not emerge via the resolution or arbitration of uncertainty. Instead, it is a highly political space, a field of negotiation in which outcomes are hard to discern, where care, tact, and skill—and attention to emerging possibilities—are what it takes to effectively invoke and/or embody the state. In this sense, we suggest that while state power has stabilizing effects, these effects are arrived at as a consequence of the affective force of ambiguity and uncertainty.

A Contested Technical Study: Plans for the Ollantaytambo Bypass

In 2005, Peru's Ministry of Foreign Trade and Tourism, MINCETUR, took out a loan of $4.8 million from the World Bank to finance the Vilcanota Valley Rehabilitation and Management Project, which was geared broadly toward improving environmental, touristic, and economic conditions in what is known as the Sacred Valley, that is, the area between Machu Picchu and the city of Cusco. In 2009, after MINCETUR had failed to make any headway with the venture, the Bank restructured the loan, diverting some 60 percent of the project components to the regional government of Cusco. This was the first time that the World Bank had granted authority for its funds to be administered by a regional government in Peru. The relationship was consolidated in May 2011 with the signing of an agreement to finance a second stage of the Vilcanota Project, this time via a direct loan of around 100 million US dollars to the regional government.

As initially conceived, the project's planned activities consisted of implementing visitor centers in the Sacred Valley, designing studies for the rehabilitation of archaeological sites, setting up a regional solid waste management system, undertaking the resettlement of households vulnerable to flooding below Machu Picchu, carrying out engineering and environmental assessments and investments in urban infrastructure, training local tourism service providers, formulating urban and rural land use plans, and offering capacity building for municipalities. In 2009, when the project was restructured and the regional government gained control of more than half of its components, a number of revisions were made. These included the insertion of a proposal to fund a technical study for the construction of a road bypass around the village of Ollantaytambo, the site of one of the most significant archaeological complexes in the region and currently also the primary embarkation point for the train that takes tourists to Machu Picchu itself.

The commitment of funds for the technical study reflected long-held anxieties about the increasing traffic through the village. Ollantaytambo is not only a key tourist destination, but also a bottleneck for interprovincial trade between lowland provinces and the departmental capital of Cusco. Heavy freight lorries currently pass through the heart of Ollantaytambo, and there are concerns that the vibrations are damaging the foundations of the Inkan-built platform that supports the archaeological complex, quite apart from the mundane dangers that heavy traffic poses to local people and to tourists. The aim of the proposed bypass was thus to resolve the problem by diverting traffic around the platform. The Tourism Ministry, based in Lima, was charged with contracting an engineering consulting firm to draw up the technical study, and in July 2009 a Peruvian-Spanish consortium, CPS-INECO, was selected for the task.

The study elicited and condensed a whole range of regulatory ambiguities, which will be examined in more detail below. However, it is also important to emphasize from the start that it was not in any way a lack of regulation that generated the problems we discuss. On the contrary, it was instead the complexity—surfeit, even—of institutional and regulatory presence that laid the grounds for the experimental engagements that this project exemplified. World Bank projects are highly structured, and this case was no exception. A great deal of effort was invested in elaborating the normative frameworks and the lines of responsibility. A lengthy document detailing the terms of reference for the study was drawn up with the participation of a wide range of stakeholders, including the municipality of Ollantaytambo. The document specified that the contractor of the technical study, and thereby its key executor, was MINCETUR, the Tourism Ministry. The Transport Ministry had institutional responsibility for declaring the project viable in technical terms. However, other aspects also had to be considered. The Culture Ministry would have to approve the archaeological study evaluating the likely impact of the planned road on the archaeological complex. Furthermore, both the local state (the municipality of Ollantaytambo) and the regional state (the regional government of Cusco) would have to consent to the proposals made by the technical study, indicating in this way the social viability of the project. In addition, the terms of reference specified that several layers of supervision would be put in place in order to ensure the project's compliance with the environmental and social safeguards required by both the World Bank and Peruvian state law. Meanwhile, a team responsible for overseeing the project in terms of World Bank safeguards was to be based in Cusco's regional government. Other actors with an interest in the technical study were to be integrated through the formation of a committee set up to monitor the project as it progressed. Apart from the key institutions already mentioned, among the actors with seats on this committee was FETRANSA, the company that manages the state-concessioned railway on which train operators run their services between Cusco and Machu Picchu.

These normative arrangements demonstrate that there was a sense in which the organization of the bypass project was—and should be—clear-cut. According to the framework at least, everybody knew, in theory, which body was to be responsible for different tasks and who was in control. The problem was that things did not turn out that way. When it came down to it, the regulatory structures did not deliver on their promise of coherence and order. This was partly due to the destabilizing effects of Peru's emergent decentralization. By virtue of the shifting configurations of power effected by this process, previously nationally owned services are being outsourced to private companies whose relation to the state remains contested and uncertain, and the jurisdiction of local and regional government bodies is thrown into question as they lay claim to greater autonomy. Further complicating matters was the lack of agreement over which problem the study should be aiming to resolve. This was a complex issue, for the problem could be posed in a number of different ways. For example, it could be seen as an issue whereby the need to preserve easy passage for interprovincial trade had to be prioritized. Alternatively, it could be framed in terms of the need to protect the local tourism economy and to preserve fragile archaeological ruins. More radically, the very fact that people were living within and gradually building into the old Inkan citadel in central Ollantaytambo was cited by some as a problem that could be resolved by moving the tourist trade associated with the embarkation to Machu Picchu out of the village.

When CPS-INECO ran a public consultation on their proposal for the bypass in November 2010, Ollantinos roundly rejected it, despite the broad consensus that a bypass should be built. What most Ollantinos objected to was not the bypass itself, but rather where and how CPS-INECO was proposing to build it. One provocation was CPS-INECO's plan to make way for the new road by pulling down several of the terraces that undergirded the Inkan platform supporting Ollantaytambo. But what stung most was that the plan proposed to cut the bypass straight through the current railway station, located some five minutes from the central square, and to build a new station at a site 3.4 kilometers outside the village. Hundreds of tourists traveled daily from Ollantaytambo's station to Machu Picchu, and the municipality argued that the implementation of CPS-INECO's recommendations would threaten the village with the loss of income from tourism and the creation of a competing 'satellite city' of hotels and restaurants owned by big investors in the area surrounding the proposed new station. Ollantinos would thus be excluded from the tourist industry on which they depended.

A new Ollantaytambo mayor took office in January 2011, and the issue of where and how to build the bypass became one of the major preoccupations of his administration. His campaign had been fought with explicit accusations against his predecessor of attempts to gain personal benefit from the relocation of the train station. Even before he had formally taken up the reins of the municipality, the new mayor had made it his priority to formulate an alternative to CPS-INECO's proposal. He wanted to alter the route of the bypass, arguing that the threat to the Inkan terraces and to the station posed by CPS-INECO plans could be avoided if the bypass were constructed along the slither of land between the existing railway and the river.

Meetings between CPS-INECO, the Tourism Ministry, and the municipality to resolve the conflict began in earnest soon after the mayor's inauguration. They were tense encounters in which it became increasingly clear that the layers of regulation designed to clarify how projects like the bypass should unfold could, within the context of a decentralizing state, instead generate uncertainty and indeterminacy. This problem was thrown into relief during a January 2011 meeting over the contested CPS-INECO study, which took place in the Tourism

Ministry in Lima. In the description that follows, we address one particular debate that occurred over the course of the meeting that demonstrates how norms and regulations open up spaces of ambiguity and doubt.

The idea behind this meeting was to evaluate reasonably what had emerged as two competing technical proposals—one presented by CPS-INECO, the other by the municipality of Ollantaytambo. CPS-INECO questioned the validity of the municipality's proposal by focusing on the risk of flooding in the area. Its representatives brought out photographs of the unexpectedly high river levels that had provoked the extensive flooding that had devastated the valley in 2010. They suggested that if this were to happen again, the bypass route proposed by the municipality would not withstand the floodwaters. One of the municipal engineers countered that this flooding had been historically exceptional, an event that might happen only once every 500 years. "Every 25 years," the CPS-INECO engineer retorted. The municipal engineer argued that there were no recorded measures that would allow them to make that projection. He said that the normal flow of the river was 400 to 500 cubic meters a second in high water season. The most extreme measurement over the course of the previous 25–50 years had been 600 cubic meters a second. In 2010, it had reached an unprecedented 1,200 cubic meters per second 30 kilometers below Ollantaytambo but not in the area in question. He also pointed out that the retaining walls constructed by the Inkas along the river shores had remained intact despite the high water volume, suggesting that this was not a vulnerable point. He looked again at the photographs presented by CPS-INECO and declared that they were misleading.

In response, the CPS-INECO engineer handed him a photograph of a different site where the retaining wall that had been protecting the train line had been carried away by the river the previous year. He stated that the figures were not definitive in this era of climate change, observing that the actual measurements were deviating from statistically generated models. But the municipal engineer argued that if they were going to deal with engineering issues, "Let's go with the numbers ... Let's always go with the statistical data." He said that when CPS-INECO engineers brought out images of flooding, they were being manipulative. "It's like showing that a building falls when an earthquake occurs," he said furiously. Another municipal engineer intervened to say that the parameters of such exceptional events should not overly restrict them, "because if in Chile they begin to construct buildings so as to resist earthquakes of 8.5 on the Richter scale, they will be super-structures. We have to work within the parameters that engineering has given us."

At this point, another engineer from CPS-INECO spoke for the first time, saying that the norms of the Peruvian state had to be verified, because he understood that new bridges, for example, had to be designed to last 500 years. Before that, he said, they had to last only 30–50 years. The two municipal engineers murmured under their breath that in fact the Peruvian norm prescribed that constructions last only 100 years. But the CPS-INECO engineer was insistent—it had to be 500 years. "I also complain," he said, "but it is a parameter that has to be taken into account because it is the Ministry of Transport that has to approve the study. It's not me or the mayor or MINCETUR that will approve it. This [regulation] has to be taken as the point of departure."

His intervention was disconcerting. The figure of 500 years seemed excessive and spurious and yet somehow authoritative. As the municipal engineers implied throughout the encounter, engineering only ever sets out to provide technical responses according to limiting parameters. Structures are built in relation to budgetary constraints and are as much a function of political will and social viability as they are of any external framings. The invocation of a time horizon of 500 years seemed far removed from the pragmatics of recognizable construction norms. Indeed, as one of the municipal engineers pointed out, if they were to work to standards such as these, they would only ever construct perfect structures, adequate not to prevailing conditions but ready to confront any eventuality. Nevertheless, despite their evident disagreement with the CPS-INECO representative's statement, the municipal engineers did not debate the issue further. Perhaps they decided that there were more important battles to fight, or maybe they were not sufficiently sure of their ground to contest his claim. Whatever the reason, the effect of the invocation of the 500-year norm was to stall the debate, the unresolved number hanging uncertainly over the proceedings that followed.

There was a suggestion that the issue might be resolved by tracking down the norm. Yet the norm was curiously absent and out of reach, and nobody followed through on this option. It also seems likely that finding the norm would simply reimpose the terms of the dispute: What would it mean to frame a structure in terms of 100 years or 500 years? What kind of change—climatic, geographical, and social—might be expected in that time? Which kinds of data should count and when? Should the fact that the railway line was compromised upriver from Ollantaytambo during the flooding of 2010 impact on the design of infrastructure for unaffected areas farther downriver? Does a photograph provide better evidence than a number? And how should the validity of past numbers compete with the possibility of radically new ones? How should engineering find a balance between uncertain futures and measurements that already exist? Who should make the decisions over these issues? Despite the meeting's premise that addressing the technical dimensions of the competing proposals would help to resolve the conflict, the invocation of the technical simply raised additional questions. It was the issue of what did and did not count as adequately technical that became the focus of discussion. A point that had seemed to turn on the achievement of technical objectivity and calculability came to turn on winning a debate over different ways of valuing regulation and risk.

These negotiations in the offices of the Tourism Ministry in Lima exemplify the open-endedness of normative and technical regulation. The example also allows us to present the basic parameters of our ethnographic field: the terms in and through which the bypass is contested, and the ways in which a distributed or partially decentralized state creates the conditions for its own unsettling. However, we are also aware that the example we have given is primarily one of discursive qualification. We have tried to evoke the uncertainties that surround the regulative apparatus, but now, having established something of what is at stake, we want to present a second ethnographic scenario in which we think the affective force of state power is more strongly in play—more implicit, less articulate, and potentially more unsettling.

The Five-Meter Rule: A Further Chapter of Unsettling Regulation

Over the course of 2011, the municipality of Ollantaytambo frequently arranged to receive visitors from key institutions with a say in the routing of the bypass in a bid to win political support for their alternative to CPS-INECO's proposal. On such occasions, visitors and municipal staff would walk the length of the site proposed for the planned bypass, alongside the railway tracks, discussing *in situ* the technical and political issues around the project. In mid-2011, the mayor and his municipal staff toured the site with a group of engineers from FETRANSA, the company that manages the railway tracks concessioned to it by the central Peruvian state. It was particularly important for the municipality to win FETRANSA's support because its chosen routing for the bypass would involve moving the railway tracks by a few meters in order to create space for the new road. Municipal staff knew that only FETRANSA had the power to endorse this move. Prior to the meeting, therefore, tensions were running rather high as the mayor, councilors, engineers, publicity staff, and administrators stood alongside the railway line, awaiting FETRANSA's arrival.

Before long, the general manager of the company appeared, accompanied by another man and a woman. As they exchanged greetings and the manager began to outline FETRANSA's position, the municipality's public relations officer whipped out his voice recorder, as was customary on these occasions, to record the conversation. However, not much had been said when the woman from FETRANSA interrupted, sharply telling the publicity officer that it was not the right moment to record: "This is just a conversation. Later, when things are more formal, it would be more appropriate to record, but not now." The rebuffed public relations officer complied, a little deferentially, and the conversation continued without further comment. But the rebuke cut through the studied politeness of the meeting, exposing unspoken tensions.

The manager of FETRANSA fluidly took up his narrative again, as though there had been no interruption. He noted that he was sympathetic to the municipality's desire to build the bypass immediately alongside the railway tracks, but there was a sticking point: a regulation required that there be a space of five meters between the track and the road. The upholding of this five-meter space was stipulated in the terms of the concession awarded to FETRANSA by the Transport Ministry. He was insistent that these were the norms imposed by the Ministry and that they were not negotiable. The faces of the mayor and his councilors were studiously impassive, but there was a palpable tension in the silence that followed his words. In order to build the road as they wished, immediately beside the railway, the municipality would need to encroach at least three meters into this five-meter space. The existence of any such regulation had not been anticipated within the municipality, and it effectively overthrew the possibility of constructing the bypass according to the mayor's plan.

One of the municipal engineers chipped in to say that there were villagers who held land in areas encompassed by this five-meter strip. He noted lugubriously that it had been difficult to persuade them to cede even the two or three meters that the municipality had asked for to build the bypass, so he was sure that they were going to reject any proposal to further extend the measure. Not only this, he added, but in some narrow sections of the gorge along which the railway runs, there were not even five meters to be had. The implications of this number seemed uncertain given its apparent legal incontrovertibility, on the one hand, and the material realities that contested its viability, on the other.

After we had walked for a few minutes in silence, the mayor, who was tramping companionably alongside the manager of FETRANSA with his hands behind his back, began to speak slowly. He observed mildly that the five-meter issue had rather poured cold water on their hopes for the road and that people in Ollantaytambo were not going to accept it. His dispassionate reiteration of the municipal engineer's words seemed to produce a shift, for the manager now said that he was open to the possibility of a bimodal bypass (one where the road would occupy the same space as the rail line) or only a two-meter gap between the bypass and the railway track in the very narrow stretches. But where land was available, even if it was titled, FETRANSA would need the space, he said. This was a subtle movement away from the company's original interpretation of the Transport Ministry's norm. FETRANSA was thinking in terms of the pragmatics of construction and in a small way distancing itself from its prior alignment with the regulative functions of the central state. The manager then went further and asserted that ultimately FETRANSA was there to make a profit. The company was interested in expanding, he said, by installing more rails alongside the existing tracks in order to attract more train companies to operate services on the railway. As FETRANSA's manager, it was his duty to facilitate this, he said. The space that the state could expropriate by law in relation to the execution of public works would offer his company potential for this kind of expansion.

This comment was surprising. Beyond the matter of the Transport Ministry's normative regulations, the manager of FETRANSA apparently considered the five-meter margin to pose an entirely different possibility. The company was not merely suggesting a pragmatic adjustment to an abstract state regulation, but was using the regulation (which it was required to uphold) to further its own commercial advantage. This acknowledgement seemed to loosen the relation between FETRANSA and state power, thus opening the possibility of a more flexible approach to the regulation. While FETRANSA was subcontracted by the state, it no longer appeared as a proxy for the state or to be acting on its behalf, as was implied earlier in the encounter.

When we reached the train station, the manager of FETRANSA slipped a further limiting factor into the conversation. Gesturing toward an area where two or three sets of tracks were laid to enable trains to pass one another, he said that the construction process itself would put pressure on this crossing zone. He seemed to be suggesting that the location of the station could not be assured whatever decision was reached on the routing of the bypass. The train companies may simply decide to move the station anyway so as not to have to deal with further interruptions from disruptive roadworks. Furthermore, at some point, in order to provide room for expansion, the station would inevitably have to be moved anyway, he said, but this process would likely be accelerated through the construction of the road. This dealt a further blow to municipal plans to keep the station in Ollantaytambo and retain control over the commercial opportunities it posed.

We walked the remaining length of the train line until we arrived at the other end of the proposed route, where we stood awkwardly in a circle. A sense of irresolution hung over the situation. It was unclear whether we were still involved in thinking through the problem, or if we were simply waiting for FETRANSA's car to reappear. Exceedingly politely, the mayor asked the manager of FETRANSA if he wanted to take the municipal car, which was parked nearby, back to the center of Ollantaytambo. His politeness seemed an attempt to maintain openness in the situation, for it was clear that FETRANSA's manager had already communicated with the company's driver. The manager said that no, he would wait for FETRANSA's car to come.

There was a tense, if cordial, pause. The manager's comments had been hypothetical and somewhat confusing. It had become difficult to read FETRANSA's position. Who did the company represent? How definitive were its prescriptions? We stood silently in a circle. The car still did not come. And we went on standing there, caught between the run-up to a gracious farewell and the desire to seek answers. This was not the friendly silence of companionship; it felt oppressive.

Finally, the manager spoke, repeating his desire that the situation be resolved and observing that his company was disposed to collaborate in order to arrive at such a resolution. It sounded like an attempt to end the meeting. But the attempt fired one of the municipal engineers to speak. A little defiantly, he asked directly if FETRANSA could move the station away from its current site if it chose to, and the manager, apparently relieved at the intervention, responded that FETRANSA itself could not, but that it could not oppose the idea if Peru Rail, the company that held the concession to the station, decided to do so. But he said it would not be convenient for FETRANSA if the station were moved any closer to Machu Picchu. The company charged the train operators a toll of $3.50 per kilometer covered by each train coach every time it traveled on the track. That was how FETRANSA made its money. "It's more advantageous to us that the station stay where it is," he said. "But it is better for the train companies to move the station as close as possible to Machu Picchu, because that way they pay less for renting the rails." A further distinction had opened up—between the interests of FETRANSA and those of the train operators. This slippage was somewhat complicated by the fact that FETRANSA and Peru Rail, the principal train operator, are both subsidiaries of the same company, Orient Express.

Another municipal engineer returned to his preoccupation about land expropriation, restating that it would be difficult to obtain the five meters due to landowners' resistance. The manager responded that he would give the cadastral map to the municipality so they could see that the five-meter provision was legal and could identify who would be affected. But the engineers protested that such a document, despite its legal status, simply did not reflect the reality. One said that some property holders had won the right to be there because they had used the land for so many years. "That's also a legal fact," the engineer said, simmering a little. The manager said that could well be the case, but that the municipality could use the cadastral map as an instrument for negotiating with the landowners in order to clarify the situation. Here he was addressing the municipality as an instance of the state, with obligations to ensure that legal norms are both understood and enforced.

But his tone shifted immediately afterward when he declared that the municipality could also ensure that the landowners had legally underwritten land titles if they wanted to reinforce their case against the imposition of the five-meter rule. But this was a matter for the municipality, not for FETRANSA. "It's not that FETRANSA is going to go off and do this kind of work with the landowners," the manager stated. "The municipality would have to be responsible for that." It was evident that he was trying to give the municipality options to play with 'off the record'. But his comments clouded FETRANSA's role still further. Was he insinuating that company interests would be served if the municipality were to contest the five-meter norm? Or was he simply trying to be helpful? At any rate, FETRANSA was no longer standing in for the state, but rather declaring an interest in supporting the municipality in its efforts to find ways to confront the imposition of state regulations by strengthening the legal basis of landowners' titles and thereby their case for compensation. The municipality had slipped from being addressed as an instance of government, a state actor that must enforce normative frameworks, to being addressed as a local entity that would work around the regulations to secure the particular interests of Ollantaytambo. The state, it now seemed, was elsewhere.

The manager then acknowledged that, in the end, the Transport Ministry would have to deal with the problem, not FETRANSA. "If you pay 100 million for a state concession, and someone local says 'No, I'm only going to give you half of what you want' [in terms of land], well the state has to resolve it." FETRANSA had already paid for its concession, and the state would have to supply it with the corresponding land extension. He added that FETRANSA was handing over 40 percent of its income to the Transport Ministry, so it was to the Ministry's advantage to sort out the situation. The Ministry would not want to lose such a large quantity of money, he implied, now posing the state not as a disinterested regulator of the common good, but rather as an entity with commercial interests of its own. Both FETRANSA and the state were being invoked as different kinds of enterprises, each concerned with the protection of its own interests.

We all continued to stand in a circle, eyes cast down. Finally, FETRANSA's car arrived, and the manager's two colleagues, who had left the party earlier, stepped out, laughing. Their arrival alleviated the tension. "They've paid you to delay!" the manager of FETRANSA smiled at them, insinuating that their long absence had provided the municipality with an opportunity to convince FETRANSA to approve its project.

We bid our farewells, and while those from FETRANSA sped away, the municipal engineers discussed the encounter. One pointed out the injustice of the state, saying that the property owners along the planned bypass already had their land titles, but that the Ministry of Transport had not consulted with them prior to handing the concession over to FETRANSA. But another hinted at the possibilities posed by the meeting, observing enigmatically that FETRANSA had given them "some guidelines for getting around the situation." He reckoned there would have to be a further exchange between the company and the municipality, although exactly what form this would take remained unclear.

Concluding Thoughts on Affect, the State, and Ethnographic Writing

In this chapter, we have explored what a focus on affect can bring into view. Kathleen Stewart (2007) makes the point that her explicit engagement with the poetics of affect allows her to portray a more direct and concrete engagement with the forces of 'neo-liberalism', 'advanced capitalism', and 'globalization' than these concepts themselves allow. The ideas are descriptive up to a point, but they also tend to the abstract and/or the generic. The ethnographic vignettes that Stewart draws for the reader set out to convey scenes of 'immanent force' and the sense of energy that runs through everyday encounters. A turn to the affective in ethnographic writing involves a shift in focus away from what might be referred to as social structure, or the "fixed conditions of possibility" (ibid.: 2), toward "lines of potential" (ibid.: 11)—an attention to emergent rather than established relations. This change in orientation challenges the ethnographer to find a way both to track and to convey that which is intrinsically uncertain—the hovering, never quite realized or only momentarily realized.

Hence, our concern has been to point to the ways in which the affective force of the state emerges, not in relation to the state's presence or absence, but rather in the shifting movement between the two. FETRANSA's relation to the state becomes increasingly ambivalent over the course of the encounter we describe, and the manager's different modes of addressing the municipality—as being aligned with state norms, at one moment, and as a defender of civil society, at another—unsettles any sense that the municipality is simply a nested layer of a decentralized state structure. It is and it is not. However, beyond this, what we wish to emphasize is that this ambivalence may itself be seen as an effect of the anticipatory space of possibility that is opened up over the course of the encounter.

If we take, for example, the moment when the manager of FETRANSA suggests that the municipality should seek ways of titling lands within the five-meter strip that forms part of the concession, it comes across as somewhat confusing. Why is the manager suddenly offering support to the municipality where it does not need to? The moment is perhaps more explicable when we consider the habitual ways in which people exceed the roles prescribed for them. FETRANSA was in no way required to offer help to the municipality, and the municipality might have been more assertive by threatening that disquiet over the bypass could lead to out-and-out protests and rail blockades, a scenario that had been seen in previous years. Instead, both parties were very attentive to one another throughout the tour of the route. Possibly against his intentions, as suggested by his tacit attempts to close the meeting when the circle formed around the municipal car at the end of the tour, the manager found himself attending to local concerns, responding to the municipality's desire for a solution that would take their needs into account. The entire encounter was shot through with small gestures of care. The very act of walking together down the tracks enabled a mutual attentiveness that opened up a sense of possibility, overturning the earlier rigidity that characterized the discussion about the five-meter provision. Indeed, the impression garnered at the end of the meeting that some kind of agreement had been reached, in the absence of any specific accord, was in itself affectively mediated.

We have here been less interested in the emotional workings of affect, choosing instead to test out the idea that the very demonstration of emotion is, to use Mazzarella's (2010) term, already a qualification of corporeal 'intensity'. Our ethnography is not about the drama of expressed emotion, then, but rather about 'ordinary affects'—the sense of energy that runs through everyday encounters. More specifically, however, we have sought to complicate the notion that affect may simply be located on one side of an emotion/sense, meaning/non-meaning duality. Rather, we have tried to show how affect emerges at the shimmering border between these categories, in the play between determinacy and indeterminacy and in the sense of anticipation, uncertainty, and possibility that underwrite minor, mundane gestures, such as a gesture of care, which open up a sense of potential. And we have sought to describe how the force of state power emerges in and through the tensions and tiny shifts in perspective when the state is neither exactly absent nor present, but unfolds indirectly as a virtual presence, a potential force held in abeyance.

Acknowledgments

We undertook this research as part of an ethnographic project entitled "Experimental States: Law, Engineering, and Regional Government in Cusco, Peru," which was funded by the Wenner-Gren Foundation, the Arts and Humanities Research Council (AHRC), the American Council for Learned Societies (ACLS), and the National Science Foundation (NSF). We would like to thank the municipality of Ollantaytambo for its willing participation in this research and the Economic and Social Research Council (ESRC) for supporting the project. We would also like to thank our co-researchers—Jimena Lynch Cisneros, Deborah Poole, and Teresa Tupayachi Mar—and the participants in the workshop "Affective States: Exploring Emotion in Political Life," held in Manchester on 17–18 May 2012, for their helpful comments on earlier versions of this chapter.

Annabel Pinker is a Leverhulme Early Career Fellow at the James Hutton Institute in Aberdeen. Her research focuses on contemporary state practices and the material politics of road and energy infrastructures. Since completing her PhD (University of Cambridge, 2010), she has held positions at the Institute of Latin American Studies at the University of London and the Centre for Research on Socio-Cultural Change (CRESC) at the University of Manchester, where she formed part of the collaborative "Experimental States" project, exploring how state power in Peru is being reconfigured through the emergent political spaces opened up by decentralization. She is currently developing research on the new coalitions of power, technology, expertise, and everyday life sparked by moves toward energy decentralization in Scotland.

Penny Harvey is a Professor of Social Anthropology at the University of Manchester. Since 2012, she has also held the position of Professor II in Social Anthropology at the University of Oslo. Her most recent work draws on ethnographic fieldwork in Peru and the United Kingdom that focuses on infrastructural projects as sites of political experimentation. Recent publications include *Infrastructure and Social Complexity* (2016, co-edited with Casper Bruun Jensen and Atsuro Morita) and *Roads: An Anthropology of Infrastructure and Expertise* (2015, with Hannah Knox). She is currently embarking on a new study of nuclear decommissioning.

References

Aretxaga, Begoña. 2005. *States of Terror: Begoña Aretxaga's Essays*. Ed. Joseba Zulaika. Reno: University of Nevada Press.

Barry, Andrew. 2002. "The Anti-political Economy." *Economy and Society* 31 (2): 268–284.

Berlant, Lauren. 2011. *Cruel Optimism*. Durham, NC: Duke University Press.

Collier, Stephen J. 2011. *Post-Soviet Social: Neoliberalism, Social Modernity, Biopolitics*. Princeton, NJ: Princeton University Press.

Connolly, William E. 2002. *Neuropolitics: Thinking, Culture, Speed*. Minneapolis: University of Minnesota Press.

Das, Veena. 2004. "The Signature of the State: The Paradox of Illegibility." In Das and Poole 2004, 225–252.

Das, Veena, and Deborah Poole, eds. 2004. *Anthropology in the Margins of the State*. Santa Fe, NM: School of American Research Press.

Harvey, Penelope. 2005. "The Materiality of State-Effects: An Ethnography of a Road in the Peruvian Andes." In *State Formation: Anthropological Perspectives*, ed. Christian Krohn-Hansen and Knut G. Nustad, 123–141. London: Pluto Press.

Kelly, Tobias. 2006. "Documented Lives: Fear and the Uncertainties of Law during the Second Palestinian *Intifada*." *Journal of the Royal Anthropological Institute* 12 (1): 89–107.

Lampland, Martha, and Susan Leigh Star, eds. 2009. *Standards and Their Stories: How Quantifying, Classifying, and Formalizing Practices Shape Everyday Life*. Ithaca, NY: Cornell University Press.

Massumi, Brian. 2002. *Parables for the Virtual: Movement, Affect, Sensation*. Durham, NC: Duke University Press.

Mazzarella, William. 2010. "Affect: What Is It Good for?" In *Enchantments of Modernity: Empire, Nation, Globalization*, ed. Saurabh Dube, 291–309. London: Routledge.

Navaro-Yashin, Yael. 2007. "Make-Believe Papers, Legal Forms and the Counterfeit: Affective Interactions between Documents and People in Britain and Cyprus." *Anthropological Theory* 7 (1): 79–98.

Navaro-Yashin, Yael. 2012. *The Make-Believe Space: Affective Geography in a Postwar Polity*. Durham, NC: Duke University Press.

Nuijten, Monique. 2003. *Power, Community and the State: The Political Anthropology of Organisation in Mexico*. London: Pluto Press.

Poole, Deborah. 2004. "Between Threat and Guarantee: Justice and Community in the Margins of the Peruvian State." In Das and Poole 2004, 35–65.

Richard, Analiese, and Daromir Rudnyckyj. 2009. "Economies of Affect." *Journal of the Royal Anthropological Institute* 15 (1): 57–77.

Riles, Annelise, ed. 2006. *Documents: Artifacts of Modern Knowledge*. Ann Arbor: University of Michigan Press.

Rose, Nikolas. 1999. *Powers of Freedom: Reframing Political Thought*. Cambridge: Cambridge University Press.

Rose, Nikolas, and Peter Miller. 1992. "Political Power beyond the State: Problematics of Government." *British Journal of Sociology* 43 (2): 173–205.

Stewart, Kathleen. 2007. *Ordinary Affects*. Durham, NC: Duke University Press.

Tarlo, Emma. 2001. "Paper Truths: The Emergency and Slum Clearance through Forgotten Files." In *The Everyday State and Society in Modern India*, ed. C. J. Fuller and Veronique Benei, 68–90. London: Hurst.

Taussig, Michael. 1992. *The Nervous System*. New York: Routledge.

Taussig, Michael. 1997. *The Magic of the State*. New York: Routledge.

Thrift, Nigel. 2008. *Non-Representational Theory: Space, Politics, Affect*. London: Routledge.

Tsing, Anna L. 2004. *Friction: An Ethnography of Global Connection*. Princeton, NJ: Princeton University Press.

Chapter 2

THE FINES AND THE SPIES
Fears of State Surveillance in Eritrea and in the Diaspora

David Bozzini

> ... the spies hide out in every corner
> But you can't touch them, no
> Cause they're all spies
> They're all spies
>
> — Coldplay, "Spies," *Parachutes* (2000)

Under the cover of anonymity, two Eritrean refugees in Switzerland described the political situation in their country to a journalist in the following way: "You cannot speak about politics in Eritrea, even within your own family circle" (Mounier-Kuhn 2009). For the last few years, Eritrea has been consistently characterized as a prison state by the media (e.g., Rice 2009) and by international agencies (e.g., Human Rights Watch 2009; International Crisis Group 2010). However, the interview with the two Eritreans not only related homeland political tension as it affected them, but also revealed how state control transcends

Notes for this chapter begin on page 46.

Eritrean national borders: "Even here, we cannot have trust in each other. All of the exiles have claimed political asylum, but nevertheless most of them refuse to denounce the current Eritrean government. They do not fear for themselves, but they have concerns about their families living in Eritrea" (Mounier-Kuhn 2009). This account is one among many similar narratives that can be collected from Eritreans living in Europe. Eritreans expect to be monitored abroad by the Eritrean state, and they fear repression in Eritrea. Many mention the presence of state spies reporting back to the Eritrean government.

This chapter discusses the fears related to the reach of the Eritrean state, both within and beyond its sovereign territory. It explores such fears by focusing on one particular state measure and its social consequences: retaliation against the relatives of deserters, who are jailed and forced to pay a fine of 50,000 nafka (about 2,500 euros). I argue that this recent measure has fostered a culture of mistrust in the Eritrean transnational social field by sending a clear signal that the state could at any time retaliate against deserters' relatives back home. This represents a substantial political gain for the current government in Eritrea. On the one hand, it has curbed dissidence in the diaspora despite the huge number of deserters living in exile. On the other, it has reshaped existing modalities of enforced transnational control by the current Eritrean leadership. I contend that emotions—and fears in particular—are constitutive of Eritrean modalities of governance that have changed over the last decades and have shaped Eritrean subjectivities in exile. This applies both to relationships between fellow citizens and to the real and imagined individual bond with the Eritrean state. Fears about the state cannot be understood as generated by state measures alone. 'State terror' is rather a diffuse and complex social phenomenon that questions the limits of the concept of governance as an intentionally planned and institutionally bounded kind of process.

The constructivist perspective on emotions in which this chapter is anchored claims that "the individual is the site, but not the source, of emotional events [and that] the learned feelings that individuals express are consonant with the ambient social order, its norms, its ideals, its structures of authority" (Reddy 1999: 259). Discourses and, more generally, social life shape emotions and the way in which they are felt or experienced, displayed and interpreted (Leavitt 1996; Lutz and Abu-Lughod 1990). But emotions are also performative: they shape selves (Rudnyckyj 2011) and play a part in defining sociality and social boundaries (Ahmed 2004; Svašek 2010). They also assert, challenge, or reinforce power or status differences (Lutz and Abu-Lughod 1990), contribute to shaping control and governance (Richard and Rudnyckyj 2009), and allow the mobilization of social movements or inhibit political activities (Jasper 2011).[1] Fear is always related to a particular object and has always to be considered in its specificity instead of as a general and abstract category. Some fears are not necessarily negative but can also be considered a conscious strategy, a moral obligation, or even a lifesaving virtue in authoritarian contexts.

After a section that briefly contextualizes post-independent Eritrean politics, I present the effects that the uneven implementation of the retaliation measures had in Eritrea in 2005 and 2006. I discuss the fears about various forms of state control and explore the role of these fears in what can be considered a despotic regime. The following two sections shed light on how these fears about the Eritrean state have translated and impacted upon social relations in the diaspora. This leads me to suggest a rethinking of Eritrean enforced transnationalism and of the role that haunting fears in general can have in authoritarian regimes and in their marginal and deterritorialized spaces.

The ethnographic material on which this chapter draws derives from research conducted in Eritrea between 2003 and 2007 and among the Eritrean diaspora in Europe since 2008. Almost all respondents in Eritrea were national service conscripts who had been assigned to state civil institutions. Most were from the Tigrinya ethnic group, and two-thirds were male. Some deserters were contacted in Sudan by telephone and through the Internet, while most Eritreans interviewed in Europe were deserters who had been granted asylum and a permanent or temporary residence permit. Names and narratives have been altered to protect anonymity.

Eritrea: Militarization and Exile

After three decades of guerrilla warfare against Ethiopian rulers (1961–1991), the Eritrean Popular Liberation Front (EPLF) constituted an independent Eritrean government and a single party, the People's Front for Democracy and Justice (PFDJ). Post-war national reconstruction was disrupted only a few years later when the bloody Ethio-Eritrean conflict raged at the turn of the century (1998–2000). Not long after the ceasefire, Isayas Afeworki, the first and current president of the State of Eritrea, suspended democratic reforms and purged from the PFDJ his main contenders, known as the G-15 (Connell 2003; Hepner 2009). Since then, an authoritarian regime constituted by the government, the army, and the PFDJ has been committed to limiting the influence of the private sector and foreign donors (Gaim Kibreab 2009) and to developing a command economy to face the economic challenges caused largely by the rupture of Eritrea's relationship with Ethiopia.

The Warsay Ykäalo Development Campaign,[2] initiated in 2002, has played a crucial role in these changes. It employs an army workforce in party companies and state institutions. National service conscription (*hagärawi agälglot*) of both male and female Eritrean citizens on reaching the legal age of 18 (GoE 1995) is the central pillar of this operation. Conscripts are assigned as simple soldiers, builders, teachers, nurses, office workers, or technical staff. For both military and civilian conscripts, national service has become indefinite: no demobilization has taken place over more than a decade. Conscripts do not hold responsibilities within state institutions, and their rights are limited. They are not allowed to own a passport or to leave the country. They cannot have land allocated to them, nor can they obtain official documents without prior formal authorization of their superiors, who are usually former freedom fighters and cadres of the former EPLF. They cannot be employed elsewhere, and their mobility inside the country is limited. Deserters and objectors are literally denied any rights. In short, national service conscripts are legally positioned as "subjected citizens" (Navaro-Yashin 2005: 112).

Alongside the militarization of education, production, and construction, the government has strengthened its surveillance techniques and its coercive measures as a means to retain conscripts in service (Bozzini 2011a). Military control and repression became rampant after the significant increase in desertion and draft objection following the launch of the Warsay Ykäạlo Development Campaign. However, attempts to strengthen control over conscripts never constituted an efficient system of bureaucratic surveillance, nor did they give rise to an all-controlling police state. Instead, these efforts have been notable for generating a widespread feeling of insecurity among conscripts (Bozzini 2011b). The despotic modality of governance and the unintended production of uncertainties that are at the center of Eritrean state interventions have persuaded many Eritreans to defect and flee to Sudan or Ethiopia. According to UNHCR statistics,[3] Eritrean exiles registering in refugee camps in these countries numbered fewer than 10,000 in 2004, but over 20,000 each year since 2009.

The Eritrean economy in general, and the state's income in particular, continues to depend heavily on diaspora remittances. This has been the case since long before the formal establishment of the current independent state, when the EPLF was already relying on diasporic financial support (Tekle Woldemikael 1991). Since independence, a 2 percent income tax has been levied on Eritreans residing abroad. Eritrean citizens who need consular services are asked to pay the tax retroactively, along with other special fees. Channeling hard currency from the Eritreans in the diaspora, who are increasingly refusing to support the state, is certainly one of the current challenges that the Eritrean leadership is facing. Since 2005, the government has been imposing fines on deserters' families who were then forced to seek additional remittances from their relatives abroad in order to comply with this new measure.

Panic and Confusion: the Uneven Implementation of Retaliation on Deserters' Families

During the summer of 2005, a wave of panic occurred in Asmara, the Eritrean capital. This time, neither a conscriptable age cohort nor a constituted group such as a church was targeted by the police, as had usually been the case in the past. A new and unforeseen repressive measure was introduced whereby the police took into custody parents whose children were alleged to have defected from the national service.[4] Before the arrests were implemented throughout Eritrea, parents were detained in rural towns of the southern region. Paying off 50,000 nakfa to the local administration was the sine qua non condition for releasing a family member from custody. However, confusion about the range, the rules, and the criteria for the arrests reigned for more than a year. This new measure generated uncertainties, fears, and distress in many families and became an expression of a distinctive despotic mode of governance.

Without any official declaration from the police or the government, the inhabitants of Asmara initially assumed that all parents of deserters were being targeted. Almost all families expected to be summoned until, several weeks later, it became known that the measure was mostly aimed at families of those who had deserted from the civilian service during the last few years. The state was not retaliating against families of wartime deserters. This 'rule' came to be understood through the collective work of interpretation, as well as intensive exchange of information and comparison of cases discussed among friends and relatives. In so doing, Asmarinos filled in the gaps of official information. However, all sorts of discordant case stories continued to circulate since there were many discrepancies in the enforcement of the measure. For instance, some detainees were released so that they could find the money, while other families were reported to have two or more relatives in custody. Above all, the maximum period of detention remained uncertain in cases when the fine (*gäbri* or *mäqsəti*) could not be secured. Within this panic and confusion stirred up by the authorities, citizens continued to try to work out the implicit new rules and the limits of the retaliation.

State inconsistencies were not the only cause of disquiet. Conflicting information, hearsay, incomplete narratives, and anticipation also contributed to making the situation more confusing. Stories of individual cases, updated on a daily basis, continually altered interpretations. Fearful predictions circulated, thus blurring even the distinction between what was the result of misunderstanding and what was instead the outcome of the state's arbitrary modus operandi. As Greenhouse (2002: 1) puts it: "[M]aintaining the illusion of states' concreteness calls for new kind of creative energy on the part of the people who inhabit these [unstable] states." Hasty interpretations were often the result of such creative energy used in Eritrea to anticipate and foresee the logics and dynamics of the state measures. However, it must be emphasized that such attempts at decoding cannot be reduced simply to cognitive processes. As Reeves argues in this book, rules have an "affective dimension" and can elicit "feelings that intensify in conditions of collective uncertainty."

Understandably, the search for rules to make sense of the arbitrariness of the authorities was hopeful but also put a strain on the nerves of the conscripts and their families. When arrests unexpectedly stopped in 2006, Asmarinos believed that the retaliation measures had been abolished—only to be plunged back into distress a few weeks later when incarcerations resumed. Rules, expectations, and explanations emerged, reassuring or terrifying conscripts and their families for some time before disappearing and sometimes reappearing later on in amended versions, thus catalyzing and amplifying emotional oscillations. Agitation was sparked off again for some weeks when rumors had it that some storekeepers had been menaced with having their commercial license revoked if one of their children was declared to be missing from national service. For some time, however, nobody was able to confirm the actual enforcement of this threat. Instead, the ceaseless circulation of conflicting information ruined any attempt to clarify the situation, thus allowing the disruptive effects of doubts and fearful projections to ripple indefinitely. As Ahmed (2004) notes, circulation is crucial for understanding the dynamics of fear: the more that rumors circulated to get rid of the deafening silence of the Eritrean state, the more that fears intensified in the capital city. The authorities' silence first set the scene, creating anxiety and anticipation for those families who had not yet been targeted by the measure. Then rumor transformed this widespread anxiety into flurries of countless fears, creating what Taussig (1992) calls a 'nervous system', an oscillation of uncertainties consisting at once of rumors of actual threats and rumors of prospective penalties.

The affective experience of the unaccountability and unpredictability of such silent and volatile governance was coupled with another silence—one that the measure promoted within the family itself. Samson, who had been serving for eight years in the PFDJ headquarters, had finally arranged his exile to Sudan just as retaliation was first taking place in Asmara. He postponed his departure but eventually decided to keep to his plan despite the guilt that he felt about what would certainly happen to his father. "Telling him my plan is now impossible! This would mean that I am telling him to prepare to go to jail," Samson confessed to me two weeks before he stepped onto a bus instead of clocking in at his office. Since it had become increasingly problematic for conscripts to disclose exile plans to their close relatives, parents were thus trapped in the fearful expectation of retaliation. In addition, suspicions and anxiety about a sudden departure also surfaced within families. Uncertainties multiplied and sparked new fears as the silence within families intensified the silence of the authorities.

Fears of Bureaucratic Control

Deserters' families also felt threatened when they encountered bureaucrats, especially at the local administration level (*mmhdar käbabi*). For Tsemainesh, who was a single mother of three children, accessing basic services became a source of considerable unease once her older daughter, of an age to be conscripted, had fled to Sudan. Tsemainesh was reluctant to access food rations even though they were essential to feed her family every month, because coupons were delivered according to the number of family members and upon request of their ID cards. Since her daughter had fled with her card, Tsemainesh feared that the administrator could easily discover the escape. Risk assessment of bureaucratic encounters thus promoted strategies of avoidance.

Circulation of fearful expectations intensified self-control. Many Asmarinos were afraid of an imminent tightening of controls through the implementation of a computerized database system within the state bureaucracy. Popular diaspora-based opposition websites published similar rumors, fueling fearful expectations in Eritrea: "It is now known that extensive lists of the so-called absent persons were prepared and given to local administrators in all of the Southern Region … Lists of missing persons have been prepared for all six regions and handed over to the authorities in each region. The campaign is, therefore, expected to be carried out in the remaining five regions as well."[5] In that sense, fear cannot always be considered a negative emotion since it can represent a useful and deliberate strategy to avoid trouble in such uncertain situations. However, as these cases show, such forms of self-control can also amplify the perception of risk. Indeed, no bureaucratic control ever rendered retaliation against deserters' families automatic. As I have argued elsewhere (Bozzini 2011b), such strategic imagination of state power and efficiency of control shielded the limits of the state surveillance apparatus and has certainly represented a partial substitute for the state's 'own' loose social and political control. This phenomenon occurs in other authoritarian regimes as well. In the case of Poland, Los (2006) argues that the fears that Poles had about the former secret service files exaggerated the efficiency of such surveillance, while in this book, Kendzior claims that Uzbek dissidents consider inevitable what seems only possible about the Uzbekistani security services. Wedeen (1998) has described this phenomenon as a politics of 'as if', which, in the context of Hafez al-Assad's Syria, was complicit with the regime.

The Anxious Fictional Reality of a Totalitarian Regime

Agitation and irritation increased considerably when Asmarinos realized that their laborious attempts to understand the implicit rules of retaliation still failed to capture the unsystematic enforcement of repression. While many families had been targeted during the year, others like Tsemainesh's were still fearfully expecting to be summoned at any moment. Acknowledgment of bureaucratic inefficiency and the confusion arising from the circulation of conflicting information gave rise to conjectures of covert surveillance and denunciation. Exacerbating pre-existing fears and suspicions about the dynamics of the security service, these conjectures offered explanations for the patchy enforcement of retaliation.

Besides well-known agents who kept an eye on neighborhoods for the local administrations, covert surveillance had several faces in Eritrea and always combined partial knowledge with fantasy or suspicions about unveiled secrets. Informers (*ezni*, or 'ear' in Tigrinya), undercover agents (*sälay*), and informal collaborators reporting back to the security service (*dhanät*) or to the local administration were assumed to be present at the university and in bars, churches, and Internet cafés, while others were said to roam the streets of the capital city. Most people assumed that a colleague, a friend, a neighbor, a relative, or a spouse could be forced to join the hidden crowd of state informers (Bozzini 2011a; Treiber 2004). If not necessarily discontinued, solidarity and trust among friends were often undermined.

Not surprisingly, the tactic of retaliation increased the vulnerability of deserters' families by catalyzing the possibility of blackmail or of being informed upon. Threats of such denunciation to the authorities were often raised during out-of-court arbitrations. I also collected several narratives of deserters' families who claimed to have been harassed by fellow citizens (Bozzini 2011a). The sudden summons from the authorities and the absence of an investigation were sometimes understood to be the result of indiscretions reported intentionally to officials, as in the case of Aron's family. Aron's father was summoned by the local administrator a few months after his son had arrived in Khartoum. The official gave Aron's father some weeks to collect the money for the fine. The whole family started to seek an explanation for such a sudden call, and their gaze turned toward their close neighbor, a veteran fighter who had recently asked about Aron. Aron's sister remembered that she once saw the neighbor speaking with the administrator, and several family friends confirmed that both men had become close friends recently, often chatting together at a café. They eventually considered their suspicion confirmed when, shortly after Aron's father paid the fine, they learned that their neighbor had just bought an apartment at a very fair price through agreements with the local administration and possibly with part of the money from the fine. Accurate or not, such interpretations caused social ruptures among fellow citizens by supporting the idea that the state could intrude into personal relations.

Both real and alleged threats accounted for the fear that infused such contexts, increasing mutual suspicion. Threats in the form of bureaucratic tools like databases, covert surveillance, or denunciation were neither the realities resulting from certain projects or modalities of state governance nor the simple explanations and beliefs that people elaborated. Rather, they constituted a complex and irreducible assemblage of what Aretxaga (2000) calls the 'fictional reality' of the state. The state, writes Aretxaga, "materializes not only through rules and bureaucratic routines (Foucault) but also through a world of fantasy thoroughly narrativized and imbued with affect, fear, and desire, that make it, in fact, a plausible reality" (ibid.: 52). If indeed "much of the potency of *the state* is in the imagination of it" (Kapferer and Taylor 2012: 1), then informers and snitches were always both presumed and real, actual and potential, hidden and revealed, thus catalyzing the fears about an arbitrary authoritarian state. Its manifestation was troublesome and terrifying because its limits, its actions, and its agents were boundless and could jeopardize at any time the remaining intimate spaces of trust and solidarity.

But denouncing the potential denouncers—that is, sharing knowledge and suspicions about potential informers—led to performances that allowed the power of the arbitrary state to endanger the reputation of rivals (Bozzini 2011a: 260–270). In giving to every citizen "direct access to the coercive apparatus of the state, unmediated by lengthy and complicated judicial procedures" (Gross 2002: 120–121), the Eritrean state instituted a dynamic that partly got away from its control but that was also still profitable for maintaining the power of its institutions. As the case of Aron's family indicates, the measure of retaliation against deserters' families in particular, and access to arbitrary state power in general, has represented for virtually every Eritrean citizen not only everlasting fearful threats but also opportunities.

From this perspective, the state appears to be an open-ended assemblage of complex, dynamic, and heterogeneous forces vested in actors, representations, emotions, and processes that largely transcend what are usually defined as state institutions, as well as their agents and their actions. The totalitarian regime promoted by the retaliations against deserters' families was composed as much by the coercive actions of state authorities as by the widespread imagination of a total and effective surveillance apparatus and the circulation of the arbitrary power of the state that was manifested in blackmail, denunciation, and defamation. In other words, a totalitarian regime cannot be understood except by taking into account official policies alongside their popular representations, fears about the state, and the consequences that these have for social relationships.

The Translation of Fears in Exile and in Europe

Fear of the Eritrean state does not stop when one has crossed the border illegally. While uncertainties due to exile and asylum seeking generate many anxieties, fear about the reach of the Eritrean state beyond its territory is a discrete category of emotion experienced by most Eritrean migrants. The fictional reality of state agents abroad is well-exemplified in Daniel Ghebreselassie's (2010) written account. When he arrived in Kassala, his contact immediately mentioned that "many Eritreans live in that area so we had to get away. It was surprising that we had to escape from nationals of our country ... He told us that we need to be careful as there are many Eritrean spies in the city [who] look to catch the newly arrived ... We were not sure whether [our contact] will help us frankly or try to deceive us. I [hated to] be suspicious of everyone we met, but we have heard of all the things that [have] happened." Later, Daniel adds: "He told us that we had frightened him the previous night. His friend [had] called him from Eritrea and told him that his regiment was sending some agents to capture him and bring him back to Eritrea. At first he thought we [had come] to arrest him" (ibid.: 19–21). Refugees in Sudan persistently speak about threats exerted by the Eritrean secret service and the Sudanese authorities with whom the secret service allegedly collaborate: "There [have] been government warnings for the foreigners to renew their permits. Those who don't could be deported. I was there myself, and I spent my last days in Khartoum confined to my house to avoid being caught. There were no large-scale *giffa* [roundups] when I was there. People were very terrified by the prospect" (Samuel, pers. comm., Sudan, February 2008).

Deportation is not merely a hypothetical threat. During the last few years, cases have been regularly reported (Geiser 2011; Human Rights Watch 2011; UNHCR 2011) in which former officials, political opponents, and national service members have been kidnapped in Khartoum and in the eastern provinces of Kassala and Gedaref (EPDP 2012; Hepner 2011). Fear of deportation is not only present in Sudan. Threats and actual deportations of groups of Eritreans have recently occurred in Egypt, South Africa, Malta, Libya, and Israel. Providing their families back home with the necessary money to pay the fines certainly extended the period of time during which deserters were subjected to these threats in Sudan.

If the fear of deportation vanishes when Eritreans arrive in Europe, fears about Eritrean state surveillance and the presence of state agents remain and take on new forms. During asylum application processes, many deserters choose to rely only on a few people and to visit a limited number of friends and relatives in order to avoid taking risks in the Eritrean local community, which they have barely joined. The historical presence of the party-state overseas is pivotal to understanding the fears experienced by deserters. Since the end of the 1970s, the EPLF (and later the PFDJ) has deeply shaped the Eritrean communities overseas (Bernal 2004). Its institutions have played a considerable role in channeling all kinds of support to the guerrilla front (Tekle Woldemikael 1991) and have represented a crucial mechanism in the EPLF's accession to state power. They have also notably undermined the power and legitimacy of its co-national contestants in the diaspora (Al-Ali et al. 2001; Conrad 2006; Hepner 2007, 2009). Maintained after independence, the dense grid of the EPLF's offices, alongside the newly established consulates and embassies, constituted the extraterritorial branches of what became a 'diasporic state' (Ruth Iyob 2000), which was able to impose an income tax on Eritrean citizens residing overseas.

Since the crackdown on protesters and the radicalization of the leadership in 2001, several new measures and institutions have been implemented in the diaspora in order to secure mobilization and tackle the increasing popular discontent with the government: party rallies and sponsored cultural activities have flourished; pre-independence mass organizations have been revived; youth branches of the PFDJ (YPFDJ) have been founded; and pressures have been exerted to promote taxation compliance and other fund-raising activities (Koser 2002). Despite the fact that, during the last decade, many Eritreans residing abroad have distanced themselves from the regime and have (re)organized into several opposition groups, the Eritrean regime still benefits from the support of a significant number of loyalists in the diaspora (Müller 2012). For these reasons, the ubiquitous power of the Eritrean state and the influence of the PFDJ (and before it the EPLF) in diaspora communities across the globe are widely acknowledged among deserters.

During discussions about the overseas influence of the state and the PFDJ among deserters who recently arrived in Switzerland, one exile declared that the party "is very good at threatening their opponents abroad." Another remembered the threatening innuendo in President Afeworki's address to Eritreans in South Africa who were protesting against the policies of the Eritrean government: "If you tie a hen with a long thread, she thinks she is free." In a similar vein, a journalist recently assaulted by loyalists in Houston declared to the press: "Wherever there are Eritreans, there are government spies who report your opinions and activities … Those [who] have opinions different than the government, they are … labeled as opposition, as against the country, as traitors" (Tedros Menghistu, quoted in Keita 2010).

The Eritrean Spies Overseas

According to my interlocutors, Eritrean spies roaming abroad are of two kinds. They are either long-time EPLF supporters who arrived in Europe during the 1980s, or they are deserters or draft evaders who initially sought asylum for political reasons but then chose to settle under the umbrella of the party-state organizations. These 'traitors of traitors' are suspected by some of my respondents of being 'false refugees' sent by the government to monitor the diaspora communities. Older supporters and loyalists are considered to be spies mainly because deserters assume that they blindly follow the government and will therefore report any information that they think will be useful to protect Eritrean sovereignty from international conspiracies. Plausible or not, these two allegations have clearly fueled a culture of mistrust and reveal the political and generational tensions unfolding in the diaspora.

The Eritrean bureaucratic form of state surveillance—but this time considered on a transnational scale—remains at the center of the stories that circulate and that reanimate fears about the state. For instance, deserters seeking asylum in Switzerland are convinced that some Eritreans close to the embassy circle are working in institutions such as the federal office for migration and with NGOs in charge of delivering welfare benefits and legal assistance for asylum seekers and indigent refugees. Translators working in these institutions are widely believed to collect asylum seekers' personal information and report it to the embassy, and rumors exchanged among deserters have it that Eritrean embassies keep files on exiled citizens in order eventually to retaliate against their families back home. Tedros, who was registered in Italy, declared that the Eritrean translator whom he met in the camp turned out to be a hidden state agent since "he advised us to ask for economic refuge, and he cheated in the interviews, giving us a bad name" (Tedros, pers. comm., Switzerland, September 2010). Such perceived vindictive actions indicate that fear and mistrust are related not only to potential retaliation against relatives back home, but also directly to the life of deserters overseas.

If loyalists did not consider exerting any form of coercion over newcomers, it remains the case that in such a context, imbued with mistrust, a simple invitation to an event or a request to sign a petition or to collect money for a development project might easily be experienced as a form of blackmail that invites deserters to comply in order to avoid all kinds of subsequent possible problems. Measures of intimidation are thus always considered to be exerted in a 'smart' and covert way. Filming has been a widespread practice of intimidation, and, inevitably, a party member was found capturing on video a demonstration that took place in Geneva in 2011. One loyalist, widely suspected to be an informer for the local branch of the PFDJ in Switzerland, confirmed to me that he liked to attend the opposition's events in order to "learn from them."

Understandably, all sorts of fears, pressures, and blackmails—but also promises of assistance by well-integrated loyalists—have led some deserters toward the transnational organizations of the single-party state despite their antipathy toward the Eritrean government. Some accounts reported in the media point to pressures and "emotional blackmail" (Selam Kidane, quoted in BBC 2010) that are used to make deserters commit to activities of the party-state (Monnat 2012; Schweri 2010). One former EPLF leader, who was active in Europe before Eritrean independence, affirmed that this had happened already: "We offered assistance to the newcomers, and they eventually knew what could possibly happen to them if they were not showing enough commitment. Now, they are even offering business licenses to relatives in Eritrea" (Tesfamariam, pers. comm., Switzerland, January 2012). More commonly, perhaps, the need of a consular service may exert sufficient pressure to force exiles eventually to honor, even retroactively, their 2 percent income tax. Neutrality and absence of commitment, whether in favor of or against the party-state, were justified also by the necessity to maintain a large spectrum of relationships in communities that remain relatively small, as in Switzerland and the Netherlands. Furthermore, some newcomers have to deal with relatives whom they have rejoined overseas and who are loyal to the PFDJ.

Because many exiles expect to be registered in the embassies or to fall under the spotlight of the party-state, only a few dare to raise their voices and commit to dissident activities. Those interlocutors who still felt guilty and ashamed about the detention of their fathers back home declared that they would not be able to bear the responsibility of another act of retaliation against their family. Eyob, for instance, indicated that he was very reluctant to join a demonstration organized in Geneva despite the organizers' declaration that this demonstration was not politically motivated against the Eritrean government: "I will become active in the opposition once I will know that my brother is safely out of Eritrea" (Eyob, pers. comm., Switzerland, June 2011). Others like Yonas, who was serving in a sensitive office until 2010, feared both state officials and opposition groups. To protect himself and his family from ill-intentioned persons, Yonas chose to blur information systematically about his place of residence. For several months, acquaintances (including myself) thought that he was living in Lausanne while he was in fact dispatched to another area by the Swiss authorities. Like his friend who fled from the same office, Yonas was even using a Facebook account (posting pictures and so forth) to deliberately deceive people about the European country where he resided.

Such retaliation measures have vividly reminded all Eritreans that the state can harm families at any moment. Fears of surveillance and potential new retaliations have clearly curbed the political commitment of deserters exiled in Europe since the measure imposing fines on deserters' families was introduced in 2005. While this still prevents any larger mobilization against the Eritrean government, deserters try nowadays to domesticate fears about the transnational state and increasingly dare to raise their voices in public and on various semi-private online platforms such as Facebook groups and chat rooms: "Everyone who is fleeing Eritrea is expecting to raise money to send to his family for this issue. Most of them have included this cost in their exile budget … 50,000 nakfa is not anymore enough to keep us silent. We start fighting even if our family has to pay" (Amanuel, pers. comm., Netherlands, April 2012). Mobilization in Europe, however, still remains extremely fragile.

Conclusion

If the power usually attributed to the state is indisputably that of producing and imposing categories of thought (Benedict Anderson 1991; Bourdieu 1999; Mitchell 1991; Spencer 2007; Trouillot 2001), it remains nevertheless necessary to highlight that authoritarian states generate rather unstable and fragile patterns of cognition and thus generate states of fearful anticipation. An abundant anthropological literature has highlighted the diversity of relationships between fear and politics specific to the political regime and the particular historical context in which they are embedded (Aretxaga 2000, 2003; Green 1994; Sluka 2000; Taussig 1984). The case of Eritrean state retaliation against deserters' families adds to this literature, highlighting ways in which emotions are at the heart of the everyday experience of authoritarian regimes. I have argued that fears are constitutive of such regimes' transnational activities. At both intimate and transnational levels, the Eritrean tentacular governance spreads fear. The role of state institutions is central to promoting these political and social dynamics through deliberate measures that induce various forms of insecurity at a distance.

However, fears about the state are not products of the Eritrean government alone. The creation, diffusion, and political use of fears are also located in various citizen practices. Fearful political imagination about the state and its reach emerges from complex dynamics that encompass not only the despotic government and its attempts to surveil, but also the multiplicity of rumors, collective efforts to decipher rules, individual discipline to avoid potential risks, and other practices such as blackmail, denunciation, and defamation. In other words, fears and unease about the state are not only the product of state inconsistencies. They are also provoked by hearsay, incomplete narratives, anticipations of total surveillance, excessive and arbitrary coercion, and threats of popular complicity. Fears and pervasive mistrust are two core elements of the fictional reality of the Eritrean regime and its perpetuation.

At a more general level, this chapter has shown how a certain modality of governance by the EPLF and the current regime has deeply and intimately rooted fear and mistrust in subjectivities. Understood as "repeated, strong interactions among major political actors including a government" (Tilly 2006: 19), the notion of regime that already allows us to consider practices that frame the life of citizens beyond the limits of state governance takes a particular dimension in socio-political contexts structured by fear. As Rev (1987: 341) underscores: "[W]hen the full force of terror is let loose, politics does not die but gets out of hand ... Politics becomes dispersed, hidden but present everywhere." Thus, virtually all actions of every Eritrean citizen have been politicized by fear. The spectral presence of the state and its tentacular reach are effects of a regime in which state power is infused throughout the whole social body. It is because state power is so decentralized that such regimes can be said to be totalitarian.

The spectral presence of the state also spreads into the Eritrean transnational field. Fearful representations and practices circulate well beyond Eritrean sovereign territory, (re)shaping the transnational experience, exile subjectivities, and relationships in the diaspora. Whether actual or fictional, covert intelligence "colonize[s] social relationships" (Verdery 2014: 26). It alters them by instilling fear, suspicion, and allegations without necessarily recruiting new informants to its transnational network. In this sense, fear can be collectively experienced.

Experiences of the police state in Eritrea, retaliation against deserters' families, and the historical presence of the EPLF in the diaspora invite those who fled national service to join the diaspora community with caution. Retaliation has revamped a culture of mistrust and suspicion that not only has defined the relationship between citizens and the state but also has deeply shaped the relationships between fellow citizens, increasing the ethnic, regional, and religious fractures that are already apparent in Eritrean society. In addition, the presumed existence of snitches loyal to the regime has, more than anything else, served to keep loyalists far from the recent asylum seekers who have deserted national service and are likely to be critical of the political and social situation in Eritrea.

In stimulating tensions and social fragmentations, retaliation against deserters' families has thus indirectly reinforced the current leadership in power despite the obviously unpopular effects of the retaliation in Eritrea and in the diaspora. In other words, the social consequences of the retaliation on deserters' families, caused especially by the fear of further potential retaliations, has allowed Eritrea's leaders to maintain their political influence over a significant part of the diaspora, despite the massive number of deserters. Maintaining political loyalty is of course crucial for the leadership's preservation of income generated by the 2 percent taxation and other financial contributions to the party-state institutions, while the fines and the partial control of illegal money transfers have become the means to channel resources from the dissidents. The circulation of political affects is thus key to an understanding of the dynamics and the evolution of such 'enforced transnationalism' (Al-Ali et al. 2001).

Referring to activities that took place during the Ethio-Eritrean war, scholars have highlighted the role that shame played in fostering Eritrean migrants' financial contributions to the war effort. Payments were made public, pressuring citizens to avoid the shame of not having contributed enough (Al-Ali et al. 2001: 593). At that time, when hard-won sovereignty was threatened, nationalistic momentum encouraged some to slander others, denying their 'Eritreanness' and accusing them of being traitors who had sided with the archenemy. Up to now, to oppose the current government has meant, for loyalists, to stand against the sovereignty of the Eritrean state. Enforced transnationalism, intimidation, and fear mongering were already plainly effective before independence, and this suggests that the current despotic governance is deeply rooted in such historical national processes (see Bozzini 2011b; Hepner 2009).

However, at that time, the legitimacy of the national heroes and their agenda was central to the financial mobilization of Eritreans residing abroad. National pride, carefully tailored by the EPLF in the diaspora, was undoubtedly what primarily stimulated the transnational activities of Eritreans at that time. Political pride, shame, and nowadays fear—although these do not have to be understood in a strictly historical sequence—can thus be seen as traces of historical forms of intimate attachment to the state. As this chapter has argued, they should therefore be interpreted less as epiphenomenal consequences of state rule than as constitutive technologies of political and economic governance.

Acknowledgments

I wish to express thanks to Jon Abbink, Victoria Bernal, Ola Söderström, Fabienne Glatthard, and Madeleine Reeves for comments on earlier drafts; the anonymous reviewers for their suggestions; and the editors of *Social Analysis*. I am grateful to the Swiss National Science Foundation for providing funding for this research.

David Bozzini's research analyzes the social and cultural dimensions of state measures and institutions, transnational governance, and social movements, with particular focus on bureaucratic procedures, practices of security and surveillance, and various forms of activism, protest, and resistance. Currently, Bozzini is working on a research project related to the security of information, hacktivism, and initiatives against digital surveillance. Before joining the Department of Social Sciences at the University of Fribourg in 2017, he held research positions at the Graduate Center, CUNY; the African Studies Centre in Leiden; the University of Applied Sciences and Arts of Western Switzerland (HES-SO), Geneva; and the University of Neuchâtel. He is the co-editor of *Tsantsa* (the journal of the Swiss Anthropological Association), and he teaches at the University of Basel.

Notes

1. The definitions of emotion, feeling, mood, and affect are largely contested, and the terms have often been used interchangeably in the social sciences (Ben Anderson 2006). In this chapter, an affective event or situation refers to moments that elicit specific feelings, moods, or emotions. Since emotions can translate feelings and moods, they can be shared. In this sense, emotions have relational, dynamic, and circulatory dimensions that recent literature has (re-)emphasized (e.g., Ahmed 2004; Clough 2008; Navaro-Yashin 2009).
2. 'Warsay Ykäạlo' refers to the conscripts as heirs (*warsay*) of the freedom fighters. The term *ykäạlo*, meaning 'brave' or 'capable' in Tigrinya, refers to the fighters' heroic deeds and resilience during the struggle for independence.
3. These statistics are available at http://www.unhcr.org/pages/4a02afce6.html.
4. This measure was not enforced after 2012.
5. See "Incarceration Threat for Parents Whose Children Evade Sawa," Gedab News, 17 June 2005 (accessed 8 May 2012).

References

Ahmed, Sara. 2004. "Affective Economies." *Social Text* 22 (2): 117–139.

Al-Ali, Nadje, Richard Black, and Khalid Koser. 2001. "The Limits to 'Transnationalism': Bosnian and Eritrean Refugees in Europe as Emerging Transnational Communities." *Ethnic and Racial Studies* 24 (4): 578–600.

Anderson, Ben. 2006. "Becoming and Being Hopeful: Towards a Theory of Affect." *Environment and Planning D: Society and Space* 24 (5): 733–752.

Anderson, Benedict. 1991. *Imagined Communities: Reflections on the Origin and Spread of Nationalism.* Rev. ed. London: Verso.

Aretxaga, Begoña. 2000. "A Fictional Reality: Paramilitary Death Squads and the Construction of State Terror in Spain." In Sluka 2000, 46–69.

Aretxaga, Begoña. 2003. "Maddening States." *Annual Review of Anthropology* 32: 393–410.

BBC. 2010. "Eritreans Rally against UN Sanctions." 22 February. http://news.bbc.co.uk/2/hi/8528007.stm (accessed 8 May 2012).

Bernal, Victoria. 2004. "Eritrea Goes Global: Reflections on Nationalism in a Transnational Era." *Cultural Anthropology* 19 (1): 3–25.

Bourdieu, Pierre. 1999. "Rethinking the State: Genesis and Structure of the Bureaucratic Field." Trans. Loïc J. D. Wacquant and Samar Farage. In *State/Culture: State-Formation after the Cultural Turn*, ed. George Steinmetz, 53–75. Ithaca, NY: Cornell University Press.

Bozzini, David. 2011a. "En état de siège: Ethnographie de la mobilisation nationale et de la surveillance en Érythrée." PhD diss., Institut d'ethnologie, Université de Neuchâtel.

Bozzini, David. 2011b. "Low-Tech State Surveillance: The Production of Uncertainty among Conscripts in Eritrea." *Surveillance and Society* 9 (1–2): 93–113.

Clough, Patricia T. 2008. "The Affective Turn: Political Economy, Biomedia and Bodies." *Theory, Culture & Society* 25 (1): 1–22.

Connell, Dan. 2003. "Enough! An Author's Statement." In *Taking on the Superpowers: Collected Articles on the Eritrean Revolution (1976–1982)*, xxiii–xxxv. Trenton, NJ: Red Sea Press.

Conrad, Bettina. 2006. "'A Culture of War and a Culture of Exile': Young Eritreans in Germany and Their Relations to Eritrea." *Revue européenne des migrations internationales* 22 (1): 59–85.

Daniel Ghebreselassie Anenia. 2010. "The Escape." New York. Unpublished.

EPDP (Eritrean People's Democratic Party). 2012. "EPDP Central Council Member Is Missing; Feared Kidnapped by the Cruel PFDJ Regime." http://www.harnnet.org/ (accessed 8 May 2012).

Gaim Kibreab. 2009. *Eritrea: A Dream Deferred.* Suffolk: James Currey.

Geiser, Alexandra. 2011. *Erythrée: Enlèvements au Soudan.* Bern: OSAR.

GoE (Government of Eritrea). 1995. *Awadj Hagerawi Agolgolot 1995/82.* Asmara: Government of Eritrea.

Green, Linda. 1994. "Fear as a Way of Life." *Cultural Anthropology* 9 (2): 227–256.

Greenhouse, Carol J. 2002. "Introduction: Altered States, Altered Lives." In *Ethnography in Unstable Places: Everyday Lives in Contexts of Dramatic Political Change*, ed. Carol J. Greenhouse, Elizabeth Mertz, and Kay B. Warren, 1–34. Durham, NC: Duke University Press.

Gross, Jan T. 2002. *Revolution from Abroad: The Soviet Conquest of Poland's Western Ukraine and Western Belorussia.* Pbk ed. Princeton, NJ: Princeton University Press. Originally published in 1988.

Hepner, Tricia R. 2007. "Transnational Political and Legal Dimensions of Emergent Eritrean Human Rights Movements." Migration Studies Working Paper Series No. 36. Forced Migration Studies Programme, University of the Witwatersrand.

Hepner, Tricia R. 2009. *Soldiers, Martyrs, Traitors, and Exiles: Political Conflict in Eritrea and the Diaspora.* Philadelphia: University of Pennsylvania Press.

Hepner, Tricia R. 2011. "Human Tsunamis." Counterpunch, 22 April. http://www. counterpunch.org/2011/04/22/human-tsunamis/ (accessed 8 May 2012).

Human Rights Watch. 2009. *Service for Life: State Repression and Indefinite Conscription in Eritrea.* 16 April. https://www.hrw.org/sites/default/files/reports/eritrea0409web_0.pdf.

Human Rights Watch. 2011. "Sudan: End Mass Summary Deportations of Eritreans." 25 October. http://www.hrw.org/news/2011/10/25/sudan-end-mass-summary-deportations-eritreans (accessed 8 May 2012).

International Crisis Group. 2010. "Eritrea: The Siege State." 21 September. http://www. crisisgroup.org/en/regions/africa/horn-of-africa/ethiopia-eritrea/163-eritrea-the-siege-state.aspx.

Jasper, James M. 2011. "Emotions and Social Movements: Twenty Years of Theory and Research." *Annual Review of Sociology* 37: 285–303.

Kapferer, Bruce, and Christopher C. Taylor. 2012. "Forces in the Production of the State." In *Contesting the State: The Dynamics of Resistance and Control,* ed. Angela Hobart and Bruce Kapferer, 1–20. Wantage: Sean Kingston Publishing.

Keita, Mohamed. 2010. "For Eritrean Expatriate Press, Intimidation in Exile." Asmarino, 18 June. http://asmarino.com/articles/705-for-eritrean-expatriate-press-intimidation -in-exile (accessed 8 May 2012).

Koser, Khalid. 2002. "Une diaspora divisée? Tranfers et transformations au sein de la diapora érythréenne." *Politique Africaine* 85: 64–74.

Leavitt, John. 1996. "Meaning and Feeling in the Anthropology of Emotions." *American Ethnologist* 23 (3): 514–539.

Los, Maria. 2006. "Looking into the Future: Surveillance, Globalization and the Totalitarian Potential." In *Theorizing Surveillance: The Panopticon and Beyond,* ed. David Lyon, 69–94. Devon: Willan Publishing.

Lutz, Catherine A., and Lila Abu-Lughod, eds. 1990. *Language and the Politics of Emotion.* Cambridge: Cambridge University Press.

Mitchell, Timothy. 1991. "The Limits of the State: Beyond Statist Approaches and Their Critics." *American Political Science Review* 85 (1): 77–96.

Monnat, Lucie. 2012. "Le régime érythréen racketterait sa diaspora." *Tribune de Genève,* 1 February. http://www.tdg.ch/suisse/Le-regime-erythreen-racketterait-sa-diaspora/story/13811628 (accessed 8 May 2012).

Mounier-Kuhn, Angélique. 2009. "L'Erythrée du président Afeworki, un Etat prison déserté en masse par ses habitants." *Le Temps,* 21 January.

Müller, Tanja R. 2012. "From Rebel Governance to State Consolidation—Dynamics of Loyalty and the Securitisation of the State in Eritrea." *Geoforum* 43 (4): 793–803.

Navaro-Yashin, Yael. 2005. "Confinement and the Imagination: Sovereignty and Subjectivity in a Quasi-State." In *Sovereign Bodies: Citizens, Migrants, and States in the Postcolonial World,* ed. Thomas Blom Hansen and Finn Stepputat, 103–119. Princeton, NJ: Princeton University Press.

Navaro-Yashin, Yael. 2009. "Affective Spaces, Melancholic Objects: Ruination and the Production of Anthropological Knowledge." *Journal of the Royal Anthropological Institute* 15 (1): 1–18.

Reddy, William M. 1999. "Emotional Liberty: Politics and History in the Anthropology of Emotions." *Cultural Anthropology* 14 (2): 256–288.

Rev, Istvan. 1987. "The Advantages of Being Atomized: How Hungarian Peasants Coped with Collectivization." *Dissent* 34 (3): 335–350.

Rice, Xan. 2009. "Eritrea 'Like a Giant Prison', Claims Human Rights Group." *Guardian*, 16 April.

Richard, Analiese, and Daromir Rudnyckyj. 2009. "Economies of Affect." *Journal of the Royal Anthropological Institute* 15 (1): 57–77.

Rudnyckyj, Daromir. 2011. "Circulating Tears and Managing Hearts: Governing through Affect in an Indonesian Steel Factory." *Anthropological Theory* 11 (1): 63–87.

Ruth Iyob. 2000. "The Ethiopian-Eritrean Conflict: Diasporic vs. Hegemonic States in the Horn of Africa, 1991–2000." *Journal of Modern African Studies* 38 (4): 659–682.

Schweri, Michel. 2010. "Plus de trois mille Erythréens mobilisés à Genève." *Le Courrier*, 23 Februrary. http://www.lecourrier.ch/plus_de_trois_mille_erythreens_mobilises_a_geneve (accessed 8 May 2012).

Sluka, Jeffrey A., ed. 2000. *Death Squad: The Anthropology of State Terror*. Philadelphia: University of Pennsylvania Press.

Spencer, Jonathan. 2007. *Anthropology, Politics, and the State: Democracy and Violence in South Asia*. Cambridge: Cambridge University Press.

Svašek, Maruška. 2010. "On the Move: Emotions and Human Mobility." *Journal of Ethnic and Migration Studies* 36 (6): 865–880.

Taussig, Michael. 1984. "Culture of Terror, Space of Death: Roger Casement's Putumayo Report and the Explanation of Torture." *Comparative Studies in Society and History* 26 (3): 467–497.

Taussig, Michael. 1992. *The Nervous System*. New York: Routledge.

Tekle Woldemikael. 1991. "Political Mobilization and Nationalist Movements: The Case of the Eritrean People's Liberation Front." *Africa Today* 38 (2): 31–42.

Tilly, Charles. 2006. *Regimes and Repertoires*. Chicago: University of Chicago Press.

Treiber, Magnus. 2004. *Der Traum vom guten Leben: Die eritreische warsay-Generation im Asmara der zweiten Nachkriegszeit*. Münster: LIT-Verlag.

Trouillot, Michel-Rolph. 2001. "The Anthropology of the State in the Age of Globalization: Close Encounters of the Deceptive Kind." *Current Anthropology* 42 (1): 125–138.

UNHCR. 2009. *UNHCR Eligibility Guidelines for Assessing the International Protection Needs of Asylum-Seekers from Eritrea*. Geneva: UNHCR. http://www.refworld.org/pdfid/49de06122.pdf.

UNHCR. 2011. "UNHCR Dismay at New Deportation of Eritreans by Sudan." 18 October. http://www.unhcr.org/refworld/docid/4e9d6b882.html (accessed 8 May 2012).

Verdery, Katherine. 2014. *Secrets and Truth: Ethnography in the Archive of Romania's Secret Police*. Budapest: Central European University Press.

Wedeen, Lisa. 1998. "Acting 'As If': Symbolic Politics and Social Control in Syria." *Comparative Studies in Society and History* 40 (3): 503–523.

Chapter 3

"RECOGNIZE THE SPIES"
Transparency and Political Power in Uzbek Cyberspace

Sarah Kendzior

On 19 May 2011, Aleksey Mitrofanov, a Russian politician and blogger, announced that a revolution was taking place in Uzbekistan. "What I said years ago would happen is finally happening—unfortunately," Mitrofanov (2011) reported on his blog for the radio station Echo Moscow. "On 18 May, 10,000 people in Tashkent and 15,000 in Ferghana and Andijon took to the streets. In Andijon and Ferghana, people were shot. The exact number of victims is not known ... External signals have been received. The internal pressure is phenomenal. Everything is ready to explode."

Uzbekistan's mass uprising came as news to the people of Uzbekistan. On 21 May, Ferghana News, an independent Central Asian news agency and website sympathetic to dissident causes, asked its readers to corroborate Mitrofanov's claims. Uzbeks responded that the streets of Uzbekistan were as quiet as ever and denounced Mitrofanov as a provocateur. But soon the topic turned to whether this rumor could ever become a reality. "Of course nothing will happen, the

Notes for this chapter begin on page 63.

Uzbeks are weak!" proclaimed one reader, adding: "There are more agents of the national security services than there are people! In the comments posted [on the Ferghana website] there is one NSS [national security service] agent after another!" Other Uzbeks agreed. "Don't go on this site if you're from Uzbekistan," cautioned one of them. "Half the people reading and writing are in the NSS." Another reader warned: "Quietly, law enforcement agencies, including the NSS, are reading and commenting on this and other sites ... use a proxy server."[1] A conversation about whether revolution was possible had turned into a conversation about whether discussing revolution online was possible. In the mind of most readers, both were ill-advised, and for the same reason—the unseen, ubiquitous presence of Uzbekistan's national security services.

In this chapter, I examine how the specter of Uzbekistan's national security services has shaped Uzbek online political discourse, curtailing prospects for activism despite the Internet's potential for fomenting political change. "In a system of ubiquitous spying ... everybody may be a police agent and each individual feels himself under constant surveillance," Hannah Arendt ([1951] 1968: 431) wrote of Stalin's totalitarian regime, a description equally apt for authoritarian post-Soviet states like Uzbekistan, whose national security services (NSS) are the literal and figurative heirs to the KGB. From 1991, when it became an independent state after the collapse of the Soviet Union, until his death in 2016, Uzbekistan was ruled by Islam Karimov, a Communist apparatchik turned nationalist dictator who retained the most pernicious aspects of Soviet rule. Obsessed with threats to his power, Karimov employed a massive security apparatus to monitor the activities of real and perceived opponents and scan the population for signs of dissent. The NSS holds jurisdiction over the Ministry of the Interior, which operates the national guard and special forces as well as the ubiquitous *militsiya* (police) forces that patrol Uzbekistan's streets. Citizens have come to fear the frequent and arbitrary arrests made by NSS agents, who, operating under no legal oversight, comprise the most powerful internal security force in Central Asia.

The Internet, at first glance, would seem to offer sanctuary from the surveillance of the state. On the Internet, Uzbeks can access censored information, debate controversial topics, and find like-minded individuals with whom to organize for political change. They can operate in secrecy, cloaking themselves in anonymous avatars, or can connect through semi-closed social media networks such as Facebook. Many Uzbeks use the Internet to voice dissent, particularly since 2005, when a government massacre of protesters in Andijon prompted Uzbekistan's journalists and dissidents to flee the country and reconnect later online.[2] Since 2005, dissidents have published censored works, written exposés on state crimes, and attempted to lay bare the secrets of one the world's most closed and brutal regimes. Such acts of transparency, as Clare Birchall (2011: 134) notes, are often lauded as a panacea for political problems, particularly when they involve the Internet, which many have cited as an ideal medium through which to incite political change.[3] "The enduring belief in transparency persists," Birchall argues, "because we like to think that revolution and transparency lead to more knowledge, to knowability, but the unknowable is always at play" (ibid.: 146). For Uzbek dissidents, the great unknowable is the NSS, which has damaged attempts to mobilize despite never being caught participating directly in Uzbek online communities. It is enough that they *seem* to be intervening, that they are certainly listening, monitoring, and recording—and that it is impossible for Uzbeks to use the Internet without accepting this as inevitable. The NSS inhibits whatever space they inhabit—physical, psychic, and virtual. Far from being a means to evade Uzbek state control, the Internet is an NSS playground.

In this chapter, I use the example of the NSS during Karimov's rule to reflect on how the psychic hold of a police state manifests itself on the Internet. Numerous scholars have examined the police as an "all-pervasive, ghostly presence" (Benjamin 1978: 287)—a shadow entity that exerts a psychic force as powerful as the physical force it wields (cf. Aretxaga 2003; Derrida 1991). "The spectral double of the police acts like the permanent body of the state, a presence interiorized as the law, at once fearful and paternalistic, familiar and strange, uncanny, a presence that one cannot shake out of oneself," writes Begoña Aretxaga (2003: 406) of this elusive yet pervasive power. What happens, then, when this 'spectral double' manifests itself in a medium renowned for its transparency, a medium that some trumpet as a veritable guarantor of democracy because it forces state secrets into the open? I contend that the psychic power of the security forces is reaffirmed online even as its physical presence—and to some degree its air of mystery—diminishes. There are two arguments for this. The first is that while the Internet may give citizens a newfound ability to interact and organize, it does not ameliorate their pre-existing fears, biases, and suspicions—in fact, it often exacerbates them. In previous works (Kendzior 2006, 2011), I discussed how the emergence of Uzbek opposition websites in 2005 reified the cynical political culture of Uzbek dissidents and furthered their internal fractiousness. In these pages, I explore cynicism's frequent partner, paranoia, and how it has similarly inhibited Uzbek political activity. Uzbek paranoia is to some extent a logical response to extreme circumstances—what George Marcus (1999) characterizes as 'paranoia within reason'—but it is also a reflection of what Jonathan Bach (2010: 288) calls "paranoia [as] a structural condition of rule." The paranoia that has structured Uzbekistan during its two decades of independent statehood does not dissolve on the Internet; rather, it is amplified and given new life.

This brings me to my second argument: that there are qualities inherent to the architecture of the Internet that breed paranoia, despite—and occasionally because of—the 'transparency' conferred by the medium. In recent years, numerous scholars have raised concerns about the erosion of online privacy (Nissenbaum 2009; Solove 2007; Zittrain 2008), the tyranny of digital memory (Lanier 2010; Mayer-Schönberger 2009), and the use of the Internet for state surveillance (Kalathil and Boas 2003; Morozov 2011). Most of these concerns have revolved around the consolidation of what was once the Internet's very human chaos into impersonal monopolies on knowledge and information, such as Google, Facebook, and Wikipedia, which are controlled by powerful corporations or faceless 'crowds'. Internet users have become anxious about personal data posted online, who accesses it, and how users can change or erase their own information—often coming to the terrible realization that they cannot. In a perceptive essay for the *New Yorker*, Adam Gopnik (2011) describes the way that "the Internet gets inside us": "Everything once inside is outside, a click away; much that used to be outside is inside, experienced in solitude. And so the peacefulness, the serenity that we feel away from the Internet ... has less to do with being no longer harried by others than with being less oppressed by the force of your own inner life." It is relief, in other words, from a kind of paranoia: an incessant patrolling of the digital self.

For Uzbek dissidents, the Internet has given rise to twin anxieties: suspicion that others are not who they say they are, but are in fact NSS agents, and unease about what the NSS will do with the digital trail they are leaving behind. Both of these fears are rooted in paranoia shaped by life in a police state, but they have become magnified by the Internet's increased orientation toward the rote display of private life. The architecture of Web 2.0, with its ceaseless imperative to reveal all (and its merciless cataloging of all that one has revealed) prompts users to stroll gaily into the panopticon only to regret it later. In a paranoid political culture, such transparency is more than just 'oversharing': it is a form of political powerlessness. In a landmark study of paranoia in politics, Elias Canetti (1973: 292) noted: "Power is impenetrable. The man who has it sees through other men, but does not allow them to see through him." As Uzbek dissidents become progressively more open online, the silence of the NSS becomes deafening, and so the NSS becomes, perversely, the object of their obsession. Online, Uzbek dissidents wrestle with competing desires: to inform other Uzbeks about their activity (in public) and to lay the groundwork for what that activity will be (in secret). Both of these goals are inhibited by the dual mechanisms of Internet and state surveillance. Much as most of us have internalized the Internet, so have Uzbeks internalized the NSS, and the combination of self-consciousness and suspiciousness that results is a serious impediment to mobilization.

In the remainder of this chapter, I discuss how the specter of the NSS shapes online Uzbek political life. First, I trace the development of Uzbekistan's paranoid political culture under Karimov and examine the NSS as an *olabo'ji*, or 'boogeyman'—a shadow entity bestowed with almost unworldly power. Second, I explore the NSS as a weapon that online dissidents use against each other in their internal politics. Here I examine the accusations of 'spying' that dissidents routinely lob to discredit each other and how the murky online presence of the NSS has exacerbated pre-existing political tensions. While frightening as a specter, the NSS is perhaps even more unnerving when its mechanisms are revealed. Warning that the power of the state does not dissipate even when 'unmasked', Aretxaga (2003: 401) writes: "On the contrary, such mystifying power often seems to be augmented by such unveiling of the state's scandalous life, triggering an endless proliferation of discourses about the state at all levels of social life." The Internet has allowed dissidents, as Aretxaga puts it, "to gaze into the labyrinthine interiority of state being" (ibid.) as never before. But these revelations do not reassure anyone of the state's inherent weakness; instead, they stoke paranoia by making a shadow force 'real' in a medium where reality is always in question, where the self is always in check.

Paranoia and the State: The NSS as Boogeyman

Before exploring the issue of paranoia in Uzbek online politics, it is important to explain how paranoia functions as a mechanism of the Uzbek state. Uzbekistan's late president, Islam Karimov, rose to power on a nationalist platform largely borrowed from the Uzbek opposition (*muxolifat*) that had emerged in the aftermath of Mikhail Gorbachev's *glasnost'* and *perestroika* reforms. When Uzbekistan became independent after the collapse of the Soviet Union—an unexpected development that many Uzbeks greeted with unease—Karimov, then first secretary of the Uzbek Communist Party, became president. He began consolidating his rule in two ways: by promoting what Andrew March (2003) calls an 'ideology of national independence', a teleological progression of the Uzbek nation-state from which Karimov's power and policies were assumed to naturally flow, and by constructing a massive security apparatus to ensure that his ideology was put into practice. (Conversely, as March notes, the ideology was used to justify Karimov's authoritarian control.) From 1992, Karimov outlawed opposition parties, censored independent media, banned foreign travel, and arrested citizens deemed inappropriately political or religious. Nick Megoran (2008) links these policies to what he describes as Karimov's 'discourse of danger', which asserted that Uzbekistan is constantly under threat from hostile forces. Karimov's written works, mandatory readings in Uzbekistan's schools and universities, warned Uzbeks that they are vulnerable to 'secret and open attacks' and that the state is their only protection. Karimov assured Uzbeks of their inherent greatness, linking it to a primordial Uzbek *ma'naviyat*, or 'morality', but he insisted that this moral fiber is in constant threat of decay due to the conspiracies of foreigners, Islamic terrorists, and any individual who can be linked with either of the two. Creatively applied, this could be almost anyone. Dissidents were routinely cast as 'enemies of the people' whose *o'zbekchilik* (Uzbekness) was always in question.

In an insightful analysis of paranoia in politics that draws on theories advanced by Canetti, Bach (2010: 294) argues that the success of a ruler can be evaluated by how effectively he or she draws the population into his delusion: "The more paranoid a ruler becomes, the more essential it is that others share the ruler's system of delusions and conspiracies. This leads to what we can identify as successful and unsuccessful paranoid rulers in Canetti's structure of rule: The *successful* paranoid ruler will make the people share his paranoia, and they will feed on it together." In this respect, Karimov can be seen as a successful paranoid ruler—in part because he succeeded in blending his national ideology so seamlessly with the manpower needed to maintain it, but also because his carefully calibrated rhetoric taps into genuine anxieties of Uzbek citizens, solidifying their notions of citizenship in the shaky aftermath of the Soviet Union's collapse. As Megoran (2008), Kendzior (2011), and others note, Karimov's propaganda reflects values—national autonomy, moderate Islam, sanctity of family—that many Uzbeks hold and want to protect, including members of the Uzbek opposition, who do not oppose state ideology but seek to make it legitimate in practice. It is not 'the state' that scares dissidents—indeed, a good number of opposition members served in the Karimov administration in the early years of Uzbekistan's independence and helped create its national ideology. Rather, they fear its shadow forces: the very forces tasked with protecting Uzbek citizens from people like them. For the opposition, the NSS is an inverted mirror of state-sanctioned paranoia.

Although always immense, the NSS has grown significantly since 2005, the same year in which the number of Uzbek dissident websites increased. On 13 May 2005, a large protest in the city of Andijon over the country's deteriorating social and political conditions was suppressed by state troops who fired indiscriminately into the crowd, killing around 800 people. As a result of the Andijon violence and the brutal crackdown on dissents that followed, most of Uzbekistan's opposition fled into exile, where they began creating anti-government websites. Back in Uzbekistan, the NSS was expanded so that it subsumed the interior ministry and the police, giving rise to a state security apparatus so enormous that in 2007 it staged its own 'Olympic' games. The NSS was also put in charge of monitoring the Internet and circumventing the sudden proliferation of dissident material. NSS officials patrol Uzbekistan's cyber cafés, curtail access with blocks and firewalls, and track and arrest users attempting to download illicit content. One Uzbek in Tashkent, who was trying to visit an opposition website in 2006, found an NSS officer at his door within minutes (IWPR 2006). Others have reported being beaten or arrested by NSS agents shortly after posting controversial content, and still others have reported that their personal e-mails and social media pages have been hacked (Front Line Defenders 2010). Already in 2011, NSS officers began confiscating laptops at the airport, checking browsing history, and interrogating anyone with a record of visiting websites critical of the government.[4]

Judging by the lengths to which the NSS goes in order to control Internet access—Uzbekistan now has some of the most severe Internet restrictions in the world, despite the small proportion of citizens online—it is clear that the regime sees the Internet as a threat. And to some degree it is, in that it enters an element of unpredictability into the veneer of state control. Yet when one examines Uzbek online works about the security services, one finds not a sense of empowerment over the ability to remark openly about government crimes but rather frustration that the NSS's enigma endures even in an era of digital transparency.

In 2009, a prominent Uzbek blogger remarked on his futile search for information about the state's shadow organs: "Every morning, I type 'national security services' [*milliy xavfsizlik xizmati*] into Google. This is like hiring a poor laborer to excavate an immense treasure trove—you can't find what you're looking for, and eventually I'm dragged downward, that is, into the place of the President of the Republic of Uzbekistan." He noted that government websites describe in detail all internal branches but one—the NSS—and added a list of questions that, in an ideal world, Uzbek journalists would be able to ask their government: How many people are in the NSS? How does it function? Who are their leaders? What are their official roles? These are basic questions, and the fact that they remain elusive in an era of unparalleled information access only highlights the NSS's impenetrability. On the Internet, the imbalance of power that persists on the ground in Uzbekistan is replicated: dissidents make themselves newly visible in order to attract adherents, while the NSS remains a cipher, listening without being heard.

Some Uzbek dissidents, unable to diminish the security services' power through exposure, focus their online efforts on critiquing the NSS's psychic hold. One such example, published in April 2006 on the no longer active dissident website Muslim Uzbekistan, is a popular article titled "Is it the Boogeyman or the *Militsiya*?" Written pseudonymously by a member of the Uzbek political opposition, the article opens with an anecdote from the author's youth. Every day, before his mother would leave for work on the collective farm, she would tell the author: "If your baby brother wakes up and cries, rock the cradle. If that doesn't work, tell him the boogeyman [*olabo'ji*] is coming, and that will make him afraid not to sleep." "Who is the boogeyman?" the author asked. "From what I know, he was some sort of shah [*podsho*], some murderous tyrant [*odamxur*]," she said. "I think he was the son or grandson of Genghis Khan. Or maybe a wild beast. I don't know, this is something we learned about from our parents. They scared us by saying the boogeyman was coming, so we would pretend to be asleep." Years later, the author was married with children of his own. One night, while his wife was putting the children to bed, he overheard her say: "Sleep, stay quiet, the *militsiya* are coming. You must sleep or else they will take you." Startled, he asked his wife why she had said this. "Why, all mothers tell this to their children," she replied. "This is how they scare their children to sleep."

"Is it the Boogeyman or the *Militsiya*?" which was widely reprinted across the Uzbek web, is notable for its assertion of tyranny as an Uzbek inevitability, positioning the state security forces as the modern incarnation of the ruthless rulers of Uzbekistan's past. Fear has always been an Uzbek weapon, one that Uzbek mothers have long wielded over their beloved children and that the Uzbek government now wields over its people. The story argues that a primal power is at work, lulling people into complacency not through its outright assertion of force, but through the subtle way it renders people unwilling to act. "The *militsiya* are our own," the article concludes sarcastically. "In an independent country, is it not good to have everything be our own? How else will mothers get their children to sleep? *Or is it time to wake up?*" Comparing the modern *militsiya* to the shahs and khans of yore—who were promoted by the Karimov administration as predecessors and role models—the author inverts the administration's ideology of national independence, portraying Uzbeks as automatons paralyzed by their own paranoia, their centuries of subjugation a natural counterpart to their rulers' unyielding power.

In 2009, I interviewed the author of this article, a well-known dissident and former Karimov administration official. He told me that his tale of the boogeyman was not the only work he had written about the state security services. In 2007, as he was hiding out in neighboring Kyrgyzstan, he published a series of online articles written under a different pseudonym—he has over a dozen—about the NSS's illegal attempts to track him down. Like the boogeyman story, these articles served no pragmatic purpose other than to attest to the perseverance and power of the police. Most Uzbeks who read them were sympathetic to the protagonist's plight, but they offered no suggestions that might help him. Instead, they merely offered their condolences as he chronicled his doom. Readers also had no idea that the articles were in fact written by the subject of the story. The author told me that he used pseudonyms to protect his family, who are still in Uzbekistan, because he feared recrimination would be worse if the NSS knew he was writing about them online. Yet he wanted his story to be told—if only to serve as a reminder that, even abroad, no Uzbek is safe. Now living out of the country, he sometimes publishes under his own name and at other times under a pseudonym, writing articles about his persecution in and outside of Uzbekistan and occasionally deciding to delete them later. He is torn between chastising Uzbeks for their cowardice and being prudent as to his own protection. In order to participate in the Internet's open environment, he must close himself off.

In a study of Stalin's legacy in Siberia, Caroline Humphrey (2003: 184–185), drawing on Freud, notes that the reason "paranoic projections and identifications are closed, that is, resistant to unraveling ... is because *there is in fact a certain truth to them.*" It is in this way that the paranoid political culture of Uzbekistan is perpetuated on the Internet even by those seeking to escape it. The aforementioned dissident writes of the *militsiya* as boogeyman to criticize how Uzbeks have internalized their oppressors, cowering like children at their grandiose power. Yet in relaying the story of his own persecution, he proves that there is good reason for this fear. Criticizing the NSS online may be an act of defiance, in that it contradicts the Uzbek government's representation of itself as just and benevolent, but it also reminds Uzbeks that they are in constant danger—that, in fact, the boogeyman is *real*.

"It is on the basis of secrecy that states work their magic," writes David Nugent (2010: 699), echoing other studies that link the control of secrecy to the establishment of social order (Penglase 2009; Taussig 1997). Ironically, as the NSS is written about online, its magic only grows, because the only 'secret' revealed is the open secret of its brutality: a fact that the Uzbek government hardly wants advertised but that every Uzbek already knows. In the next section, I address how the specter of the security services has damaged relationships between dissidents, who must not only grapple with the NSS's looming online presence, but also learn to deal with those who leverage it for personal and political gain.

Paranoia in the Opposition: The NSS as a Weapon

In February 2007, Isyonkor, a popular Uzbek dissident website that became inactive in 2008, published an article titled "Josuslarni tanib oling!" (Recognize the Spies!). The author, a prominent dissident living in the United States, called upon members of the opposition to free themselves from "NSS games" by becoming more vigilant in their online environment. He described three spies who frequent Uzbek opposition websites ("a master at computers," "a man close to an opposition leader," "a person who knows almost everyone in every opposition group"), but he gave no names. Immediately, the comments section was filled with speculation about who the spies might be. Among the suggested culprits were the editor of the website, the writer of the article, and several of the commenters. Other readers decried the article, wondering why Isyonkor, at that time the most influential of Uzbek websites, would publish such an inflammatory piece.

An accusation of spying is one of the most effective ways to sabotage an Uzbek opposition member or group. Since I began reading Uzbek dissident websites in 2006, such allegations have appeared with increasing frequency. Dissidents are routinely denounced as *josuslar* (spies), *SNBchi/MXX xodimlari* (NSS officers), or *maxsus xizmatchilar* (secret agents), sometimes in articles written by other dissidents, but more often in comments left by anonymous readers. To some extent, the accusations of spying are a by-product of the long-standing fractiousness of the Uzbek opposition, which has been at war with itself since it emerged in the late 1980s. In 1990, Birlik (Unity), the first Uzbek opposition group, split when dissatisfied dissidents left to form Erk (Will), a rival group. Both were outlawed in the early 1990s, and many of their members were jailed or forced into exile. Since the Andijon events of 2005 and the simultaneous rise of Uzbek political websites, a number of new opposition groups have emerged, but they have been as plagued with infighting and as politically ineffective as past groups.

In a previous work (Kendzior 2011), I argued that the Internet strengthens the cynical culture of Uzbek dissidents because the qualities that make online communities so attractive—the ability to speak freely, to post anonymously, to enter uninvited and disappear without warning—are the very features that foster internal contention. The same can be said about the Uzbek political culture of paranoia. Uzbek dissidents assume that their online environment is being monitored and that what they say can be used against them. Some dissidents use pseudonyms and comment anonymously in order to protect themselves. However, they are aware that others are also acting under aliases and that agents of the NSS may be among them. 'Outing' another dissident as an agent can be an act of loyalty to other dissidents, an act of personal vengeance against a political rival, or itself an act of NSS deception—that is, an NSS agent posing as a dissident accuses a dissident of posing as an NSS agent. On the Internet, there is no way to tell. Furthermore, there is no need to tell—the rumor itself is the problem.

Several scholars have noted the way that rumor constructs an 'alternative public sphere' (Perice 1997), which gains salience when the rumors are presented in a written form (Bubant 2008; Herriman 2010). For Uzbek dissidents growing up in a propagandistic police state, the 'alternative public sphere' has long been the *only* public sphere, a claim that could arguably be made for many post-Soviet authoritarian states (Komaromi 2008). Uzbek news travels through *mish-mish* (gossip) as pervasively as through official channels, but the assumption that all information is unreliable, and all sources biased, has had the perverse effect of ensuring that all rumor is taken seriously. This is not to say all rumor is believed—on the contrary, most information is received with skepticism—but that it is shared, parsed, and discussed to a degree belying its dubious origins. Rumors that spies are posing as dissidents have a particular insidiousness because they exacerbate paranoia about the omnipresence of the NSS as well as a general inclination to distrust fellow dissidents. To spread such a rumor is to exploit a weakness in Internet culture that inherently favors the state. After all, there is no doubt that the NSS is spying on everyone—the only question left is, who are its agents? That is an inflammatory question when expressed orally, but expressed on the Internet, where it is endlessly copied and cached, it is a question that stops attempts at political organization dead in their tracks.

In the aftermath of the 2011 Arab uprisings, two new Uzbek opposition groups emerged, vowing to capitalize on the revolutionary fervor and foment similar events in Uzbekistan. The first group, Yetar (Enough), which described itself as a youth group, planned to organize a massive rally in Tashkent in July 2011. Its plans were announced via a memo e-mailed to Yangi Dunyo—a popular news site and the successor to the aforementioned Isyonkor—on the unfortunate date of 1 April. The Uzbeks who did not believe it to be an April Fool's Day joke immediately presumed it to be a government plot and asked Yetar to identify its leadership. Yetar, whose e-mail address was the unhelpful etar2011@gmail.com, responded by saying it could not reveal any information about its membership online because doing so would jeopardize its operation.

The transparency of the Internet was what allowed a fledgling dissident group like Yetar to attract public attention, and it was also the very thing that made the group operate in secret. This was both plausible and completely infuriating (infuriating, in a sense, because it was so plausible), and dissidents devoted a great deal of time trying to ascertain the legitimacy of the group. In late May 2011, a Yetar representative announced, via dissident websites and Facebook, that the group was canceling its July protest "due to incredible measures taken against our peaceful protest by the Uzbek authorities, who put our own people involved in the organization in the country under suspicion, and Karimov's willingness to use weapons against peaceful demonstrators."[5] Readers responded to this news by again raising the specter of the NSS. Some claimed that the NSS was responsible for spying on Yetar online and ruining their revolution; others reiterated the claim that Yetar was in fact the NSS and that the whole thing had been devised by the Uzbek government to make uprisings seem unfeasible.

Both of these are reasonable but also paranoid assumptions, and, in the end, they are damaging. Yetar's emergence coincided with the formation of a second new group, O'zbekiston Xalq Harakati (O'XH, People's Movement of Uzbekistan), a merger of several pre-existing Uzbek dissident groups headed by Uzbekistan's most famous dissident, Muhammad Salih, a poet, the Erk leader, and a former presidential candidate. Because Yetar and the O'XH appeared at the same time—the same time, notably, that the aforementioned Russian politician Mitrofanov was fabricating stories about violently suppressed protests—many readers of Uzbek websites expressed suspicion that the sudden appearance of both parties was part of a government plot to lure dissidents into

NSS-patrolled groups. Unlike with Yetar, few dissidents doubted the O'XH's veracity—some of its members are quite famous—but they did doubt the group's motivation and remained skeptical of its plans for revolution. Whether or not Yetar existed, the fact that it announced its goals on the Internet, and then renounced them as untenable, made similar announcements from other groups seem dubious as well. Was Yetar real? Was the O'XH a government plot? It almost does not matter because the Internet flattens the distance between accusation and information, making rumors as meaningful as the reality. From June 2011 to April 2012, the first entry about the O'XH in Google was not the group's own website, but a popular article published on multiple dissident websites titled "The People's Party of Uzbekistan Is a Secret NSS Operation."[6] There was nothing anyone could do to change that.[7]

Allegations of NSS involvement are damaging when aimed at groups, but are particularly pernicious when they concern the reputation of individual dissidents. This brings me to a scandal that emerged in the online dissident community in the spring of 2011. To some degree, I am hesitant to relate it, as any attempt to chronicle interpersonal conflict on the Internet has the potential to worsen it by duplicating, and reifying, spurious accusations. Although the information I cite is publicly available, I am not using names so as to avoid the damage incurred when one's Google results designate one as a traitor or a spy. Such is the paradox of writing an article about political rumor on the Internet: in trying to understand the rules, you inevitably become part of the game.

In February 2011, the editor of an Uzbek website accused a prominent dissident of being a member of the NSS. Both parties were exiles living close to each other abroad, and when the editor hurt his hand in a car accident, he enlisted the help of the dissident to run his website. During his tenure, the dissident published articles in which he accused various asylum-seeking Uzbek refugees of being Islamic terrorists. The editor, incensed by what he thought was the smearing of vulnerable parties, announced that this confirmed his suspicion that the dissident was actually a regime agent, adding that he had witnessed the dissident spying on Uzbeks abroad and reporting his findings to government agents. He accused the dissident of purposefully trying to stir up trouble in the opposition and endangering Uzbek refugees.[8]

According to the editor, the dissident responded to these accusations by threatening to hurt the editor's relatives in Uzbekistan, and the editor went to the police of the European country in which they both lived. The police promised to look into it, and in the meantime the editor published a series of articles detailing the various ways that the opposition had been compromised by the traitor in their midst. These allegations were echoed by readers in the comments section of his and other websites—but along with them came new allegations against the editor. Since 2005, the editor has also been accused of being in the NSS numerous times, in part because his brother-in-law had worked briefly for the security services. The editor and his wife have protested those who have said that this means they, too, are guilty of NSS involvement, claiming that the brother-in-law had enlisted only to investigate the murder of his father, a Soviet-era dissident who had been murdered by the KGB from the inside.

This anecdote likely strikes those unfamiliar with Uzbek politics as unduly dramatic, gossipy, and conspiratorial—but what is important to note is that underlying each accusation is vulnerability about the Uzbek virtual environment and the people who inhabit it. Each claim has the ring of truth and precedent: the Karimov regime had, in fact, used the Internet to smear innocent people as terrorists, and dissidents have, in the past, shifted their allegiances to the government while in exile. There is no reason *not* to believe anything, and so it falls on the accused to build a case for their innocence, not by defending their own honor—for who would believe them?—but by publicly speculating on the nature of their accusers and, most notably, on the nature of the Internet itself.

In March 2011, the accused dissident attempted to clear his name in an article published on another website. First noting that for the Uzbek opposition, "the words 'secret agent' and 'informer' have come to mean much more than the words 'fight, freedom, and the future of the people,'" he goes on to ask his readers to "think logically about what an agent is." The first task of an agent, he states, is to infiltrate parties, find out who their leaders are, and learn their ideas. Since the Uzbek opposition has no functional parties, leaders, or ideas, he continues sarcastically, they are immune in this respect. The second task is to keep track of developments. This is a ridiculous task, he implies, since Uzbeks exaggerate everything they are doing and use online aliases to make their ranks seem larger. The third task of an agent is to infiltrate the dissident community by making friends through e-mail and Skype. Here the dissident's snarky tone disappears, and he becomes reflective:

> Ask yourself: How do I know [dissident's name]? And then you will realize that they [his accusers] do not, and that you have become a 'victim' of Internet provocateurs, who impose their opinions and personal hatred on others, namely, you. The result is that you become a 'zombie' who struggles not just with the dictatorship, but with your colleagues. Subjected to others' opinions, you start to hate people whom you have never seen. Only the Uzbek opposition, with the aid of Internet journalism, would make a hero out of a former agent of the NSS[9] and check those who escaped for validity, accusing their former friends and colleagues of being agents of the NSS and MVD [Ministry of Internal Affairs]. So it is best not to believe the gossip, and always try to talk with someone if possible.

What is notable about this response is that the dissident accuses the Internet, as a medium, of creating the same paranoid conditions that the NSS is said to intentionally provoke. Much as a fellow Uzbek writer drew a comparison between the boogeyman and the *militsiya*, here Uzbek Internet users are rendered as 'zombies', manipulated by a torrent of information that they can never verify, but which seems to confirm all their worst suspicions. The Internet, in other words, does the NSS's dirty work for it. To some degree, this is an unfair reification of an impersonal medium—but it is the impersonal nature of the medium, combined with the very personal accusations of the people who use it, that makes it so perilous. Participants in Uzbek online communities face the scrutiny not only of amorphous regime agents, but of their peers, who clock and catalogue their suspicions. This dissident's discomfiting declaration—that the illusion of the NSS is as effective as the reality—shows how hard it is for Uzbek activists to build the trusting relationships on which political action is premised.

Conclusion

For Uzbek dissidents, the Internet is not a revolution but an evolution, whereby the long-standing political culture of cynicism and paranoia has been shifted into a medium that both circumvents the conditions that generated it—the Uzbek state—and strengthens its most pernicious aspects. Praising the Internet's potential to augur political transparency fails to account for what 'transparency' means to the people who use it. Uzbek dissidents who expose the corruption of the Uzbek state are never liberated from its control, not only because of the pervasive psychological hold the state wields, but also because of the Internet itself. Individuals who fear being watched or followed have voluntarily placed themselves in a medium that allows people to watch or follow them. While the Internet offers the opportunity for connection, it also allows for pseudonymity and anonymity that bolster internal suspicions. The architecture of Web 2.0 lends itself well to organizations like the NSS despite the best efforts of dissidents to use the medium to their advantage.

Aretxaga (2003: 397) notes how security apparatuses lock the "state's own citizens in a paranoiac gaze that curtails civil rights and extends terror through the social field." Although the Internet has been heralded as a sanctuary from repressive regimes, for Uzbeks fleeing the NSS, it provides little relief. Whether online or offline, the 'social field' of Uzbeks is comprised of social relationships based on a shared experience of cynical and paranoid political culture. The Internet reaffirms the police state's panopticon: one does not know who is watching or why—only that one is being watched. The digital gaze of the NSS is both external and internal, frightening in its presence and unnerving in its absence. That Uzbeks may be watched by those with whom they have established direct interpersonal relationships—agents posing as dissidents, or dissidents suspected of being agents—further complicates the idea of the Internet as a venue for 'free' expression. The experience of Uzbek dissidents scattered around the world suggests that when the state's "powerful insubstantiality" (Taussig 1992: 113) is technologically amplified by the Internet, its threatening force is able to inhibit whatever space the citizens inhabit—physical, psychic, and virtual. The affect of fear and paranoia created by interaction between citizens and real or imagined agents of the state follows them even into exile or refuge, far beyond the state's physical borders (cf. Bozzini, this book). The Internet, rather than freeing dissidents from fear of the state, amplifies and extends the reach of its gaze across not only social spaces, but physical ones as well.

Acknowledgments

The author would like to thank Madeleine Reeves and other participants of the workshop "Affective States: Exploring Emotion in Political Life," held in 2012 at the University of Manchester, for their helpful feedback on an earlier draft of this chapter.

Sarah Kendzior is an award-winning independent journalist, writer, researcher, and critic whose multifaceted work focuses mainly on US and Central Asian politics. She received her PhD in Anthropology from Washington University in St. Louis. Currently, she is an op-ed columnist for the *Globe and Mail*. She has written for outlets such as Al Jazeera English and Radio Free Europe, and her articles have appeared in the *Guardian*, *New York Times*, *Chicago Tribune*, and *La Stampa*, as well as academic journals that include *American Ethnologist*, *Central Asian Survey*, and *Nationalities Papers*. She recently published a collection of essays, *The View from the Flyover Country* (2015).

Notes

1. See "Uzbekistan: Rumors of Mass Unrest in Several Cities Have Not Been Confirmed," Ferghana News Agency, 20 May 2011, http://www.fergananews.com/news.php?id = 16758&mode = snews.
2. See Kendzior (2006) and Megoran (2008) for more on the Andijon events and Kendzior (2011) for more on Uzbek dissident websites.
3. See Shirky (2008) for a representative example.
4. "Farg'ona aeroportida yo'lovchilar noutbuki tekshirilmoqda" [Visitors to the Ferghana Airport Are Having Their Laptop Computers Searched], Ozodlik Radio, 6 June 2011, http://www.ozodlik.org/content/fargona_aeroportida_yolovchilar_noutbuki_tekshirilmoqda/24212860.html.
5. See Yetar's Facebook page at https://www.facebook.com/#!/pages/%D0%95%D1%82%D0%B0%D1%80%D0%9F%D0%BE%D1%80%D0%B0We-demand-the-dismissal-of-Islam-Karimov/179071258811897.
6. The search conducted to obtain this result was "O'zbekiston xalq harakati." I have conducted this search monthly since June 2011, and the result is always the same—and potentially very damaging to the group.
7. Bach (2010: 297) has noted how the "disaggregation of the self into data alters boundaries of public and private and leads to a radical reconfiguration of agency and individual autonomy." Google and other algorithmic search engines are a prime example of this phenomenon.
8. In 2008, another website had accused this dissident of being in the NSS. In addition, the dissident himself had published a very popular article in 2005 speculating that yet another dissident group was a cover for an NSS operation.
9. This reference is to Ikrom Yakubov, an alleged NSS officer who defected and went into widely publicized exile in 2008, unnerving both the state and its opponents in the process.

References

Arendt, Hannah. (1951) 1968. *The Origins of Totalitarianism*. New York: Harcourt.

Aretxaga, Begoña. 2003. "Maddening States." *Annual Review of Anthropology* 32: 393–410.

Bach, Jonathan. 2010. "Power, Secrecy, Paranoia: Technologies of Governance and the Structure of Rule." *Cultural Politics* 6 (3): 287–302.

Benjamin, Walter. 1978. "Critique of Violence." In *Reflections: Essays, Aphorisms, Autobiographical Writings*, ed. Peter Demetz, 277–301. San Diego: Harcourt Brace Jovanovich.

Birchall, Clare. 2011. "'There's Been Too Much Secrecy in This City': The False Choice between Secrecy and Transparency in US Politics." *Cultural Politics: An International Journal* 7 (1): 133–156.

Bubant, Nils. 2008. "Rumors, Pamphlets, and the Politics of Paranoia in Indonesia." *Journal of Asian Studies* 67 (3): 789–817.

Canetti, Elias. 1973. *Crowds and Power*. Trans. Carol Stewart. New York: Continuum. First published in 1960 as *Masse und Macht*.

Derrida, Jacques. 1991. "Force of Law: The 'Mystical Foundations of Authority.'" *Cardozo Law Review* 11: 921–1045.

Front Line Defenders. 2010. "Uzbekistan: Physical Attack against Human Rights Defender Mr Dmitry Tikhonov." 26 February. http://www.frontlinedefenders.org/node/2387.

Gopnik, Adam. 2011. "The Information: How the Internet Gets Inside of Us." *New Yorker*, 14 February.

Herriman, Nicholas. 2010. "The Great Rumor Mill: Gossip, Mass Media, and the Ninja Fear." *Journal of Asian Studies* 69 (3): 723–748.

Humphrey, Caroline. 2003. "Stalin and the Blue Elephant: Paranoia and Complicity in Post-Communist Metahistories." In *Transparency and Conspiracy: Ethnographies of Suspicion in the New World Order*, ed. Harry G. West and Todd Sanders, 175–203. Durham, NC: Duke University Press.

IWPR (Institute for War and Peace Reporting). 2006. "Uzbekistan: Internet under Surveillance." RCA Issue No. 461, 17 August. http://iwpr.net/report-news/uzbekistan-internet-under-surveillance.

Kalathil, Shanthi, and Taylor C. Boas. 2003. *Open Networks, Closed Regimes: The Impact of the Internet on Authoritarian Rule*. Washington, DC: Carnegie Endowment for International Peace.

Kendzior, Sarah. 2006. "Inventing Akromiya: The Role of Uzbek Propagandists in the Andijon Massacre." *Demokratizatsiya: The Journal of Post-Soviet Democratization* 14 (4): 545–562.

Kendzior, Sarah. 2011. "Digital Distrust: Uzbek Cynicism and Solidarity in the Internet Age." *American Ethnologist* 38 (3): 559–575.

Komaromi, Ann. 2008. "Samizdat as Extra-Gutenberg Phenomenon." *Poetics Today* 29 (4): 629–667.

Lanier, Jaron. 2010. *You Are Not a Gadget: A Manifesto*. New York: Knopf.

March, Andrew F. 2003. "State Ideology and the Legitimation of Authoritarianism: The Case of Post-Soviet Uzbekistan." *Journal of Political Ideologies* 8 (2): 209–232.

Marcus, George E. 1999. "Introduction: The Paranoid Style Now." In *Paranoia within Reason: A Casebook on Conspiracy as Explanation*, ed. George Marcus, 1–12. Chicago: University of Chicago Press.

Mayer-Schönberger, Viktor. 2009. *Delete: The Virtue of Forgetting in the Digital Age*. Princeton, NJ: Princeton University Press.

Megoran, Nick. 2008. "Framing Andijon, Narrating the Nation: Islam Karimov's Account of the Events of 13 May 2005." *Central Asian Survey* 27 (1): 15–31.

Mitrofanov, Aleksey. 2011. "In Uzbekistan, It Has Begun: In Russia, They Do Not React." Echo Moscow. http://www.echo.msk.ru/blog/mitrofanov/776427-echo/.

Morozov, Evgeny. 2011. *The Net Delusion: The Dark Side of Internet Freedom.* New York: PublicAffairs.

Nissenbaum, Helen. 2009. *Privacy in Context: Technology, Policy, and the Integrity of Social Life.* Stanford, CA: Stanford University Press.

Nugent, David. 2010. "States, Secrecy, Subversives: APRA and Political Fantasy in Mid-20th-Century Peru." *American Ethnologist* 37 (4): 681–702.

Penglase, Ben. 2009. "States of Insecurity: Everyday Emergencies, Public Secrets, and Drug Trafficker Power in a Brazilian *Favela.*" *PoLAR: Political and Legal Anthropology Review* 32 (1): 47–63.

Perice, Glen A. 1997. "Rumors and Politics in Haiti." *Anthropology Quarterly* 70 (1): 1–10.

Shirky, Clay. 2008. *Here Comes Everybody: The Power of Organizing without Organizations.* New York: Penguin Press.

Solove, Daniel J. 2007. *The Future of Reputation: Gossip, Rumor, and Privacy on the Internet.* New Haven, CT: Yale University Press.

Taussig, Michael. 1992. *The Nervous System.* New York: Routledge.

Taussig, Michael. 1997. *The Magic of the State.* New York: Routledge.

Zittrain, Jonathan. 2008. *The Future of the Internet—and How to Stop It.* New Haven, CT: Yale University Press.

Chapter 4

MORAL SUBJECTIVITY AND AFFECTIVE DEFICIT IN THE TRANSITIONAL STATE
On Claiming Land in South Africa

Christiaan Beyers

> ... there were people ... that never took it in their minds that this thing would
> go this far, you know, they thought it's a dream, it can never happen, forget-
> ting that this is a new government. I think they had it in their minds that this
> is still the old government, and that is why they didn't come, most of them.
> (Interview, 30 May 2002)

In November 2000, a ceremony took place to mark the formal transfer of land
from the state to claimants in Cape Town's District Six. Attended by President
Thabo Mbeki, it drew considerable media attention. In the interview quoted
above, a woman forcibly removed from the city center reflects upon the discontent felt by many of her fellow former residents at having been 'excluded'
from the South African land restitution process. Despite widespread publicity
during the program's first five years, they, as well as most people who qualified

for restitution, failed to submit claims by the December 1998 deadline. This happened largely because they did not believe that anything would come of the process or, at a more basic level, that the new regime would be any different from the old one.

Alongside South Africa's more famous Truth and Reconciliation Commission (TRC), the Commission on Restitution of Land Rights (CRLR) was set up as a transitional justice mechanism to provide redress for victims of apartheid- and colonial-era forced removals. In recent decades, transitional justice measures—including criminal prosecutions, truth telling, reparations, and administrative reform—have gained prominence as a means to re-establish the rule of law in the context of the transition from authoritarianism or conflict to formal democracy, and to legitimize the state by persuading citizens of its ability to provide justice, peace, and stability (de Greiff 2012). The state is represented as a force for the good, capable of, among other things, punishing perpetrators of past human rights abuses and providing redress for their victims.

How do people come to believe in a transitional state as something essentially different from its previous incarnation? This chapter addresses this question by considering how the state becomes realized as a 'social fact' in popular representations of justice. Generally, the social factuality of the state consists in its symbolic construction as an objective and unitary entity, a construct that comes to structure social reality and exercise a force of social constraint upon individuals. Transitional justice works compellingly to refigure the state by interpellating victims of past wrongs as moral subjects of the (new) state. It attempts to engender an attachment to the very idea of a new and just state. I focus on one specific bureaucratic technology, the land claim form, and study how it elicits emotional responses and, in the process, how it 'captures' and 'stores' the affects associated with the experiences of apartheid-era forced removals. By turning private suffering and trauma into evidence by which to constitute a category of victims to whom state officials must administer compensation, the claim form provides a privileged site for observing a direct encounter between the newly constituted citizen and the transitional state. Claimants assert moral agency by demanding recognition and by expressing those demands in collective action.

My analysis draws mainly on the narrative portions of 320 claim forms for District Six in central Cape Town. For the would-be claimant, filling out a claim form typically marks the beginning of a process of what is very often an unprecedented emotional investment in the state. However, claim forms are processed according to the narrow evidential requirements of law, and while claimants are encouraged to include expressions of emotional trauma, both material compensation and symbolic recognition are indefinitely forestalled, leading to claimants' rising frustration. In claimant communities, this 'affective deficit' and the desire for recognition are channeled into collective projects aimed at achieving and expanding claims settlements. Continuing hopes—not only for claims settlements, but also for a wider transformation of the state—are evident in testimonies that incorporate elements of a national narrative of liberation, juxtaposing the 'evil' old regime with the 'good' new regime. However, these testimonies seldom come without a dose of cynicism about the persistently alienating character of state power. This is confirmed by the lack of adequate redress, which in turn gives rise to a sense of disillusionment, but also to some claimants' renewed commitment to realize the promise of recognition.

The Transitional State as Social Fact

Although not a revolutionary state, the transitional state is 'new' in the sense that it typically rests on novel structures—a new constitution, new institutions of government, new legislation and decision-making procedures, and so forth. A starting question for theories of transitional justice is how to re-establish the rule of law by building upon a continuity with aspects of the previous legal order that are amenable to democratic governance, while breaking with its illiberal aspects (Teitel 2000). Informed by traditional liberal political theory, such scholarship generally assumes a hard distinction between state and society and treats legitimation as a second-order problem of statecraft.

Rejecting this sharp state-society divide, Timothy Mitchell (2006) redirects analysis to the 'state effect': a multitude of practices and processes by which the distinction is produced "internally, *within* the network of institutional mechanisms through which a social and political order is maintained" (ibid.: 170). Mitchell's approach is salient in transitional contexts, where the state-society distinction is particularly indeterminate and where the very existence and viability of the state is often palpably at stake. At the same time, and in light of the contested nature of state boundaries, it is important to consider the agency of individuals as 'subjects' of state-building projects and, indeed, the ability of the subjects targeted by agencies acting in the name of the state to constitute themselves in different terms (Nustad 2005). Such agency is often expressed through the passionate assertion of moral claims.

In tracking state effects in relation to emergent moral subjectivities, the classic concept of the 'social fact' is analytically useful because of its moral, affective, and emotional connotations. Social facts can be seen as resulting in part from the 'structural effects' that Mitchell highlights, but the key issue is how they come to resonate with individuals by drawing upon cogent socio-cultural sources and, crucially, on affects relating to personal experiences. In what sense is the state itself a social fact? Following John Searle (2010), the state can be seen as ontologically subjective because it exists as an entity only insofar as people believe it does; however, it is epistemically objective "because its truth or falsity can be ascertained independently of the attitudes and opinions of observers" (ibid.: 18). The basic importance of the social fact of the state derives from its status as "the ultimate repository of deontic powers in a society" (ibid.: 164), namely, "rights, duties, obligations, authorizations, permissions, privileges, authority, and the like" (ibid.). This formulation is useful for its clarity, but it only begins to answer why, beyond rational reasons, this particular social fact is so compelling. It is worth recalling Durkheim's (1995) work on religion in which collective representations, such as 'God', capture for the group the emotional intensity of times of collective effervescence and embody a great deal of emotional investment, which is essential to the constitution of a social fact.

Charged with affects, emotions, and moral assumptions, popular beliefs in 'the state' give it an irrational basis beyond the purported rationality of its systemic components and processes. However, this 'foundation' shifts as core collective representations of statehood embody new moral claims and incorporate new affective material. Recent work on affect in a post-structuralist vein (e.g., Ruddick 2010) is particularly fruitful for delving beneath the symbolic character of collective representations (and related subjectivities) and into the semi-conscious affective layer underpinning it. However, by relegating subject formation to the determination of extrinsic forces and affects, such accounts often risk undermining the possibility of moral agency. I therefore wish to preserve a more phenomenological notion of intention, while nonetheless insisting that the subject is inherently and always decentered because it is constituted through interaction with other subjects and objects (Bakhtin 1993). A core theoretical claim of this chapter follows from this: affect becomes socially significant only by being articulated as feeling or emotion in the process of 'dialogical' subject formation.

Here I am interested in the apparently mundane site of the state's inscription in land claim forms—or, more precisely, its co-inscription by officials and claimants. The state is constituted as a particular kind of social fact with subjective attributes. As we shall see, narratives in claim forms respond to official questions as if to a moral subject and even a speaking personality. How are affects marshaled alongside rationality in the life of the state at this point of co-inscription? In addressing this question, I follow Mazzarella (2009: 299), who urges us to take the categories by which we are interpellated into the state construct (e.g., 'citizen', 'subject', 'claimant') "not only as vitality-denying ideological obfuscations but as affectively-imbued, compellingly flawed social facts." He argues that although such categories are always partial, failed constructs and always frustrate our desire, we nonetheless continue to try to realize these promised identities because they are compelling to us, even in their perpetual forestallment. Through such categories, affect comes to reside at the very heart of the state construct, in deeply held beliefs about the make-up of social life as anchored in, underpinned by, or ruled over by the state. The analytical problem is not merely to understand the state as a kind of fiction, but to understand how that fiction is taken up very seriously by people—in other words, to understand the way in which the state is actually much more than a fiction (cf. Aretxaga 2003).

South African Land Restitution: To Claim or Not To Claim?

For people standing before trucks onto which they and their families had to summarily pack their belongings or in front of the remains of their demolished homes, there would have been little question about the *reality* of 'the state'. Like many inner-city neighborhoods, District Six was targeted under the Group Areas Act, which mandated residential segregation. After District Six was declared a 'white area' in 1966, its buildings were gradually demolished and its people progressively evicted over more than a dozen years. Some former residents were cajoled into accepting alternative accommodations in far-flung townships and suburbs, while others were shifted into recently vacated homes, thus dividing and diffusing potential resistance. An Afrikaans-speaking woman, who said she "loved District Six," described the process of removal as a drawn-out, agonizing shuffle:

> They throw one, one building apart. It's so sad. Every time when I visit my sister on a Sunday, because she was still staying in the house … there was a house gone … the Group Areas shift the people from one house, then you must go and stay there with those other people. They give you a rent card, but you must stay with the other people in that house. That's what they did! You understand? And every time, you stay in that small house now it's a broken house, now they condemn that house, hey! (Interview, 28 May 2001)

What emerges in this narrative is the way that the state and the law—and the demolishers—are imaged in the figure of a distant and impersonal entity, here "the Group Areas," the memory of which continues to inspire indignation.

It is this kind of injustice that restitution was intended to redress. The Restitution Act provides that a person or 'community' qualifies for restitution if they had been dispossessed of a right in land "after 19 June 1913[1] as a result of past racially discriminatory laws or practices."[2] Direct descendants of deceased victims of forcible removals are also allowed to submit claims: claimants are entitled to land restoration or monetary compensation.[3] Thus far, most have opted for the latter due to difficulties in locating and developing land, but also because many claimants did not want to resettle and so be 'uprooted' a second time. However, monetary settlement has seemed paltry and inappropriate in relation to what was lost. District Six claims, as well as the consolidated claims of Port Elizabeth upon which this chapter also draws, involve the restoration of substantial tracts of land (Beyers 2013). This has heightened the sense of what is collectively at stake and has led to a complex and often fraught process involving many stakeholders and layers of regulation and procedure.[4]

After finding out about the possibility of lodging a claim—either through the media or by word of mouth—the would-be claimant gathers the necessary documentation, such as school report cards, bank account statements, and insurance books. Once submitted, the claim is subject to a series of cataloguing and filing procedures, research processes involving property records and cadastral surveys, determinations of the legal standing of oral testimonies, family genealogies, 'community' histories, and so on. Throughout this process, the claimant takes part in restitution meetings, which provide a context for socializing with other claimant families.

Attendant to the claims process, there is a process of identity formation based on a sense of collective injury whereby victims of forced removals come together to form groups that strive for special rights as 'wounded communities' (cf. Ahmed 2004: 32–33; Brown 1995). This collective dimension in turn helps to maintain a buoyant feeling through the early stages of the claims process.

Within and across these fields—narratives in claim forms and group mobilization—the state appears as something worthy of tremendous emotional, intellectual, and material investment. Symbolically, the state is continually becoming a 'thing' that is 'out there', with which feelings of diverse subjects are made to connect. This externality provides a target for political action and contention. It thereby also provides a basis for solidarity for social groups that come together to gain something vis-à-vis 'the state'.

Thus far I have examined how victims of forced removals are interpellated as claimants and drawn into an emergent set of state structures, around which they increasingly come to orient their lives. However, it is critical to bear in mind that despite wide-ranging information campaigns and direct recruitment efforts, particularly in District Six (Beyers 2007), the majority of people eligible for restitution simply failed to submit a claim in the five-year period up to the deadline of December 1998. A major reason for this failure, I suggest, was a lack of belief in the 'new' state. Many would-be claimants mistrusted the state, which they had only ever known to deny their rights. As one woman, whose brother had been elected to the 'Coloured' representative structure within the apartheid government,[5] intimated:

> There's some people, has got a fear to come forward … With the apartheid era, if those officials from the Group Areas came to knock on our door … you know, they [i.e., neighbors in District Six] had a fear of the white man. They say, "No, but if the white man says we must go we must go." Now it is the same thing here, they say, "*Ag*, but why must we go back there?" They think that in turn they will be thrown out one day again. (Interview, 21 May 2001)

Skeptics saw restitution, at best, as an exceptional measure designed to reinstitute the relative privilege of a select group of former property owners and, at worst, as a "gimmick just to get votes." Many of those who did submit claims argue that they did so in spite of considerable skepticism that anything would come of the process. According to a Muslim man in his mid-forties living in the low-income, predominantly 'coloured' area of Hanover Park, a notorious gang area renamed after the main street in the former District Six:

> Now for them being here, very late claimants, it is a type of life that you lead here in Hanover Park, because not everybody here that can afford a newspaper. Now a lot of people don't know about it because they don't read the newspaper. And people are 50 years old, 60, 70, 80, 90 years old, they don't worry about this stuff, because they only go by ear; right now, "oh, there's District Six back again, and what's happening now?" But in the meantime, it is going to be too late for their claim. *Ja*, you see? … There was enough time to claim, like I say. Maybe because of lack of knowledge, *ja*, lack of knowledge, meaning, *ag*, like, "it will never happen." You hear a lot of people say, "that will never happen." But after the meeting here with Thabo, with Thabo Mbeki, here in District Six, then the people realized, hey, there's now movement here. And then they started with meetings and then they started to realize now it's, *ja*, that we can get involved here. (Interview 23 May 2001)

It is noteworthy that disbelief (here rendered as "lack of knowledge") was overcome only after the personified state, in the person of President Mbeki, conducted a meeting with prospective claimants. In the popular representations considered here, personification is the main form for attributing social factuality to the state. More than myth or mask, this could be seen as one way in which the state is abstracted from the social, thus enabling the constitution of legal subjecthood of both government and citizen (Asad 2004: 282). However, as we shall see in claimant narratives, personification might also be viewed as a way to bring the state into the fold of social connection among people.

What Is in a Claim Form?

The CRLR claim forms archive represents the first and most important way in which victims of past forced removals become institutionally inscribed in the state as land restitution claimants. Claim forms channel memories that were part of the oral culture of communities from which claimants come and concentrate these in a written form, which is stored within the archival reserves of the state. More precisely, testimonies are 'held' in the name of the state by the Commission, serving as raw material for a series of procedures designed to administer transitional justice and thus to establish the state as just (cf. Stoler 2002).

The requirements of the claim form are extensive. The form consists of four pages with nine questions, many with subsections. Among other things, it asks for details about the property where the claimant resided (street address, specific plot identification number, length of residence/ownership, etc.), dispossession (date of, and state agency responsible for), compensation provided at the time of dispossession, and principal agents claiming within the family. Question six solicits a background statement in which the claimant is to include information about the history of the property in question, its current use, and the relationship of the claimant to the dispossessed person. It also asks for "The history of the dispossession and the role apartheid had in it" and "The hardship caused (since forced removal or forced resettlement)." Extensive supporting documentation is required, including certified copies of identity documents, birth and death certificates, title deeds, and will statements of the dispossessed.

When I visited claimants' homes, they would often produce for me copies of their claim forms and supporting documents, giving me the impression that these were prized articles that validated a special status. While this attests to certain affects associated with the materiality of the documents themselves, I am more interested in the way that the claimants' overall capacity for affectation is enhanced by their capture of affects associated with forced removals under the 'old' state, and how these serve as a resource for the normative construction of the 'new' state and for collective social action. Furthermore, in wishing to preserve the intentions of subjects, I want to link the affective charge of forms to claimants' emotional-volitional responses to the possibility of redress.

It is useful to view documents as textual forms in Dorothy Smith's (2001) sense: as extra-temporal forms of representation within institutions that serve to objectify knowledge and fix meanings across diverse contexts. Claim forms enable subjects to anchor themselves in the institutional existence of the state through time and to extend the documented self into the future as someone who is entitled to a certain relationship to 'the state'.[6] By bringing together a string of documents—from birth certificates or passports to lesser documents such as rental receipts, monthly bills, and newspaper clippings—claim forms serve to collect and record claimants' past lives as a factual chronology. For the claimant, in addition to recording officially the moment of displacement, these documents testify to and stand in for a previous life, one that was destroyed in the process of forced removals. The claim form also obviously marks another key moment in the individual's life, that is, becoming a claimant, a particular kind of subject-citizen. The source of both moments is the state—then tyrannous, now apparently beneficent.

This juxtaposition of images of the state is dramatically charged with affect, which is present as emotion in the act of telling the story and is inscribed in more raw affective form within the narration. More than through legitimation according to standards of political reason, the state here comes to be founded in popular sentiment of outrage at the brutality of the former regime and positioned as the culmination of a revolutionary historical project. Claim forms frequently include direct statements of outrage, along with broader emotional expressions relating to experiences of suffering and injury as well as the desire for redress. When these kinds of messages are subsequently repeated and elaborated in more public forums, they incite sympathy and an accompanying sense of indignation, so that in this sense the claimant becomes not just a direct agent of state legitimation, but a medium for the transitional state as a newly established social fact.

A Surplus of Emotion

In filling out the claim form, the claimant is taken from a public world of ex-resident reunions, restitution meetings, rallies, and marches into a textual world where the minutiae of her or his private life are to be disclosed (Mesthrie 1998: 253–257). The affective charge surrounding the claims process is reflected in claim form narratives. Thus, most claimants do not restrict themselves to the kinds of responses officially sought. Particularly noteworthy is that at some point in the course of filling out the form, the claimant very often provides a narrative that is highly emotional in content and sometimes extends well beyond the claim form onto attached pages. Such narratives bring palpable feeling to references to the former neighborhood's "family unity," safety and security, and "culture and friends," which were destroyed at the hands of "barbaric apartheid laws." They speak of the subsequent depression, loneliness, illness, and "total loss of joy" suffered in the areas to which people were removed.

Not surprisingly, descriptions of the moment of eviction are particularly emphatic. Consider this brief response to the instruction "Write what you know of what happened from the time the dispossessed was informed about the eviction until the time he/she had to leave the house":

> I cried I was heartsore, my eyes get sore, got glucoma from the shock of the day, I almost got blind. And when we moved the day was the hardest day of my life. I didn't know what to do, everybody was gone.

Such responses do not answer the question on the form in the terms that it is laid out, namely, a request for an objective account of events at the time of removal. Instead, they present traumatic memories of the removal. Here is an excerpt from a letter one claimant attached to the form entitled "Hardships suffered because of the Group Areas Act." It starts as follows:

> Apartheid is something that took a long time to forgive. Why us? What crime did we do? We never harmed anyone. What was to happen to our children? How will we survive?

After a nostalgic account of life in District Six, where "We were all one big happy family and felt like we belonged," the letter proceeds to the fateful time:

> All this happiness and comfort was shattered when the bulldozes [sic] came in and drove us out of what was ours! Who gave the government the right to throw us out? ... We were thrown out ... like animals that were set loose in the wild while the 'BAAS' [boss] took over what belonged to us. We were just 'Coolies'. The pain and suffering my wife had to endure is unbearable. A loving mother who always wanted the best for her children, just had to pack her bags and leave. All the dreams we had for our children just vanished. They respected us, but now how could they still look up to us as parents? They could not understand why we had to move and why they had to say goodbye to their friends. Many nights was spent shedding tears, but there was no- [sic]
> We had to be strong for the sake of our children. Our tears were hidden and the pain in our hearts only us knew ... For my children's sake the anger in my heart still at times linger on as I reflect on how rich their lives would have been if we were not thrown out! My wife's health deteriorated during this period, as everyone had to work harder.
> Who know what ever happened to our neighbours? Where are their children now? Did they get an education or did they end up behind bars?

At this point the letter concludes with the following statement, which makes clear the response desired—something the new government must do in order to distinguish itself from the old government:

> Nothing will bring back "the Good old days," but all we can hope for is that the wrong done to us is somehow compensated for. If not for us, at least for our children. I don't wish the hardship and cries that we had to endure on even my worst enemy!

Eventual settlement of the claim in itself may of course be considered a 'response', and in this regard the question is whether compensation could be considered proportionate to the harm suffered. But there is surely more that is going on here. These narratives do not supply primarily factual evidence but instead contain some essence of personal being. They attempt to communicate to a representative of the state (an official or bureaucrat reading the form) who is thus implicated not only as an official conferring rightful compensation, but as someone with compassion. If we consider the outwardly dialogical form of the utterances (Bakhtin 1986) provided on the forms, what is implicitly sought is a commensurate emotional-volitional response that recognizes the affective content of what is communicated. Indeed, any compensation received may be judged more adequate if it is felt to issue genuinely from such recognition. This is made explicit in the following testimony of one woman who was fortunate to end up in Crawford, a middle-class area not far from the center of Cape Town. She writes of being "shocked" at being evicted and concludes her background statement as follows:

> In reading this affidavit, I hope you share my sentiments and see that I was not properly consulted, [that I was] forced, and against my will forced to sell my property at an unfair price ... I request you to sympathise with me and compensate me by giving my land back with at least a dwelling, or compensate in cash me for my loss and inconveniences I had to bear.
>
> Yours faithfully,

Claimants posit personal experiences and memories of suffering not only for catharsis, but also as a basis for entitlement. Such experiences can even be reframed as something meriting a 'reward', as was directly articulated in a group interview after one elderly woman justified her decision to take immediate monetary compensation rather than wait for land restoration, which might not come about before she dies. One of her friends agreed emphatically: "It's your suffering! Eat up your money!" Another chimed in: "Enjoy your suffering."

The Event and Its Affects

In line with the wider emphasis on reconciliation within restitution, emotional expression was encouraged as part of the 'healing' process (Walker 2008). But more than elicit emotional expression, claim forms 'capture' affects (Massumi 1995) relating to the event of forced removals and the socio-political process of land restitution, channeling their transmission in ways that are amenable to the establishment and reproduction of a new political regime. Affects can then be worked with to ground the state, anchoring its normative principles and hence delineating past and future. If the claimant 'collects' these affects and thus constitutes an emotional response in the claim form, this is only partially the product of individual agency; it is also the result of the interpellation of the individual as claimant—that is, as a subject of justice in the new state.

But the forms also contain affects that seem to evade capture and do not easily attach to any 'voice' or readily identifiable subject position. If testimonial descriptions of the moment of forced removals are naturally infused with emotion, they also carry the palpable affects of the day in a way that reveals the continuing 'charge' or 'inertia' of these affects. Consider these excerpts from three different claim forms:

THE SMILES ON THE FACES OF DISTRICT SIX WERE WIPED OFF BY THE GROUP AREAS ACT'S DECISION TO DECLARE DISTRICT SIX A "WHITE" AREA AND GLOOM TURNED TO FEAR WHEN THE LITTLE CAR WITH TWO MEN INSIDE WOULD DRIVE UP THE ROAD, STOP AT AN ADDRESS, AND DELIVER NOTICES OF REALLOCATION TO THE OCCUPANTS. WHEN IT WAS MY TURN I REFUSED ... (Capitals in the original)

They were starting to break down the [houses on the] road and there was a bad feeling. You know that you will be the next ... The old people dies as a result.

Whites came with letters and keys for new houses. Most of the people were getting sick and heart attacks. They call us "Hottentots." It was terrible. People were crying on the streets. We fighting them.

Embedded within emotional expression, which is to say, expression that processes affects subjectively, are more raw affects, present in more inchoate, incipient sensory form, such as the immanent fear and dread "that you will be next," or the glum atmosphere created by the ruins and squalid remains of buildings—the rubble of which continues to affect the mood of the central city today (cf. Street 2012)—and the sickness and shock that settled upon those remaining in the neighborhood. Evident here are what Kai Erikson (1989: 237) describes as the two forms of "communal trauma," namely, "damage to the tissues that hold human groups intact and the creation of social climates, communal moods, that come to dominate a group's spirit." Such affects are evident in a kind of record of the event that is unprocessed by reflection—the undigested remnants of physical, psychological, and social impact. To be sure, the reader of such testimonies senses these affects as an effect of representation, but it is as if the writers have not been able to take full possession of themselves before the monstrosity of what they are representing.

Such narratives also convey the effect of the events and its effects upon others. In a testimony to the terrifying power of the former regime, a recurrent theme is how loved ones "died of a broken heart." Old people, in particular, could not take the shock and trauma of being violently uprooted, and so many did not live long. The affect accompanying the event was overwhelming for them, and in many ways it continues to be overwhelming for the living who, among other things, had to witness the demise of their loved ones.

In most narratives, emotional expressions of traumatic memories are at least in part strategically crafted in order to frame entitlement. However, some testimonies are overpowered by traumatic affect:

[W]e told to move out account of Group Act in 1959 ... got wood and iron house in Rylands Est, where my house got burned out on 11th/1960, my two sons age 5/6 was Burned to Death, and shock of the Fire I lost the 8 months twins, I lost

4 children in one day, and also lost everything and had no home for a long time I really can't remember much, of all this happying I had a neverest break down, in the Fire I lost everything and all my papers, I can't remember anymore, I don't want to look at the Passed everything, I write in This Letter it's the Truth[.] I only got a snap to show of my sons and the house where we lived ... what ever happens I don't look Forward to Except anything its in Gods hand. Thanking you.

For this person—let's call her Muriel—the initial shock of being forced to move brought about other disasters, which came with their own shocks, compounding one another. Muriel is able to convert affect into named emotion and thus exercise some degree of will, even if only by making a speech act. However, there is much in that act that exceeds her conscious intention.

In sum, the would-be claimant brings to the site of her or his interpellation a tangle of experiences, memories, traumas, and aspirations. These, in turn, come with their own transmitted affects—digested to varying extents, carried along in malleable form to be attached to new signs and symbols, but nevertheless semantically organized under the auspices of certain deeply resonant collective representations. Moreover, when personal struggles and losses are marshaled as evidence and aligned with the institutional categories provided on the claim forms, there is often an implicit sense that restitution may bring the key ingredient to transforming a life and getting it back on track—or at least, that it may give meaning to hardships endured. Even affects that arise in a way that eludes conscious control are perhaps now at least brought into relation with a bigger story that culminates in a present act that is of personal, social, and historical significance.

An 'Affective Deficit'

Muriel's utterance above is addressed to the face of the state, 'who' is thanked directly when she signs off, presumably for reading and 'hearing' her statement. Direct official responses to such expressions on claim forms have been limited to verifying facts and requesting further information; for the most part, there has been no significant recognition of their emotional and affective content. Unlike the TRC, where there were hearings that brought state representatives and citizens into dialogue on a public stage, restitution claimants' experiences were usually communicated only to other claimants. There is, then, a large discrepancy between the desire manifested in narratives inscribed on claim forms and what the claims process yields—between what is 'said' and what is effectively 'heard' and 'said' in return. This does not play out as an immediate crisis for the claimant; it is rather that the sense of anticipation in filling out forms is met with flat nothingness over time. The dialogic flow of affectivity in language meets a dead end—an alienating effect characterized by an 'affective deficit'.

This is not to say that officials working in land claims offices are not impacted by such testimonies; in fact, my experience is that some officials take such indications of suffering very personally. However, in their capacity as state officials, they seldom respond, and whatever personal impact they might feel is rarely communicated to the claimants. To be sure, recognition as acknowledgement of harm, loss, and suffering has a range of meanings on the juridical and political plane that are not reducible to its meaning within interpersonal communication. Nonetheless, as their testimonies bear out, claimants think of recognition on this plane as simulating mutual recognition in an interpersonal situation, or at least as involving such an aspect. Indeed, this corresponds in part to the logic of processes of public mourning, official apologies, and commemoration, which generate a certain kind of affective intensity that allows victims of past wrongs to feel validated in their moral claims. However, for such symbolic recognition to have effect, it needs to go beyond rhetorically embellished speeches and statements by politicians and public figures at expedient times, such as during ceremonies that celebrate the formal transfer of land (which is still a long way away from substantive transfer to the claimant or settlement of his or her claim) or during election campaigns. These momentary expressions of support give hope, but when unmatched by material delivery, they come to be viewed as strategic and manipulative.

Due to the slow and uncertain unfolding of the restitution program and the acrimonious stakeholder politics that hinder the restoration and development of land, initial expectations are inevitably frustrated. The tremendous sense of hope thus gives way to a more ambivalent and realistic view that restitution is part of an ongoing calculus of state power. As one claimant submitting a claim for land in Port Elizabeth told me in an interview in a small rundown cottage in the township of Zwide, where he has lived since being removed:

> It's all about *their* [i.e., those in power] choices: to remove us, *their* choice; to build for us, is their choice. And now the rents, it's *their* choice. And allocating these national lands to us, it's also *their* choice! And what to do in those lands, it's also *their* choice! What is ours? In other words, we are living the lives of what the other people want us to live. (Italics indicate emphasis in speech)

When I asked if there was no difference between the current government and the apartheid government, he responded: "It's a different government, but it is still the government … It's still the power which we just have to accept." It is not surprising that for claimants, who have known only a severely repressive state for most of their lives, trusting a new government is not simply a rational decision. As seen here, cynicism does not reflect any doubt about the existence of the state (*pace* Navaro-Yashin 2002). Rather, it results from the realization of the continuing overwhelming force of the state, which after an initial period of idealism comes to be seen as something essentially oppressive, something that changes hands or is 'inherited'.

At stake is whether the state can become an object of emotional attachment by being fundamentally redefined as a force for the good in people's everyday lives. The affective deficit is itself productive in a sense, since the desire for recognition is sustained by its deferment. Or again, to borrow from Ahmed (2004: 131), affect intensified as a lack of reciprocity is met by an "extension of [emotional] investment ... to maintain the ideal [sought after] through its deferral into the future."

Conclusion: Hope and Disillusionment

As a transitional justice program, South African land restitution was designed not merely to shore up support for a new government, but more fundamentally—and in concert with other programmatic state initiatives—to help reconstitute the state as social fact and thereby to redefine what it means to be a citizen. Beyond rational persuasion, this has come about by working with affect and emotion. Individual claimants and co-claimants within a family have been called upon to constitute themselves simultaneously as legal subjects with rights to precise redress as prescribed by law and as moral subjects deserving full recognition for harms suffered under the *ancien régime*.

Submitting a claim involves a willingness to enter into a categorically new type of relationship with 'the state'. In many cases, this entails a considerable personal reorientation, a leap of faith that brings one to act in the belief that the state can be drastically different in character, despite the overwhelming evidence to the contrary within one's personal experience. Claimants thus come to inscribe emotional narratives that posit suffering (and the affects associated with its experience) as a basis for entitlement. However, over time it seems that early skepticism about the claims process was warranted, as those who actually submitted claims are still waiting for the process to unfold, while the machinery of the state sputters, balks, and stalls (cf. Poole 2004: 60). Very often claimants cannot understand why the process of restitution should be so complicated and bureaucratic, because, in moral terms, it ought to be a simple matter of giving back what was 'stolen' from them. The view of the state as something that persists in the instrumental accumulation of power and centralization of violence is thus underscored by its failure to deliver on promises of redress, by frequent reports of narrow ambition and corruption in government, and by incidents of state repression and brutality that occur in a wider frame. At some point after the initial submission of claims, therefore, optimism increasingly gives way to discouragement and eventually cynicism.

Waiting for the bureaucratic and political process to unfold is not as prosaic as it may sound, for the story contains the core elements of suspense in drama—a plot that one feels has to be resolved before the certainty of an ever-advancing finality. Most claimants are elderly, and frequent comments to the effect of "if God spares me" tell of their waiting amid uncertainty about how much time they have left to live. In a 1999 missive to the Land Claims Department that contains a combination of hope and rising cynicism, a District Six claimant writes about her as yet unrewarded journey through the labyrinth of bureaucracy:

> I don't want to make a nuisance of myself by continually making enquiries at the Claims Dept. but time is of the essence. I have worked hard at great expense on the above claims and have now reached the ripe old age of 80 (eighty) and

before I leave this world I would like to leave it in a happy and peaceful state and not have the sword of Damocles over my head because I feel that I should be rewarded for my research and time taken up in visits to the Deeds Office, Land Survey and Master's Office for copies of Wills etc.

The letter was written over 15 years ago, and to date a tiny fraction of claimants have returned to District Six.

Much as the claims process is designed to capture affects and direct them in certain ways, they circulate, concentrate, and morph into new affects indeterminately, and their political impact is thus uncertain. A broader question that can only be touched upon here is how affects are taken up within the wider process of group mobilization beyond claim forms (see Beyers 2007, 2009). Particularly in the early stages of the claims process, group mobilization involves intense mourning and memory work; the rekindling of old friendships, acquaintances, and social connections; and the formation of new social networks. Over time, frustration at the lack of progress finds expression in public demands that government agencies meet their obligations in claims settlement and related processes. The affective deficit observed in the claim forms is to a certain extent assuaged within the claimant group, the identity of which is based on the attribution of individual or family sufferings to the collective. It thus works to establish the 'wounded community' as an enduring context within which mutual recognition becomes possible. However, as in District Six, eventually disillusionment sets in, as collective action is able to achieve only modest gains. Nonetheless, disillusion begins with illusion, and lest it convert to more generalized disaffection and despair, claimants persist with some level of emotional investment in the process, if only because for them so much depends on its outcome.

Acknowledgments

I wish to thank Pradeep Bandyopadhyay for sharing stimulating conversations that informed this chapter, as well as two anonymous reviewers for their valuable comments.

Christiaan Beyers is an Associate Professor of International Development Studies and of the doctoral program in Cultural Studies at Trent University (Ontario, Canada) and a Lecturer at the Alice Salomon University of Applied Sciences Berlin. His research focuses on rights claims, forced displacement and migration, and memory and memorialization in South Africa. He has also written on the Russian literary theorist Mikhail Bakhtin and more recently on forced migration in Ecuador. Journals in which his work appears include *Development and Change, African Affairs, Journal of Southern African Studies, Canadian Journal of International Development, Journal of Contemporary African Studies*, and *Anthropologica*.

Notes

1. The 1913 Native's Land Act laid the foundation for territorial segregation until the advent of formal democracy in 1994.
2. See Restitution of Land Rights Act, No. 22 of 1994, Republic of South Africa, http://www.justice.gov.za/lcc/docs/1994-022.pdf.
3. New legislation was passed in July 2014 that has reopened the claims process for nearly another five years. Claims currently being lodged will be verified only after the new deadline. The ethnographic research for this article pre-dates this legislation.
4. The cases considered here consist of individual claims that have been aggregated as 'group' claims, to be processed together but settled individually, and are socially framed as a struggle for justice by a collectivity.
5. Set up in 1984, the Tricameral Parliament included elected 'Coloured' and 'Indian' houses, which had limited powers, alongside the existing 'White' house. However, there was no representation for the African majority.
6. In land restitution, those with ready access to such documentation are favored, as well as those who are more literate and competent to deal with such matters. In general, former property owners are thus well-positioned compared to former tenants, who, in turn, are better off than sub-tenants (see Beyers 2007; James 2007).

References

Ahmed, Sara. 2004. *The Cultural Politics of Emotion*. Edinburgh: Edinburgh University Press.

Aretxaga, Begoña. 2003. "Maddening States." *Annual Review of Anthropology* 32: 393–410.

Asad, Talal. 2004. "Where Are the Margins of the State?" In Das and Poole 2004, 279–288.

Bakhtin, Mikhail M. 1986. *Speech Genres and Other Late Essays*. Trans. Vern W. McGee; ed. Carol Emerson and Michael Holquist. Austin: University of Texas Press.

Bakhtin, Mikhail M. 1993. *Toward a Philosophy of the Act*. Trans. Vadim Liapunov; ed. Vadim Liapunov and Michael Holquist. Austin: University of Texas Press.

Beyers, Christiaan. 2007. "Land Restitution's 'Rights Communities': The District Six Case." *Journal of Southern African Studies* 33 (2): 267–285.

Beyers, Christiaan. 2009. "The Will-to-Community: Between Loss and Reclamation in Cape Town." In *The Rights and Wrongs of Land Restitution: 'Restoring What Was Ours'*, ed. Derick Fay and Deborah James, 141–162. London: Routledge.

Beyers, Christiaan. 2013. "Urban Land Restitution and the Struggle for Social Citizenship in South Africa." *Development and Change* 44 (4): 965–989.

Brown, Wendy. 1995. *States of Injury: Power and Freedom in Late Modernity*. Princeton, NJ: Princeton University Press.

Das, Veena, and Deborah Poole, eds. 2004. *Anthropology in the Margins of the State*. Santa Fe: School of American Research Press.

de Greiff, Pablo. 2012. "Theorizing Transitional Justice." In *Transitional Justice: NOMOS LI*, ed. Melissa S. Williams, Rosemary Nagy, and Jon Elster, 31–77. New York: New York University Press.

Durkheim, Emile. 1995. *The Elementary Forms of Religious Life*. Trans. Karen E. Fields. New York: Free Press.

Erikson, Kai. 1989. *A New Species of Trouble: The Human Experience of Modern Disasters*. New York: W. W. Norton.

James, Deborah. 2007. *Gaining Ground? 'Rights' and 'Property' in South African Land Reform*. New York: Routledge-Cavendish.

Massumi, Brian. 1995. "The Autonomy of Affect." *Cultural Critique* 31: 83–109.

Mazzarella, William. 2009. "Affect: What Is It Good for?" In *Enchantments of Modernity: Empire, Nation, Globalization*, ed. Saurabh Dube, 291–309. London: Routledge.

Mesthrie, Uma S. 1998. "Land Restitution in Cape Town: Public Displays and Private Meanings." *Kronos* 25: 239–258.

Mitchell, Timothy. 2006. "Society, Economy, and the State Effect." In *The Anthropology of the State: A Reader*, ed. Aradhana Sharma and Anil Gupta, 169–186. Oxford: Blackwell Publishing.

Navaro-Yashin, Yael. 2002. *Faces of the State: Secularism and Public Life in Turkey*. Princeton, NJ: Princeton University Press.

Nustad, Knut G. 2005. "State Formation through Development in Post-apartheid South Africa." In *State Formation: Anthropological Perspectives*, ed. Christian Krohn-Hansen and Knut G. Nustad, 79–95. London: Pluto Press.

Poole, Deborah. 2004. "Between Threat and Guarantee: Justice and Community in the Margins of the Peruvian State." In Das and Poole 2004, 35–66.

Ruddick, Susan. 2010. "The Politics of Affect: Spinoza in the Work of Negri and Deleuze." *Theory, Culture & Society* 27 (4): 21–45.

Searle, John R. 2010. *Making the Social World: The Structure of Human Civilization*. New York: Oxford University Press.

Smith, Dorothy E. 2001. "Texts and the Ontology of Organizations and Institutions." *Culture and Organization* 7 (2): 159–198.

Stoler, Ann L. 2002. "Colonial Archives and the Arts of Governance." *Archival Science* 2: 87–109.

Street, Alice. 2012. "Affective Infrastructure: Hospital Landscapes of Hope and Failure." *Space and Culture* 15 (1): 44–56.

Teitel, Ruti G. 2000. *Transitional Justice*. Oxford: Oxford University Press.

Walker, Cherryl. 2008. *Landmarked: Land Claims and Land Restitution in South Africa*. Athens: Ohio University Press.

Chapter 5

'FATHER MAO' AND THE COUNTRY-FAMILY
Mixed Feelings for Fathers, Officials, and Leaders in China

Hans Steinmüller

To avoid therefore the evils of inconstancy and versatility, ten thousand times worse than those of obstinacy and the blindest prejudice, we have consecrated the state, that no man should approach to look into its defects or corruptions but with due caution; that he should never dream of beginning its reformation by its subversion; that he should approach to the faults of the state as to the wounds of a father, with pious awe and trembling solicitude. By this wise prejudice we are taught to look with horror on those children of their country, who are prompt rashly to hack that aged parent in pieces, and put him into the kettle of magicians, in hopes that by their poisonous weeds, and wild incantations, they may regenerate the paternal constitution, and renovate their father's life. (Burke 1906: 206–207)

In farmhouses in the Enshi region of Hubei province, the clearly defined center of the house is the back wall of the central room. This is the place of the house altar or shrine (E. *jiashen*, P. *shenkan*),[1] which is now often replaced by a poster of Mao Zedong. In the past, people in villages of the township of Bashan[2] placed a scroll in the house altar with Chinese characters saying "The position of Heaven, Earth, Ruler, Kin, and Teachers" (*tian di jun qin shi wei*). This scroll neatly embodies some core tenets of popular Confucian cosmology: the respect toward the principles of the cosmos (heaven and earth), the polity (ruler), and the (male) authority in local society (kin and teachers). Embodied in the paper scroll and enacted in ritual are a number of metaphors for authority and hierarchy, at the center of which stands the principle of filial piety (*xiao*). Classical references from the Confucian canon point out the metaphorical equivalence between the ways that the cosmos, the emperor, and parental authority should be dealt with.

Notes for this chapter begin on page 97.

During the Maoist era, these house altars were taken away and replaced with pictures or posters of Mao Zedong and other revolutionary leaders.[3] At least the position of the Mao poster—which is still there in many farmhouses in Hubei—would suggest that Mao has replaced the emperor and a series of traditional fatherly authorities. The way in which people in this region of central China refer to Mao suggests not only paternal authority, but also parental intimacy. Mao Zedong is popularly called 'Father Mao' (E. *Mao Laohan'r*). Comparable to 'Old Mao' (*Lao Mao* in standard Mandarin), this expression can be translated as 'My Old Man Mao'. Both imply familiarity and closeness, but while 'Old Mao' could also imply a kind of belittling informality, 'My Old Man Mao' clearly confers respect and reverence.

In Enshi and in the neighboring regions of Chongqing and Hunan, the term *lao-han'r* is generally used to refer to one's own father. Mao Zedong is the only famous person to whom this title is commonly attached. People sometimes use the term for other well-known leaders, such as Liu Shaoqi or Deng Xiaoping, but not as frequently or as spontaneously as they do for Mao. And the term is certainly never used to refer to the emperors of the past or to contemporary leaders.

What does it mean if people refer to Mao Zedong as 'Father Mao' and if they put a poster of Mao in the place of the scroll at the house altar, that is, the place of the ancestors and the emperor? I take this question as a starting point to explore changing ideas of the leader as a father and of the country as a family in China, and on this basis I want to make some suggestions about the emotional relationships of ordinary people to the Chinese state.

In the following I describe the historical transformations of a set of metaphors in which the parent-child relationship stands in for the relationship between ruler and subject in China. I first trace the metaphorical equivalences between the father of the family and the emperor in the Confucian classics and tentatively describe a Confucian 'order of the father'. Then I outline in broad strokes some of the changes this order underwent in Republican and Communist China in the twentieth century. Against this historical backdrop, I discuss current and ongoing changes in family life and in the relationship of ordinary people to local officials and national leaders.

I look at the affective dimension of the Chinese state through core kinship metaphors such as the father and the family. These metaphors, and the emotions they imply, are manipulated and negotiated in Confucian treatises on filial piety, in Maoist campaigns, and in the contemporary propaganda discourse on 'the Chinese Dream'.[4] As emotion and sentiment, they belong to specific power relations in families and in wider society. Ultimately, I am interested in understanding the intersubjective intensities of such relations—what 'flashes up' and 'resonates' when people call Mao 'My Old Man'—and, in this sense, in affect as a constitutive dimension of the social. But I am skeptical about suspending this dimension into a realm that is pre-subjective, pre-discursive, and pre-representational, as suggested by various writers in the growing literature on affect (e.g., Massumi 1995; Mazzarella 2010; see also the introduction to this volume). Hence, I try to grasp something of these emotional intensities through a description of the historical background of these family metaphors and through an analysis of their equivalences in various scales of politics and power relations in contemporary China.[5] Emphasizing the historical and social context of emotion and sentiment (similar to Abu-Lughod and Lutz 1990), most of my examples will be from emotional discourse and discourses on emotions. The general approach of this chapter is therefore a 'narrative' and linguistic approach to emotion and sentiment (cf. Beatty 2014).

A Chinese 'Order of the Father/Son'

The notion of 'affective states' (Stoler 2004), or the concern with sentiments and management of emotions by state power, has a long-standing history in China. Many debates of the Mandarin elites centered on the effective harnessing of emotions for the sake of governance. Such elite discussions of the 'Great Tradition' were transmitted through various channels into the 'Little Tradition' of ordinary commoners' everyday life. In this context, the propagation of ancestor worship and popular ritual and its transmission and rectification by lineage elders and local intellectuals played a particularly important role (Faure 2007).

As mentioned previously, a paper scroll with the inscription 'Heaven, Earth, Ruler, Kin, and Teachers' was commonly put at the center of the house altar in many regions of central China. When interpreting the inscription in the houses of commoners, Chinese intellectuals such as the Confucian philosopher Yu Yingshi have referred to the following often-repeated lines from the book of Xunzi, a Confucian classic, as quoted in Wu Yu ([1917] 1985: 110) and Yu Yingshi (1996: 101):

> Ritual principles [*li*] have three roots: heaven and earth are the root of life, the ancestors are the root of commonality, rulers and teachers are the root of order. If there were no heaven and earth, how could there be life? If there were no rulers and teachers, how could there be order? If only one of those three is missing, there is no peace and security for humankind. Hence rituals [*li*] follow the heaven above and the earth below; they venerate the ancestors and exact rulers and teachers, since these are the three roots of all ritual principles [*li*].

In such descriptions of Chinese ritual, symbolic equivalences are established between the rules of the cosmos and the behavior toward the ruler, kin, and teachers—precisely the references that are given on the paper scroll. When burning incense in front of the scroll and bowing toward it, the same ritual act extends toward the cosmos, the polity, and the family and separates above and below, inside and outside. When ritual (*li*) is performed in appropriate ways in all those realms, it is accompanied by and reproduces emotional dispositions, the most fundamental of which is *xiao*, filial piety. If *xiao* is first the disposition of a son to his father, it has been frequently said to be at the root of the attitude and action toward superiors and rulers. The fifth chapter of the *Classic of Filial Piety* (*Xiao Jing*), titled "Filial Piety of Inferior Officials," explains this as follows:

> As they serve their fathers, so they serve their mothers, and they love them equally. As they serve their fathers, so they serve their rulers, and they reverence them equally. Hence love is what is chiefly rendered to the mother, and

reverence is what is chiefly rendered to the ruler, while both of these things are given to the father. Therefore, when they serve their ruler with filial piety, they are loyal; when they serve their superiors with reverence, they are obedient. Not failing in this loyalty and obedience in serving those above them, they are then able to preserve their emoluments and positions, and to maintain their sacrifices. This is the filial piety of inferior officers. It is said in the Book of Poetry: Rising early and going to sleep late, do not disgrace those who gave you birth.[6]

In this text, as in many other classical texts of the Confucian tradition, the relationship between son and father and subject and emperor is equalized symbolically. While the relationship between this elite textual tradition and the everyday social life of commoners is perhaps the most important question of the history of late Imperial China, there is no doubt that the ideal of filial piety and the metaphorical series extending from fathers to officials and emperors were of crucial importance in the ideology of government.[7]

Elsewhere, anthropologists and other social scientists have described similar metaphorical systems as an 'order of the father': a symbolic order that metaphorically equates the father figures in families, politics, and religion (see, e.g., Borneman 2004; Delaney 1995; Mitscherlich 1963, 1969). Typically, this might be described as the series of 'father in heaven', 'father of the country', and 'father of the family' (in German: *Gottvater, Landesvater, Familienvater*; cf. Borneman 2004).

Mitscherlich, Delaney, and Borneman write about Turkey and Germany, contexts that were shaped by Abrahamitic religions. In the quotes above and embodied in the paper scrolls in farmhouses in Hubei, we have seen a similar metaphoric series in which the relationships of subjects to rulers and sons to fathers are equated. But there are also notable differences between the Abrahamitic 'order of the father' and the Chinese one, and I suggest at least two main distinctions. First, the Chinese 'order of the father' is not grounded in transcendence, that is, in the existence of god-the-father; instead, it is viewed as immanent, based on the functioning and practical necessities of families and communities. Second, rather than the power of the father, the Chinese order emphasizes the obedience of the son. For both arguments, my reference is Gary Hamilton (1990), who maintains that patriarchy and patrimonialism in China and in Europe mean quite different things. According to Hamilton, in Europe patriarchy refers to the personal power of the father (*patria potestas*), which is justified transcendentally. In China, patriarchy is the power of a role, justified immanently through the workings of a family or a polity. Perhaps risking a gross simplification, Hamilton contrasts the power of the father in Western patriarchy with the obedience of the son in Chinese patriarchy (see also Hamilton 1985).

But the 'order of the father/son' in China is far from timeless. All elements of this order (the authority of the father and the emperor, the cosmological links between them, the principle of filial piety and its ritual enactment) have been subject to intense attacks by elite intellectuals since the late Qing dynasty. Systematic criticism and condemnation of these discourses were an integral part of the Communist Revolution. Nevertheless, elements of this order survived in popular practice and ritual. While fighting the older 'order of the father', the modern state in China also relied in various ways on the metaphorical equivalence between the father at home and the father in politics.

As elsewhere (cf. Benei 2008; Carsten 2004; Delaney 1995), the vocabulary and metaphors of kinship have been crucially important for producing the sense of national belonging in China (e.g., Duara 1996: 45–46). The influential translator and intellectual Yan Fu, for instance, wrote in 1914 that nationalism, or 'love of the country', should derive from traditional Chinese familism (*jiating zhuyi*) and its basic principle of filial piety (*xiao*) (Nakayama Kujiro, quoted in Levenson 1969: 106). Since the last years of the Qing dynasty, nationalism—that is, the attachment to one's country—has been defined in a new and more emotional way. Instead of being 'loyal' to a dynasty, people should 'love' the country-family. This is reflected in the Chinese words for nationalism or patriotism, *aiguozhuyi* (love-countryism), and the nation-state, *guojia* (country-family).

The Communist Revolution further intensified the emotional links to the party-state via family metaphors, promoting new radical ideas of popular sovereignty and mass representation. Party cadres and officials in the new mass organizations were supposed to 'serve the people' and be present in their everyday lives. Whereas previously the term 'public servants' (*gongpu*) was used for *yamen* runners and other 'servants' of local offices, now it was a term to be used for everyone in the hierarchies of state and party. From local peasant officials up to national leaders, everybody should be a 'public servant' and 'serve the people'.

The notion that local officials should be like parents to the people (*fumuguan*) had existed long before the Communist Revolution. In this ideal, the hierarchical relationship between officials and people both replicated and encompassed the relationship between parents and children. However, the Revolution brought local officials much closer to ordinary people. First of all, officials were more present at the grassroots level, and there were more of them when compared with the Republican era or the empire. According to official ideology, the new rural cadres should 'eat, live, and work together with the peasants' (*yu nongmin tong chi, tong zhu, tong laodong*). Ordinary people, cadres, and national leaders were supposed to be united in the revolutionary spirit of comradeship,[8] self-sacrifice, and modesty. Constantly rehearsed in campaign meetings, the new language of comradeship and Revolution came to permeate everyday life in the countryside.

Chairman Mao was worshipped as the 'great leader' (*weida lingxiu*) and the 'red sun' (*hong taiyang*), but he was also a 'comrade' (*tongzhi*) who stood with the 'masses of the people' (*renmin qunchong*). Against this background, it makes sense that villagers in central China would refer to Mao Zedong as their 'Old Man' (*laohan'r*). This local expression captures well the combination of hierarchical and egalitarian elements in the political persona of Mao. He was the chairman and great leader, but he was not exactly a 'traditional' father or an emperor, being emotionally much closer to ordinary people.

Like the other leaders of the Communist Revolution, Mao was to be addressed by his professional title (chairman) and his common name. This was quite different when compared with the emperors of Chinese history. No one would have dared to address an emperor directly by his name; in fact, people were not even allowed to speak his name, unless using honorific titles.[9] Mao was also not the stern Confucian father. This tradition had emphasized respect and obedience in the relationship with one's father, as in the expression a 'strict father and a loving mother' (*yan fu ci mu*). Surely, Mao also inspired respect and obedience, but perhaps more importantly his public representation relied on the emotional bonds created by the suffering he endured with and for 'the people'.

As a form of governance, Maoism relied fundamentally on mass mobilization, in contrast to Stalinism, which emphasized institution building and bureaucracy.[10] The engineering and management of emotions were of crucial importance for Maoist mobilization. This kind of 'emotion work' has been described by Liu (2010) as a combination of new themes and new discursive techniques. Core themes, such as victimization, redemption, and emancipation, were rehearsed using specific techniques of propagation, including personalization, magnification, and moralization (Liu 2010). Accordingly, family and kinship metaphors played important roles in both the discursive and the organizational innovations of Maoist governance.

While the history of these kinship metaphors (and the emotions felt for the state that they imply) is very complex, for the sake of argument I want to emphasize that the Communist Revolution and modern nationalism signaled a departure from the previous 'order of the father/son'. It seems to me that there are three obvious differences. First, the previous 'order', including all of its elements and the principles of filial piety (*xiao*) and ritual (*li*), was condemned. But even though the previous 'order' was attacked as 'feudal', it still continued to influence the way people structured their ordinary everyday practices (e.g., the house altar), and in some ways it also influenced the new discourses of socialist governance, whereby rulers became 'parents' and the state 'a family'.

Second, the new metaphors of the state-family came in a new vernacular language that was markedly different from classical Chinese. In Imperial China, the metaphorical equivalence was primarily expressed in classical Chinese, although there were certainly vernacular discourses that also drew similar equivalences (as shown in the paper scroll mentioned above). After the Revolution, the metaphors were given in the vernacular print language of the nation-state, which was cleared of formal expressions and honorifics. The introduction of a standardized national language (*putonghua*), modern schooling, and mass literacy; the spread of the mass media (radio, cinema, newspapers); and, perhaps most importantly, the extension of the state bureaucracy to the village level—all these innovations came together with a qualitative change in the language, the 'world structure', of family and nation.

Lastly, there was a qualitative difference in the way that the metaphor was emotionalized. This qualitative difference could be called a 'sentimentalization' of the metaphor. In the past, the metaphor also stood for the emotions between parents and children, but the kind of emotions referred to and specifically the way in which these emotions were evoked changed. While in the past the focus was more on propriety, obedience, and protection, now it was often about moral indebtedness and emotional attachment: a language of love, really, or, as in modern nationalism, 'love-countryism' (*aiguozhuyi*). And this language was more emotionally expressive, linked as it was to the new institutions of the nation-state, from flag-raising ceremonies to parades to Communist campaigns.

Compared to the empire, the unquestionable hierarchy of ruler and subject has been transformed into an emotionalized link between the party, its leaders, and the people. Both the imperial and the Communist relationships are based on affective debts between the two sides, yet the language and character of the relationship has changed. The imperial hierarchy can be described in its manifestations as a series of exchanges in rituals, tributes, and vows (cf. Gibeault, n.d.). The emotional effect of these exchanges has been called *en* in Chinese, meaning both the benevolence shown by the ruler and the gratitude of the subject. *En* is also the ideal attitude between the state and the people in the People's Republic of China, but the Communist Revolution further emphasized the emotional character of mutual indebtedness. In other words, the currency of the exchange has become affective, as the parental relationship to the state became vernacularized and sentimentalized.

All the violent denial of tradition notwithstanding, Mao and the Communist Revolution could not start from nothing. They had to insert themselves into an existing system and discourse. In doing so, they created a whole new world, with new categories, new timelines, new stories (cf. Apter 1993; Apter and Saich 1994; Liu 2009: 133–171). Yet at the same time, the previous system and discourse—including its core metaphors—also transformed Maoism. More than 30 years have passed since the death of Mao, and the era of Reform and Opening has seen further changes in family structures, as well as in the meanings of family metaphors in public life. In contemporary China, the social relationships between fathers, officials, and leaders are different from those of the past. They are now characterized by a heightened sense of ambivalence, which is perhaps best called 'mixed feelings'. In the following I describe some of the changes that have taken place since the 1980s with examples from my fieldwork in Bashan in Hubei province.

Mixed Feelings for Fathers, Officials, and Leaders

The Father at Home

In Bashan, the place where I did fieldwork between 2005 and 2007, most young people do not work on the farms of their parents any longer. Some have found jobs in the local tea industry or as small traders, but the majority of young men and women leave their homes for some time to work in cities, often far away in Beijing, Shanghai, Guangzhou, or Shenzhen.

Only in the most exceptional circumstances are marriages still arranged by parents. There might be an uncle who acts as a 'go-between' (*meiren*), but often this role is only for the ritual purposes of the wedding, after the young people have found each other and sometimes even lived together for a while, usually outside the village. At such crucial occasions as family and house divisions, the young tend to be much more assertive than in the past. Part of the reason is that most of them are earning their own money away from home now.

Here I will not go into detail about the changes in family life and marriage decisions in particular in Bashan.[11] What is safe to assume is that the most striking difference from the past is that children spend less time together with their parents and have more space to make their own decisions, especially in terms of marriage, but also in other spheres. Corresponding to this is an increased sense of the negotiability of emotions. Younger people have especially become much more expressive. Yan Yunxiang (2003: chap. 3) describes this change in relationship to romantic love. The relationship of children to their parents has undergone a parallel change in which more emphasis is put on the conscious expression of emotional attachment.

Writing about the importance of conjugal love, parental love, and filial piety with regard to the problem of suicide, Wu Fei (2009: 45) compares the old hierarchy of neo-Confucian roles with contemporary family relationships:

> In traditional China, the hierarchy in a family helped family members to live a stable family life. When a father acts like a father, a son acts like a son, a husband acts like a husband, and a wife acts like a wife, everyone gets the authority and respect that he or she is supposed to get, so the family is in harmony and justice is maintained. While there is no such hierarchy in the modern Chinese family, familial love is as important as ever. Without the protection of the traditional hierarchy, justice in the family is maintained through subtle games of power. In such games, familial love is not only the beginning and end of domestic justice, but it is also often used as moral capital.

The development Wu Fei paints moves from a more unconscious hierarchy toward a more conscious negotiation of power, in which 'love' becomes an aspect of the transactions. Parallel to these transformations of emotional relationships between parents and children in families, the control and influence exercised by local officials have also changed considerably.

Local Officials

As mentioned above, there is a long-standing Chinese tradition of the 'good official' who delivers justice to the people and who is like 'a parent' (*fumu guan*). Contemporary officials, however, are only rarely described in these terms. Up until 2003, most cadres in Bashan were ordinary farmers from the village. They were usually older men, who were also respected as men of standing in the village. They often acted as coordinators at family celebrations, such as weddings, funerals, and house inaugurations. Younger cadres who started working in the last 10 years generally do not live in the village. They participate only rarely in any such family celebrations and obviously do not have close links to the people in the village.

Clearly, the standards according to which these village cadres are evaluated locally are also extremely different. Whereas the older cadres had to appeal to the judgment, gossip, and respect of villagers, the younger cadres are mainly responsible to their superiors in the government hierarchies. In addition to the old peasant cadres and the new, full-time professional cadres, there is now a new type of official commonly found in rural China: the farmer who is both a successful businessman and a local official.

The village mayor of Zhongba is a particular example in this respect. In 2006, Zhu Yuan was the first woman to be elected village mayor of Zhongba, following one year when there was no mayor in office. When I asked villagers about the elections, most of them told me that they are meaningless since it is the cadres themselves who will choose the village mayor. Zhu Yuan married into the village here, and her husband Yi Hongyun is a relatively wealthy man. He is the boss of two small tea factories and one of the bigger tea traders in Zhongba.[12]

Zhu and Yi command a very prestigious position in the village community. Many networks of kin, friends, and colleagues come together in their families, and it is there that the necessary links between the locals of the village and higher government are formed. Ordinary villagers would much rather approach them than officials who are outsiders to the village and are not so familiar with the locals. To act as go-betweens and to 'get things done', local officials such as Yi Hongyun and Zhu Yuan need to maintain a wide network of personal relationships with officials, businesspeople, and villagers. To accomplish this, they need to be relatively well-off; otherwise, they could not engage in the necessary give-and-take relationships that are required.

In the networks of this 'power couple', there are also some businesspeople and men who have somewhat dubious reputations. For instance, Kang 'the second' (lao'er) is an ex-convict who lives in a big house in the township and runs a restaurant there. Kang has served several prison sentences for various crimes, including robbery and assault and battery. He claims that he is now 'retired' and lives an ordinary life as a family man and restaurant owner in the township. But according to gossip, he still has a lot of influence in local affairs, mainly because government officials and the police are 'afraid' of him.

Another frequent guest in Zhu and Yi's house is their neighbor Fang, who had been a soldier in the People's Liberation Army and had participated in the Vietnam War when he was young. Now he is a farmer and does some tea business, but he is also a notorious fist fighter: if you are concerned about your security in Bashan, he is the man to ask. At a birthday celebration in the mayor's house, we had a long chat, and over tea and cigarettes he told me stories about fights he had in the past and how to handle a brawl at family celebrations. In fact, the mayor had asked him to take care of 'security' at this birthday party.

Local officials such as Yi Hongyun and Zhu Yuan might indicate not the return but rather the emergence of 'the broker' of classical anthropological literature (cf. James 2011). The rise of brokers in local politics bespeaks a transformation of power relations that is very different from paternalistic forms that might have been more common even in Maoist China. Various Chinese sociologists and anthropologists have written about the differences between the former peasant officials and the new farmer-businessman officials. Dong Leiming (2008) and Tan Tongxue (2010: 71ff.) describe the rise of 'elite politics' (yingying zhengzhi) and the 'rule of power' (lizhi zhengzhi) in rural China.[13] Comparing the present situation with a (perhaps idealized) past in which there was a 'rule of elders' (*zhanglao tongzhi*), both refer to Fei Xiaotong's ([1946] 1999) classic portrait of rural China, *Xiangtu Zhongguo* (China from the Soil). The volume includes a chapter on the 'rule of elders' (ibid.: 368–371) in which Fei describes paternal power as the most important form of power in local communities in rural China. Exercised neither by force nor by consent, it is "a kind of power that emerges in social reproduction, educational power, or fatherly power (*babashi quanli*), what in English is called *paternalism*" (ibid.: 368–371).[14] This kind of 'fatherly power' is not only the power of fathers in families, but also the power of elders in local communities, which, according to Fei, are traditionally governed by a 'rule of elders'. The ethnographers Dong and Tan describe a transformation in which the local 'rule of elders' à la Fei has shifted toward 'elite politics' and the 'rule of power'. They contrast a respect for seniority according to traditional Chinese notions of moral propriety with contemporary governance in rural China in which wealth, the manipulation of human relations, and sometimes the threat and exercise of violence play decisive roles.

Bifurcation

Villagers, especially those who were not so well-off, often compared the likes of Yi Hongyun and Zhu Yuan with the 'good officials' of the past, that is, not only respected elders who managed community affairs, but especially revolutionary officials. As mentioned above, revolutionary cadres were supposed 'to eat, live, and work together with the peasants', as the revolutionary formula had it. This formula was still intended to apply to the officials of the working groups implementing the New Countryside programs in 2006,[15] but those officials almost never ate with farmers, let alone live and work with them. Actually, local officials rarely visited farmhouses at all, especially those that were located farther away from the single tarmac road that runs through Bashan. When complaining about the corruption of local officials, people often noted the difference from the revolutionary cadres of the past, who had shared their meals with the peasants. Now the township officials "are fat, rich, and 'full of tricks,'" a farmer would declare with indignation, "and they certainly have never come to my house."

Local officials in Bashan are judged poorly not only when contrasted with the good officials of the past. They are also compared negatively to present-day higher officials and national leaders. Many villagers imagine these higher levels of government to be just and benevolent. Let me give an example.

Zhao Mucai is in his early thirties, and we became friendly early on in my fieldwork. Mucai had been married, but the previous year his wife and baby son had been killed in an accident. Since then he has been living at home, working with his father. He had been working on construction sites in Fujian and Guangzhou, but now his greatest worry is to buy a new house of brick and concrete and find another bride for himself. His father is not very well-liked by most neighbors in their hamlet, and he has had many arguments and fights, mostly concerning the borders of his fields and the expansion of the public road that passes through one of them. His mother used to write many petition letters, and, thanks to their notoriety, they made it twice into the newspaper of Enshi city. Many neighbors think they are troublemakers.

During the evenings I spent at their home, Zhao Mucai's mother often told me about the suffering they had to endure at the hands of their neighbors and local officials and about the overall corruption and malice of the local cadres. She even showed me a story that had been published about their case in the *Enshi Daily* newspaper. I read that she had met the head of the Enshi prefecture in person in a session that he had held for people who were coming to petition. He had received her, and she had told him about the injustices that they had to suffer in the village. The chairman immediately sent a group of officials to her village to investigate the case. The officials duly arrived, but when I visited the family for the last time half a year later, the legal issues remained unresolved. "This is a capitalist society, a society for corrupt officials," the mother said to me. At the same time, she emphasized that the officials on the higher level of government are generally highly educated. They are civilized and have a "high population quality" (*suzhi gao*), meaning that they are good and benevolent. She backed that up by saying that she had met many officials on all levels— from the village to the prefecture level—and the best official she had ever met was the head of the entire prefecture of Enshi.

Such a state of affairs—in which local officials are thought of as malicious and corrupt, whereas higher levels of government are imagined as benevolent and good—has been described by Guo Xiaolin (2001) as a 'bifurcated state'. Whereas people have closer material relations with local officials, leaders higher up in the hierarchy stand in a more 'symbolic' relation to everyday concerns. This separation of high and low officials resonates with ancient hopes for the 'good local official', embodied, for instance, in the semi-mythical figure of Judge Bao. Numerous stories exist about the figure of Bao Zheng, who was a government official in the Song dynasty. In plays, novels, and folk tales, Bao persecutes criminals and corrupt officials and brings justice to ordinary people who have been wronged. One main difference between local officials in the time of Bao and in contemporary China is simply their numbers. Since the establishment of the People's Republic, the local state has expanded continuously, and the numbers of local officials in villages and townships is now much higher than in Imperial China (cf. Hamilton 1989). Together with increased numbers has come a much closer engagement between local populations and government officials. And with this deeper engagement, the possibilities of disappointment have also increased.

At the same time, the symbolic and emotional relationship to the national leader as a paternal figure has been transformed substantially. As I have pointed out above, the kinship metaphors used for national leaders were vernacularized and sentimentalized in Maoist campaigns, and this process continues today in propaganda practice and in schooling. The more sentimental and colloquial way in which ordinary people refer to national leaders since the establishment of the People's Republic further intensifies the bifurcation between the leaders high above and the local officials down below: the former are distant yet emotionally close, whereas the latter are close yet emotionally distant. And the management of political sentiment is still a core feature of propaganda and patriotic education in the People's Republic.

The National Leader

Most schoolchildren in Bashan know one poem about Prime Minister Zhou Enlai: "Prime Minister Zhou, Where Are You?" (*zhou zongli, ni zai nali?*).[16] Composed after Zhou Enlai's death, the poem commemorates the deceased leader in an extremely sentimental tone as the 'good prime minister of the people' (*renmin de hao zongli*) who visited the soldiers and the peasants and the workers and shared their joys and sufferings. The poem is said to be a tribute made by the 'sons and daughters of China' to their leader. When prompted, many of my younger friends in Bashan could recite parts of the poem and would readily admit that they felt very moved when reciting the poem and thinking about Zhou Enlai, the good prime minister.

This kind of sentimental education in schools is an example of the careful management of emotions in education and propaganda. Such management still aims at the construction of familiar identifications with the state and its representatives (cf. Stafford 1995: chap. 6). But the sentimentality expressed toward Zhou Enlai—the great leader of the past who really cared about the people—now also has nostalgic overtones. Such sentiment, again, often contrasts the older generation of past leaders with the mediocre leaders of today and the higher levels of government with the lower levels. Paradoxically, the familiarity and emotional closeness felt toward the high and dead contrasts with the distance and sometimes hatred felt toward local leaders.

Contemporary leaders are also sometimes called by kinship terms. Chairman Xi Jinping is known as 'Xi Dada' ('Big Daddy Xi' or 'Uncle Xi), and Wen Jiabao, the former prime minister of the People's Republic, was frequently called 'Wen Yeye' ('Grandfather Wen'). The image Wen presented when he appeared on television was often that of a 'man of the people': he played basketball with schoolchildren, ate with students in the university canteen, and shared his meal with workers in the factory. He also appeared in disaster areas, such as the Sichuan earthquake of 2008,[17] or on sites of major social problems, such as the milk powder scandal of 2008.[18] The imagery he invoked was frequently that of a benevolent parental authority.

Wen Jiabao's appearance with children who had been orphaned in the Sichuan earthquake was particularly emotional. In one scene, widely broadcast on national television, Wen comforted a weeping nine-year-old girl who had lost both parents in the earthquake. In a makeshift tent and surrounded by other children and government officials, the prime minister, himself close to tears, promised that the government would take care of the girl, both now and in the future. Many Chinese friends in Bashan and elsewhere in China recounted that they felt very moved when watching this scene. However, younger people who told me that they were moved by the prime minister's tears and called him 'Grandfather' seemed to distance themselves from such statements at the same time. In general, when I asked people whether they thought that Wen Jiabao was a good leader and what they felt about his performance following the Sichuan earthquake, they often said that they were moved by Wen Jiabao and that he seemed to be a 'good prime minister' (which might be reminiscent of Zhou Enlai, who was commonly called the 'good prime minister of the people'). At the same time, others were quick to point out that the prime minister's appearance with the children could be looked on as a staged public relations event. The assessments of Wen Jiabao seemed tinged with a touch of self-awareness and indirection, which could easily turn into a negative appraisal of the prime minister's actions.

The current chairman of party and state, Xi Jinping, seems to be more successful in convincing people of the sincerity of his publicly shown emotions. The promotion of Xi as a strong but modest father figure and leader, with a popular first lady at his side, is backed up by a concentration of power unprecedented since Mao and an ideological focus on his persona as the 'core' of party ideology. In particular, his crackdown on official corruption—catching both the 'tigers' (high-level leaders) and the 'flies' (lower-level officials)—is widely popular, especially in the countryside, and helpful to convince people of Xi's intentions and care for the ordinary people of China. But Xi's public persona is not seamless: the doubt that such emotional politics are just public relations and meant to conceal factional struggle behind the scenes is still lingering. Particularly among wealthier urbanites, there is scepticism about Xi's populism and the intensification of ideological work in party units. And even within the party, there are tendencies to limit a re-emergence of Mao-style populism: in 2016 official media units have been instructed to stop using Xi Jinping's widely used nickname 'Xi Dada' ('Uncle Xi') (Phillips 2016).

This is very different from the way in which Mao Zedong is addressed and remembered. Turning away from television programs and listening to the older generation, one can hear sentences such as "Old Man Mao wouldn't have it that way" in stories about the Great Helmsman's heroic politics. Here the kinship address and the intentionality of the leader could never be doubted, as they could for 'Grandfather Wen' and 'Uncle Xi'. Or at least the implication of (unavoidable) self-reflection was not present to the same extent.

Calling Wen Jiabao 'Grandfather Wen' and 'Uncle Xi' is not quite the same as calling Mao Zedong 'My Old Man'. 'Grandfather Wen' tends to be more a public relations image: children on television might call the prime minister 'Grandfather'. In early 2011, some young people sent text messages for the New Year or other occasions that used puns of the first names of Prime Minister Wen Jiabao and Chairman Hu Jintao. These included, for instance, *baobao*, which literally means 'treasure' but is also part of Wen Jiabao's first name, and 'Brother Tao' (*taoge*), which refers to Hu Jintao. There were even websites for the 'fans of the assorted eight treasures rice pudding' (*shijin babao fan*), a wordplay on the first names of Hu and Wen. Under Xi Jinping, a whole new genre of 'Uncle Xi' songs and Internet memes about Xi and First Lady Peng Liyuan appeared. While such expressions also convey some kind of emotional closeness to national leaders, most people would agree that they are 'just for fun' (*haowan'r*). They are more frequently used by the younger generation, who make more active use of text messaging and the Internet.

Wen and Xi are not thought of as father figures in the way that Mao Zedong is. When people mention them in everyday talk in Bashan, they certainly do not use the colloquial terms for father and grandfather. Whereas for Wen Jiabao, the common address was his standard professional title of 'prime minister' (*zongli*), many people in the village also call Xi Jinping 'Xi Dada'—but this is clearly inspired by his media performance, *dada* being a northern Chinese dialect expression for uncle that is not used in colloquial southern Chinese. Villagers also frequently criticize the 'fakeness' and 'superficial performance' of politicians, including national leaders. Although there is still an ongoing project of sentimentalization of politics, in the last few decades ordinary people have become increasingly worried about the sincerity of the intentions and feelings expressed by higher leaders. If the sentimentalization of Mao was experienced as inevitable, in today's China, where there are a multitude of possible choices in every sphere, feelings are always potentially insincere and affective bonds potentially fake.

Conclusion: A Changing 'Order of the Father'

This chapter has dealt with the historical transformations of family metaphors—in particular, the parent-child relationship—in China. Many of my examples have been from discourses about emotions and emotional discourse, broadly following a narrative approach (Beatty 2014). Yet like most anthropologists writing about emotions, I have attempted to contextualize and historicize these emotions (Abu-Lughod and Lutz 1990), that is, I have tried to put these narratives in the context of social changes in modern China. Through a description of the mixed feelings for fathers at home, for local officials, and for national leaders, I suggest that it is possible to grasp something of the affective intensities experienced in these relations, especially those modeled on the father-son and family metaphors.

This historical and social background, then, provides some of the vectors of the emotions felt by people in their everyday lives in rural China toward Mao and other representatives of the central government. In many ways, I am seeking to achieve something very similar to what others in this book have done using notions of 'desire' and 'affect'. But I am very cautious about suggesting anything beyond the outline of an affective environment that I have provided here. In this sense, I have tried to delineate some of the boundaries of what is said and what is done about an emotional discourse and a discourse on emotions that link the family and the state.

It is evident that in contemporary China, metaphors applied to national leaders and the state, such as the father and the family, continue to be salient. Sometimes they appear to directly contradict the self-interested actions of local officials. One way to avoid cognitive dissonance between the hopes for parental benevolence and the reality of less-than-benevolent local officials is to further bifurcate the state, with father-like leaders higher up in the government and non-parental leaders on the local level.

So when a farmer talks about township officials being corrupt and 'full of tricks', he implicitly also denies them their claim to being 'parental officials'. Yet the metaphorical equivalence of fathers and leaders can also be doubted for those on top, for instance when the emotions shown by national leaders are described as PR performances. These comments point to a complex field of affective engagements with the state and its representatives. In this chapter, I have tried to relate this field to historical transformations of kinship metaphors in Chinese politics and to changing power relations in Chinese society. Both form the background on which the 'affect' of calling Mao 'My Old Man' might be understood—and felt.

Acknowledgments

This chapter has been presented on numerous occasions: in the panel "Between Thrill and Disillusion: Ethnography and the Affective Life of the State," at the American Anthropological Association Annual Meeting, Montreal; at the Institute of Chinese Studies, Oxford; at the School of Oriental and African Studies, University of London; at the Institute of Anthropology, University of Kent; and at the Department of Anthropology, Goldsmiths, University of London. Many colleagues offered their comments, and I am particularly grateful to Maurice Bloch, Judith Bovensiepen, Stephan Feuchtwang, Julieta Gaztañaga, Mateusz Laszczkowski, Anna Lora-Wainwright, Magnus Marsden, Madeleine Reeves, Alpa Shah, Charles Stafford, and the anonymous reviewers for their suggestions. It is my fault alone if I did not heed their advice.

Hans Steinmüller is a specialist in the anthropology of China. He has conducted long-term fieldwork in the Enshi region of Hubei province in central China, focusing on family, work, ritual, and the local state. The main focus of his research is the ethics of everyday life in rural China, but he has also written on topics such as gambling, rural development, and Chinese geomancy (*feng shui*). He is the author of *Communities of Complicity: Everyday Ethics in Rural China* (2013) and co-editor of *Irony, Cynicism and the Chinese State* (2016, with Susanne Brandtstädter).

Notes

1. Throughout the text, Chinese words are italicized in the standard pinyin form. Words in the Enshi dialect that differ markedly in pronunciation and meaning from standard Mandarin Chinese I have marked with an 'E'. All other Chinese words in italics are part of the vocabulary of standard Mandarin. They are marked with a 'P' (for *putonghua*, i.e., standard Mandarin Chinese) only if it was necessary to distinguish them from the Enshi dialect (e.g., 'street' is 'E. *gai*' and 'P. *jie*'). Unless otherwise indicated, all translations are mine.

2. I conducted fieldwork in Bashan between 2005 and 2007 and revisited it in 2011.

3. In another publication (Steinmüller 2010), I explore the significance of this replacement and the potential awkwardness of the popular Confucianism embodied in the paper scroll and the rituals directed toward it.

4. 'The Chinese Dream' is a key term in the official discourse of China's current regime. Its meaning is extremely broad, but it is supposed to include both the aspirations of individuals and the goals of the Chinese nation. Soon after he took office as general secretary of the Communist Party, Xi Jinping used the phrase in a high-profile visit to the National Museum in Beijing in November 2012. Since then, it has been used widely in official documents and speeches.

5. In this sense, I find myself in agreement with Mathijs Pelkmans (2013), who emphasizes the difficulties of ethnographies using 'affect theory' in accounting for variation and specific power arrangements.

6. This is the translation by James Legge (1879: 470–471), which is available online at http://ctext.org/xiao-jing (accessed 25 November 2011).

7. See, for instance, David Faure's (2007) book on the history of state and lineage in Guangzhou, which has the programmatic title *Emperor and Ancestor*.

8. For the rise of comradeship in Communist China, see Vogel (1965).

9. Such titles included 'the holy and exalted' (*shengshang*), 'your majesty' (*bixia*), and 'the son of heaven' (*tianzi*). There were complicated sets of honorifics to refer to the emperor's health ('the dragon's body', or *longti*) and his feelings ('the emperor's face', or *longyan*).

10. Mass mobilization, including the management of political sentiment, did play an important role in the Soviet Union (see, e.g., Kharkhordin 1999; Kotkin 1995). But Stalinism was more successful than Maoism in establishing new bureaucracies of government and industry, and after the Stalinist purges, the government did not mobilize the entire population in mass campaigns comparable to the Great Leap Forward or the Cultural Revolution in China.

11. My observations are broadly in line with the accounts given by Yan Yunxiang (1997, 2003, 2010) and others about the rise of the conjugal family in rural China in the Reform era.

12. Several of the journalist teams that have visited Zhongba have also reported this household as a model of economic success in Zhongba. According to one report published in a national magazine, Yi Hongyun makes an annual income of 150,000 yuan from his tea plantations and tea production business.

13. Tan Tongxue (2010: 185–198, 403–404, 423–426) describes political situations in which local power holders, who are often gangsters as well, use force and sometimes violence to govern.

14. Gary Hamilton and Wang Zheng translate the same phrase as "power generated through education and through patriarchal privilege, or what is normally called 'paternalism'" (Fei 1992: 114). It is interesting to note that in the original Chinese text, Fei refers directly to the English notion of paternalism and provides the Chinese translation for this social scientific concept, rather than pointing to the numerous references on filial piety in the Confucian canon.

15. One of the documents outlining the objectives of the working group in Zhongba reads as follows: "The members of the working group are supposed to eat, live, and work together with the peasants." See Enshi City Government, 27 April 2007, http://old.hbenshi.gov.cn/news/xnc/2007/426/07426134928H57KH8DC3G2IDG08 59F6.shtml (accessed 1 January 2016).

16. The Chinese text of the poem can be viewed at http://sincereandys.blog.163.com/blog/static/8584963820090965116150/.

17. For an analysis of Wen Jiabao's performance during the Sichuan earthquake, see Xu Bin (2012).
18. One company, Sanlu, had adulterated the milk powder formula with the chemical compound melamine.

References

Abu-Lughod, Lila, and Catherine Lutz. 1990. "Introduction: Emotion, Discourse, and the Politics of Everyday Life." In *Language and the Politics of Emotion*, ed. Catherine Lutz and Lila Abu-Lughod, 1–23. Cambridge: Cambridge University Press.

Apter, David E. 1993."Yan'an and the Narrative Reconstruction of Reality." *Daedalus* 122 (2): 207–232.

Apter, David E., and Tony Saich. 1994. *Revolutionary Discourse in Mao's Republic*. Cambridge, MA: Harvard University Press.

Beatty, Andrew. 2014. "Anthropology and Emotion." *Journal of the Royal Anthropological Institute* 20 (3): 545–563.

Benei, Véronique. 2008. *Schooling Passions: Nation, History, and Language in Contemporary Western India*. Stanford, CA: Stanford University Press.

Borneman, John. 2004. "Gottvater, Landesvater, Familienvater: Identification and Authority in Germany." In *Death of the Father: An Anthropology of the End in Political Authority*, ed. John Borneman, 63–103. New York: Berghahn Books.

Burke, Edmund 1906. *Works*. Vol. 5. Oxford: Oxford University Press.

Carsten, Janet. 2004. *After Kinship*. Cambridge: Cambridge University Press.

Delaney, Carol. 1995. "Father State, Motherland, and the Birth of Modern Turkey." In *Naturalizing Power: Essays in Feminist Cultural Analysis*, ed. Sylvie Yanagisako and Carol Delaney, 177–200. London: Routledge.

Dong Leiming. 2008. *Songcun de Tiaojie: Jubian Shidan de Quanweiyu Zhixu* [Mediation in Song Village: Power and Order in a Time of Radical Change]. Beijing: Falü Chubanshe.

Duara, Prasenjit. 1996. "De-Constructing the Chinese Nation." In *Chinese Nationalism*, ed. Jonathan Unger, 31–55. New York: M. E. Sharpe.

Faure, David. 2007. *Emperor and Ancestor: State and Lineage in South China*. Stanford, CA: Stanford University Press.

Fei Xiaotong. (1946) 1999. *Xiangtu Zhongguo* [China from the Soil]. Beijing: Qunyan Chubanshe.

Fei, Xiaotong. 1992. *From the Soil, the Foundations of Chinese Society: A Translation of Fei Xiaotong's Xiangtu Zhongguo, with an Introduction and Epilogue*. Berkeley: University of California Press.

Gibeault, David. n.d. "L'autorité comme échange: La Chine." Unpublished manuscript.

Guo, Xiaolin. 2001. "Land Expropriation and Rural Conflicts in China." *China Quarterly* 166: 422–439.

Hamilton, Gary G. 1985. "Patriarchalism in Imperial China and Western Europe: A Revision of Weber's Sociology of Domination." *Theory and Society* 13 (3): 393–425.

Hamilton, Gary G. 1989. "Heaven Is High and the Emperor Is Far Away." *Revue européenne des sciences sociales* 27 (84): 141–167.

Hamilton, Gary G. 1990. "Patriarchy, Patrimonialism, and Filial Piety: A Comparison of China and Western Europe." *British Journal of Sociology* 41 (1): 77–104.

James, Deborah. 2011. "The Return of the Broker: Consensus, Hierarchy, and Choice in South African Land Reform." *Journal of the Royal Anthropological Institute* 17 (2): 318–338.

Kharkhordin, Oleg. 1999. *The Collective and the Individual in Russia: A Study of Practices.* Berkeley: University of California Press.

Kotkin, Stephen. 1995. *Magnetic Mountain: Stalinism as a Civilization.* Berkeley: University of California Press.

Legge, James, trans. 1879. *The Shû King, Shih King and Hsiâo King, in Sacred Books of the East, Vol. 3.* Oxford: Oxford University Press.

Levenson, Joseph R. 1969. *Confucian China and Its Modern Fate.* Berkeley: University of California Press.

Liu, Xin. 2009. *The Mirage of China: Anti-Humanism, Narcissism, and Corporeality of the Contemporary World.* New York: Berghahn Books.

Liu, Yu. 2010. "Maoist Discourse and the Mobilization of Emotions in Revolutionary China." *Modern China* 36 (3): 329–362.

Massumi, Brian. 1995. "The Autonomy of Affect." *Cultural Critique* 31: 83–109.

Mazzarella, William. 2010. "Affect: What Is It Good For?" In *Enchantments of Modernity: Empire, Nation, Globalization*, ed. Saurabh Dube, 291–309. London: Routledge.

Mitscherlich, Alexander. 1963. *Auf dem Weg zur vaterlosen Gesellschaft: Ideen zur Sozialpsychologie.* Munich: Piper.

Mitscherlich, Alexander. 1969. *Society without the Father: A Contribution to Social Psychology.* Trans. Eric Mosbacher. London: Tavistock.

Pelkmans, Mathijs. 2013. "The Affect Effect." *Anthropology of This Century*, no. 7. http://aotcpress.com/articles/affect-effect/.

Phillips, Tom. 2016. "'Big Daddy Xi' No More? Chinese President's Nickname Nixed." *Guardian*, 3 May. https://www.theguardian.com/world/2016/may/03/big-daddy-xi-no-more-chinese-presidents-nickname-nixed.

Stafford, Charles. 1995. *The Roads of Chinese Childhood: Learning and Identification in Angang.* Cambridge: Cambridge University Press.

Steinmüller, Hans. 2010. "How Popular Confucianism Became Embarrassing: On the Spatial and Moral Center of the House in Rural China." *Focaal* 58: 81–96.

Stoler, Ann L. 2004. "Affective States." In *A Companion to the Anthropology of Politics*, ed. David Nugent and Joan Vincent, 4–20. Oxford: Blackwell.

Tan Tongxue. 2010. *Qiaocun You Dao: Zhuanxing Xiangcun de Daode, Quanli, yu Shehui Jiegou* [Moral Life in Bridge Village: Morality, Power, and Social Structure in a Changing Countryside]. Beijing: Sanlian Shudian.

Vogel, Ezra F. 1965. "From Friendship to Comradeship: The Change in Personal Relations in Communist China." *China Quarterly* 21: 46–60.

Wu, Fei. 2009. *Suicide and Justice: A Chinese Perspective.* New York: Routledge.

Wu Yu. (1917) 1985. "Du 'Xunzi' Shu Hou.'" [After Reading Xunzi] In *Wu Yu Ji* [Collected Works of Wu Yu], 110. Chengdu: Sichuan Renmin Chubanshe.

Xu, Bin. 2012. "Grandpa Wen: Scene and Political Performance." *Sociological Theory* 30 (2): 114–129.

Yan, Yunxiang. 1997. "The Triumph of Conjugality: Structural Transformation of Family Relations in a Chinese Village." *Ethnology* 36 (3): 191–212.

Yan, Yunxiang. 2003. *Private Life under Socialism: Love, Intimacy, and Family Change in a Chinese Village, 1949–1999.* Stanford, CA: Stanford University Press.

Yan, Yunxiang. 2010. *The Individualization of Chinese Society.* Oxford: Berg Publishers.

Yu Yingshi. 1996. "Tan 'Tian Di Jun Qin Shi' de Qiyuan." [About the Origins of 'Heaven, Earth, Ruler, Parents, and Teachers']. In *Xiandai Ruxuelun* [On Contemporary Confucianism], 101. Taipei: Global Publishing.

Chapter 6

THE TURN OF THE OFFENDED
Clientelism in the Wake of El Salvador's 2009 Elections

Ainhoa Montoya

> ... Ahora es la hora de mi turno
> El turno del ofendido por años silencioso
> A pesar de los gritos ...
>
> [... Now it's my turn
> The turn of the offended after years of silence
> In spite of the screams ...]
>
> — "El turno del ofendido," Roque Dalton (1962)

On the evening of 15 March 2009, former journalist and Salvadoran presidential candidate Mauricio Funes announced publicly the results of El Salvador's fourth democratic presidential election: the party he represented, the Farabundo Martí National Liberation Front (FMLN), had won. The FMLN originated as a

Notes for this chapter begin on page 117.

Marxist-Leninist coalition of guerrilla organizations in 1980 and became a legalized party at the end of the 12-year civil war between the FMLN and the Salvadoran state that ravaged El Salvador during the 1980s. The FMLN's electoral victory had no precedent in a country ruled by military dictatorships and elite governments throughout the twentieth century. Since 1989, the right-wing, anticommunist, and pro-elite Nationalist Republican Alliance (ARENA) party had governed El Salvador, with the FMLN being the primary opposition force beginning with the 1994 elections. For many, the 2009 FMLN victory represented a potential watershed in the country's economic and political situation. Although far from a landslide, the outcome sparked exhilaration among the many Salvadorans advocating political change. In San Salvador, El Salvador's capital, waves of people dressed in red, the FMLN's color, and waved red flags with the party's logo, flooding the central streets until late at night. Jubilant after the victory, a vast array of FMLN supporters—young, old, mothers and fathers with children in their arms—screamed, laughed, and chanted in unison, "El pueblo unido jamás sera vencido" (The people united will never be defeated). Some people turned on their car radios, from which blared the FMLN's election theme songs, featuring refrains such as "Nace la esperanza, viene el cambio" (Hope is being born, change is coming).

The optimism pervading the massive celebrations in San Salvador's streets echoed the sentiment that characterized the celebrations that took place in 1992 at the end of the civil war (Murray 1997: 2–3). On 16 January 1992, 200,000 Salvadorans gathered at San Salvador's central plaza, Gerardo Barrios, singing the insurgents' anthem, *Sombrero Azul* (Blue Hat), to celebrate the signing of Peace Accords by representatives of the United Nations, the Salvadoran government, and FMLN commanders in Chapultepec, Mexico. Large red flags and FMLN banners, hitherto outlawed, had been laid over the façade of the National Palace and the Metropolitan Cathedral, two of the main buildings surrounding the plaza. The Peace Accords signified for many the positive outcome of a civil war that had devastated the country economically and had seen the death or disappearance of more than 75,000 Salvadorans.

Although the signing of the Chapultepec Accords stirred great expectations among Salvadorans, during the negotiations preceding the accords, the FMLN relinquished its commitment to economic reform in order to concentrate on political and institutional changes, thereby allowing successive ARENA governments to continue their implementation of an intense neo-liberal agenda that was to transform El Salvador from a monoculture export economy into one based on finance, exacerbating the country's long-standing problem of rural poverty (Segovia 2002: 178–182). Meanwhile, during the post-war era homicide rates have escalated relative to the last stages of the war (Cruz 1998a: 6; Ramos 2000: 9). Disaffection and disillusionment among ordinary Salvadorans have steadily intensified during the two decades since the war's end as everyday economic and public insecurities became ever more acute (Cruz 1998b, 2001; Moodie 2010: 145; Silber 2011).

I juxtapose these two celebratory moments in the history of El Salvador to raise questions about how hopes stemming from specific political imaginaries are born, maintained, and exhausted. Drawing on my research in the predominantly rural Santiago Nonualco, the second-largest *municipio* in El Salvador's La Paz region, I seek to elucidate how Salvadorans conceive of and relate to the state after their country's 'transition' to democracy. Despite the generalized disaffection and distrust among ordinary Salvadorans vis-à-vis state officials and institutions in the late 2000s, a large portion of El Salvador's population participated actively and passionately in the 2009 elections.[1] In the region where I did my research, many left-wing and disaffected Salvadorans who had placed their hopes in the FMLN regarded this party's victory as an opportunity for redress and began engaging the state through clientelist networks following the election. The ways in which ordinary people took part in political networks, I argue, evidence the degree to which Salvadorans conceive of the state as a legitimate interlocutor, notwithstanding their disillusionment and disaffection with democracy. In other words, Salvadorans have exhibited a genuine aspiration for engagement with the state that runs parallel to their disaffection vis-à-vis the *actually existing* state.

A Sense of Possibility

In order to examine popular participation in party politics during El Salvador's elections and their aftermath and to understand the relevance of this participation to state-citizenry relations in a country that has undergone a 'transition' to democracy, I invoke Verdery's (1999: 26) appeal "to animate or enchant the study of politics." Verdery suggests that we animate the study of politics by "energizing it with something more than the opinion polls, surveys, analyses of 'democratization indices,' and game-theoretic formulations that dominate so much of the field of comparative politics" (ibid.). Accordingly, even as I focus in this chapter on formal political arenas, elections, and routine party politics, I do so by concentrating first on the passion that pervaded the 2009 elections and then on the sentiment of aggrievement that surfaced soon after.

Elections and clientelism are two arenas of party politics that appear intimately related in El Salvador as well as in many other Latin American countries (see Auyero 2000; Gay 1999; Lazar 2004; McDonald 1997). Electoral processes in El Salvador have involved the mobilization of material resources and the exchange of favors—especially by ARENA, the governing party until 2009—so as to maintain more or less permanent political clienteles. Clientelism in El Salvador is part of routine politics since this mobilization of resources and exchange of favors does not begin or end with electoral campaigns. In this chapter, I am particularly interested in the frenzied activation of these networks through the FMLN party and the new FMLN-led government in the aftermath of the 2009 elections. Following election day, many ordinary Salvadorans in Santiago enthusiastically approached party leaders and state officials with various requests and demands. While this may not seem unusual, these Salvadorans, as I will show later, relied on clientelism due to a generalized sentiment of having been wronged (historically as well as recently) and with the goal of seeking redress for various kinds of exclusions.

The 2009 presidential election brought to the fore the relevance of ritualized elements and affective dynamics. As underscored by recent ethnographic research on the procedural elements and party politics of other democratic polities (see Banerjee 2007; Coles 2004; Lazar 2004; McDonald 1997; McLeod 1999), these rituals and dynamics—overlooked in previous analyses of elections—shed light on the processes by which voters calculate their stakes in elections. Abstention, which had predominated in El Salvador's elections until 2004,[2] has typically been explained as a symptom of cynicism and disillusionment (Cruz 1998b, 2001). However, starting in 2004, ARENA's active mobilization of war-related discourse and symbols ignited latent conflicts and passions among many Salvadorans (Montoya 2013). This exacerbation of ongoing friction is rooted in El Salvador's civil war—a domestic episode that evolved into a Cold War battle. While it was eventually brought to an end with peace negotiations brokered by the United Nations, the civil war nonetheless remains a source of deep social and political division.

I suggest that the unprecedented degree to which the Salvadoran population actively participated in the 2009 elections can be attributed to a complex intersection of passionate feeling and an emerging sense of possibility for political change. In her research on the emergence, development, and demise of an AIDS activist group in the United States, Gould (2009: 3) suggests that affect, emotions, and feelings can inform us about "political imaginaries and their conditions of possibility," helping us to understand what motivates people toward political action or inaction. Building on Massumi, Gould (ibid.: 23–26, 31) contends that affect denotes the visceral yet presupposes sociality. Affect allows for an exploration of ambivalence and contradiction that a focus solely on emotions and feelings as qualified and structured states eclipses. Yet, in contrast to Gould (ibid.: 32), I do not invoke here the concept of affect as a relatively autonomous force; rather, I propose that affect is a felt intensity or charge suffusing a particular milieu or environment. This understanding of affect is akin to that advanced in works that have underscored the relationship between subjects and their environments (see Navaro-Yashin 2012: 17–27; Richard and Rudnyckyj 2009: 73). This chapter thus contributes to the study of an 'affective milieu' and its relationship to an emerging sense among Salvadorans that specific political imaginaries might actually come about. In other words, I explore how the passions on display in El Salvador's 2009 elections were related to a renewed sense of possibility—to the opening of a new 'political horizon'—for how Salvadorans imagined their relationship with the state.

In examining the relationship between democracy and the collective sentiment of hope, Appadurai (2007) concludes that democracy must be built on hope in order to achieve a 'mass politics' and to distance itself from tyranny. Within a democratic context, Appadurai suggests that we view hope as emerging from the space between utopia, on the one hand, and pragmatism and policy, on the other. Building upon this delineation that considers hope to be "about possibilities rather than about probabilities" (ibid.: 30), I contend that deep post-war disillusionment in El Salvador had gradually eclipsed the intermediate realm of hope. A sense of possibility, however, re-emerged—albeit only temporarily—during the 2009 elections. The emotionally saturated nature of the elections and of clientelist engagements with the FMLN's state officials and party leaders evidenced an aspiration to a state that would provide redress for wartime and post-war offenses and exclusions.

I argue that a focus on both the passion and the deep-rooted sense of indignation and aggrievement among those involved in routine politics in El Salvador can serve as a lens through which to understand Salvadorans' participation in clientelist networks subsequent to the 2009 elections. Specifically, I seek to elucidate how this sudden embrace of clientelism is related to the opening up of a political horizon enabled by the affective milieu of the elections. In the two sections that follow, I depict the affective milieu of the 2009 presidential election and its aftermath and suggest why it can be analytically fruitful to bring this to the fore. In the remainder of the chapter, I propose that the surge in political clientelism through the FMLN that occurred after the 2009 elections might evidence a deep-seated desire for engagement with the state, and I trace the historical origins of this desire.

The 2009 Elections

On the eve of a visit by ARENA presidential candidate Rodrigo Ávila to Santiago Nonualco on 19 September 2008, I saw a large group of young men sporting T-shirts with ARENA's logo heading out toward the rural areas that surround the *municipio*. Through a window at my host family's house, I watched as they painted all the lampposts on the central Avenida Anastasio Aquino with the blue-white-red of ARENA's tri-color flag and plastered walls and house fronts with posters of their candidate. This occurred despite the obvious disgruntlement of residents in Barrio El Ángel, who are overwhelmingly FMLN loyalists. About half an hour later, a couple of my neighbors arrived at the house to swap impressions about an incident that had just occurred nearby. An ARENA member had ripped a poster of FMLN candidate Mauricio Funes off a house front and replaced it with one of Rodrigo Ávila. Irritated, the owner of the house had come out to complain and had begun shouting at the ARENA members until one of them threatened him at gunpoint. My neighbors speculated that the armed men accompanying the ARENA contingent had been hired directly by the regional ARENA deputy, a local from Santiago who was connected by rumors to various violent episodes, especially during elections.

Later that evening, a few neighbors, likewise resentful about the new colors imposed on their street and house fronts, claimed that the ARENA propaganda would not last long. By 6:00 AM the next morning, the lampposts, the curb of the sidewalk, walls, and even rocks and tree trunks on the Anastasio Aquino Avenue were covered with red paint, symbolizing the FMLN. Posters of Mauricio Funes and FMLN flags had reappeared. I asked a neighbor about the chameleonic transformation of the street that had occurred overnight. He explained that ARENA members had been guarding their work until midnight. FMLN loyalists had waited until they left and then proceeded to paint over ARENA's work, burn the ARENA flags, and plaster posters of Mauricio Funes over those of Rodrigo Ávila. "El Barrio El Ángel es *zona liberada*" (The El Ángel neighborhood is a *liberated zone*), this neighbor declared proudly, using an expression employed by guerrillas during El Salvador's civil war to denote FMLN strongholds. This confrontation over the color of the neighborhood was not an isolated incident in Santiago, occurring ever more frequently as the 2009 elections approached. Tensions escalated to the point of fights and gunfire, as recounted publicly by those involved on both sides. National media outlets reported similar incidents nationwide. This election-related violence was not unprecedented in Santiago: during the campaign of the 2004 presidential election, two ARENA loyalists had been run over and killed while plastering their party's propaganda throughout the Coastal Road that crosses the *municipio*.[3]

In 2008 and 2009, I closely followed the elections in Santiago Nonualco. Observing the electoral strategies of the various parties often entailed traveling with their leaders and constituents to various sectors of Santiago as well as to neighboring *municipios* and San Salvador, thereby allowing me to draw comparisons among different *municipios* and regions. When I arrived in El Salvador on 1 August 2008, the electoral campaign for the municipal and legislative elections to be held on 18 January 2009 and the presidential election on 15 March had not yet officially commenced. However, the main parties' constituencies had already been campaigning for two years, their frantic activity and fervor steadily gaining momentum as the elections approached. ARENA and FMLN constituents had been organizing support groups in urban and rural areas to secure votes and volunteers for the coming elections. Their work, as described above, often incurred tension and conflicts as members of both parties sought to dominate and win votes in neighborhoods and *municipios* whose residents lacked clearly defined political allegiances. Much of the tension stemmed from the fact that ARENA and the FMLN represented the opposing sides of El Salvador's civil war in the 1980s. This wartime parallel was evident in some of the incidents I witnessed during and after the electoral campaign.

A few months before the presidential election, Marta,[4] the 70-year-old who heads my host family, was chatting with a friend below a prominent poster of Mauricio Funes that she had strategically placed so that it could be seen from the street. Pointing to the poster, her friend remarked in a low voice: "If Ávila wins the election, you may regret this. You should be careful." Rodrigo Ávila, one of El Salvador's former police directors, was rumored to have participated in death squads during the war, and many speculated on the repression he might unleash against FMLN supporters if ARENA won the election. Marta appeared to disregard her friend's advice. However, in the intimacy of her home, she would repeatedly insist that we all—her son, daughters, and me as well—have our passports ready. "If this man [Ávila] wins the election, there is going to be *matazón* [slaughter]," she would say. This was consistent with rumors exchanged among other FMLN loyalists about gunmen hired by ARENA to kill FMLN leaders during the electoral campaign. Indeed, many insisted that a significant number of the daily homicides in El Salvador were politically motivated.

Meanwhile, rumors circulated among ARENA loyalists about the dire consequences of an FMLN regime. Immediately after the FMLN victory in the 2009 presidential election, I learned about several old women from various sectors of Santiago who had literally fallen sick with worry over what the FMLN would do with those no longer able to work. ARENA members had disseminated rumors that a communist regime would conduct a purge of the elders. A relative of my host family from a rural sector told of her neighbor's 80-year-old mother who remained bedridden and hysterical over what she feared the new government would do with her. Interestingly, so pervasive was the anxiety about the electoral outcome that I identified similar fears among FMLN supporters as well. At a post-election meeting of the local FMLN leadership, a clearly distressed man, who owns a profitable business that imports vehicles from the United States, asked one of the party's regional deputies whether the FMLN would actually enact a socialist regime and intervene to take private property away from people. The deputy calmed him down, explaining that no private property would be touched and that this FMLN government would only give impetus to the possibility of a future socialist state.

Both FMLN and ARENA loyalists thus participated in the affective dynamics at work during the 2009 elections when hope and fear became a popular currency of relations on both the left and the right. Yet in order to understand what underlies contemporary El Salvador's political polarization in the context of the 2009 elections and the clientelist relationships that developed afterward, a historical excursus is in order. The two political parties originated in the midst of the Cold War and were inspired by the Manichaean discourse and political identities of that era. The FMLN was born in October 1980 out of the union of five political-military organizations that had formed and developed in El Salvador throughout the 1970s in response to growing economic and political exclusion (Almeida 2008). Their militarization was also encouraged by the Cubans' overthrow of Batista's regime in 1959 and later by the triumph of the Sandinista Revolution in Nicaragua at the close of the 1970s. The aim of uniting the disparate organizations into the FMLN was to defeat the Salvadoran government militarily and eventually enact a socialist regime. The FMLN embraced Marxism-Leninism, conceiving of the state as an elite instrument and democracy as a mere façade under which the country's military and economic elites pursued their own interests through the state (Martín Álvarez 2010: 11). The option of reforming capitalism was rejected. FMLN leaders instead called for armed revolution as the path to socialism, with a vanguard of intellectuals playing a fundamental role in unleashing this revolution. In rural areas particularly, it was the influence of 'liberation theology'[5] that led much of the population to join and support the armed struggle (Peterson 1997).

The founding of ARENA in 1981 stemmed from discontent among members of El Salvador's landed elite over the agricultural reforms enacted by the governing Christian Democratic Party, which had followed the failed reformist-minded military junta formed after the 1979 coup. ARENA was conceived as an anti-communist conservative party. It supported harsh US-funded counter-insurgency measures during the war, and the party's main leader, Major Roberto

D'Aubuisson, was held responsible for the creation of death squads and the orchestration of political assassinations. Economically, ARENA embraced a neo-liberal agenda that transferred wealth into finance, thereby facilitating a great degree of elite recomposition after the collapse of the agro-export model of accumulation (Segovia 2002).

ARENA won its first presidential election in 1989. This victory, along with control of El Salvador's Legislative Assembly, allowed its members to put into place an intense neo-liberal agenda that oversaw the country's gradual dollarization since 2001 and the deregulation and privatization of state-owned sectors, including public utilities. The widespread disfavor that greeted these measures notwithstanding, ARENA amassed a significant number of votes from the country's rural populations in ensuing post-war elections. The party's success at the polls stemmed partly from the political clientelism it practiced in rural areas, specifically, the hiring of political allies and the distribution of goods among those who showed allegiance during electoral campaigns. While disaffection and abstention have predominated in the post-war elections, both ARENA and the FMLN have managed to maintain core constituencies through, on the one hand, ideological affinity and wartime family experiences and, on the other, clientelism.

Since the 2004 elections, the support ARENA has received from rural populations in regions like La Paz has also been rooted in fears about the FMLN. As of 2004, ARENA's mobilization of anti-communist discourse and symbols, along with the FMLN's own dogmatism, has fed anxiety about an FMLN victory in the presidential election. Yet despite ARENA's support from rural voters, a popular view has remained—on both the right and the left—of the ARENA-ruled state as elitist and standing in opposition to the poor masses. This view is rooted partly in the Marxist analyses popularized in the 1970s and 1980s by political and military organizations and by popular movements led by progressive priests who espoused liberation theology. These analyses have crystallized in the reference to the ARENA-ruled state as 'the 14 families', which denotes the concentration of economic and political capital among a small elite.

El Salvador's 2004 and 2009 presidential elections, in short, marked a significant increase in the emotions and fear experienced by party loyalists and opponents. The strategies and passions associated with the 2009 electoral campaign amounted to a re-enactment of the war that stirred wartime memories and unresolved tensions among significant segments of the Salvadoran population (Montoya 2013). Not only was the 2009 election more disputed than prior ones, but it also managed to engage a large portion of the Salvadoran population. Certainly, the politics of fear practiced by ARENA in 2009 and the unsettled wartime conflicts that this politics evoked played an important part in inciting passionate political participation. At least among core FMLN constituencies, a sentiment of aggrievement predominated, stemming from the 20 years of consecutive ARENA governments that had ruled the country since the war. In the eyes of many FMLN supporters, these governments were the embodiment of wartime repression and the power of an elite that had historically accumulated wealth through labor-intensive agriculture.

Yet the FMLN did not win the 2009 presidential election simply by capitalizing on wartime grievances and anxieties and by solidifying the support of its core constituencies. Rather, it won by amassing the votes of Salvadorans who were disillusioned by the persistent inequality and daily homicides of the post-war era. It is necessary to underscore the tremendous sense of promise represented by the FMLN, which until 2009 had been unable to govern and hence to disappoint, and which for many represented the possibility of a radically different political project. FMLN presidential candidate Mauricio Funes played a crucial role in the party's popularity. A charismatic left-wing journalist and human rights advocate, Funes had had no prior attachment to the FMLN. In addition to representing a position independent of the FMLN, he addressed pressing social and economic issues during the campaign. In a speech delivered in Santiago on 10 March 2009, Funes stressed his commitment to, among other things, providing credit and assistance to those working the land, as well as social housing and other subsidies for poor families. These were important concerns for largely rural *municipios* like Santiago. His candidacy thus symbolized for many the possibility of significant change and, as I will show next, the opportunity to demand redress for previous offenses, whether rooted in the civil war or the post-war era.

"It's Our Turn Now"

The day after the 2009 presidential election, Mauricio Funes addressed a massive audience of FMLN loyalists celebrating their victory in San Salvador with the following declaration: "Ahora es el turno del ofendido, ahora es la oportunidad de los excluidos, ahora es la oportunidad de los marginados, ahora es la oportunidad de los auténticos demócratas" (Now it's the turn of the offended, now it's the opportunity of the excluded, now it's the opportunity of the marginalized, now it's the opportunity of the authentic democrats).[6] His paraphrasing of Salvadoran poet Roque Dalton was consistent with the rhetoric of change that had typified the FMLN 2009 electoral campaign. During the campaign, Funes and the FMLN had criticized the deepening of economic and public insecurity that had occurred during the 20 years of ARENA rule. Rather than proclaiming a transition to socialism or the reversal of ARENA's neo-liberal agenda, Funes had proposed a greater inclusiveness. Funes and the FMLN had presented themselves as 'el partido del pueblo' (the party of the people) in direct opposition to the elitist party ARENA. In this sense, Funes's utterances the day after the election emphasized that the FMLN victory was more than just the replacement of one party by another: it marked an opportunity for inclusion of those who had been excluded, both historically and during the ARENA governments.

In the days and months that followed, I noted events, actions, and conversations in Santiago suggesting that ordinary disaffected and left-wing people perceived the FMLN victory in much the same way that Funes had suggested in his telling speech, that is, as an opportunity for redress. Soon after the election, my friend Elena, a middle-aged woman I had known since my first visit to Santiago in 2001, turned her celebratory mood into pro-active efforts to shift control of the public hospital at which she worked from pro-ARENA doctors and administrators to those supportive of the FMLN. She and some of her colleagues at the Santa Teresa Hospital in Zacatecoluca, La Paz's regional capital located a 20-minute drive away from Santiago, joined forces to appoint a new director. "You don't know what the Areneros [ARENA members and loyalists] have done to the hospital," she would say to me. "They have pilfered the hospital's medicines and materials to cater to their own private clinics in San Salvador. Do you remember the case I mentioned to you of a poor 70-year-old woman who had surgery to receive a prosthesis implant? She bought the prosthesis, and the doctor who did the surgery implanted her with an old prosthesis that he had removed from another patient. Within a few days, the woman stopped walking and ended up in San Salvador, in El Rosales [Hospital]. The relatives told me that at some point they had suspected some irregularity during the surgery, and I couldn't help but tell them what I had learned about the prosthesis replacement from the nurse who had assisted the doctor during the surgery. These Areneros have no shame about taking advantage of the very poorest!" she exclaimed acrimoniously.

Complaints from Elena and her colleagues were also directed at the alleged corruption surrounding the reconstruction of the hospital, still unfinished in 2009. The Santa Teresa Hospital had been severely damaged by two earthquakes that struck La Paz in 2001. The building was abandoned thereafter, aside from a few administrative offices that remained on the ground floor. All patients, practice and surgery rooms, and machines were relocated to insalubrious portable cabins, where they remained in 2009. Although the ARENA government had received funding from the Inter-American Development Bank to rebuild the hospital by 2009, the funds had been exhausted and the work halted by 2008 before the building had been finished.[7] Given these circumstances, Elena and her colleagues saw the FMLN victory as an opportunity to subvert the Areneros's political control of the hospital. In the months following the election, they wrote petition letters to the health minister and met with various FMLN leaders they knew in La Paz, one of whom arranged a meeting with the minister. Elena and her colleagues saw the meeting as an opportunity to explain in person to the minister why they wanted her to appoint a new hospital director and to hand over to her the hundreds of signatures they had collected in support of the appointment of one of their colleagues, an FMLN member, as hospital director. Weeks after the meeting, the minister acceded to their request.

Similar excitement characterized the expectations of many Santiagueños regarding the FMLN's opportunity to capsize ARENA's control and partisan management of the state-funded program Semilla Mejorada (Improved Seed). Launched in 2006 with the goal of alleviating the debts incurred by small-scale peasants, Semilla Mejorada had in practice operated as a local patronage project. ARENA party leaders, rather than state institutions, distributed agricultural consumables, thus employing the program to remunerate those rural dwellers who had actively supported the party and to court others in hopes of securing their votes. Santiago is a predominantly rural *municipio*, with nearly half of its population employed in agriculture—the country's lowest-paying economic activity, along with domestic labor. This being the case, the distribution of seeds and fertilizer effectively granted ARENA a large political clientele, while excluding political opponents from the program.

In the months leading up to the presidential election, I overheard many conversations about ARENA's distribution of goods to those joining the party and attending its weekly public meetings in Santiago on Sundays. I witnessed one of those famed Semilla Mejorada distributions. On my way to the *municipio* market, I saw one day that a crowd had gathered around the ARENA headquarters. Inside, there was a large pile of two-pound bags of beans. An ARENA leader explained to me that the party was concerned about the welfare of the country's rural populations and that Semilla Mejorada was ARENA's program to assist the poorest citizens. Immediately thereafter, I heard another ARENA leader explain to a 60-year-old man wearing a typical peasant hat that only ARENA members would be receiving the beans. The ARENA leader suggested that this man join the party so as to become eligible for future distributions of agricultural consumables. Following his advice, the man joined a queue consisting mainly of middle-aged and elderly men wearing similar peasant-like garb.

While the partisan nature of this program had been widely criticized by FMLN supporters during the election, after the FMLN victory many of them began harboring the hope that it would now be their turn to benefit from Semilla Mejorada and other such programs. To communicate their pressing needs, these disaffected and left-wing Santiagueños met with local FMLN leaders, invited FMLN deputies to their neighborhoods and communities, or visited ministers and other FMLN state officials in their offices so as to make them aware of the public works most urgently needed in their communities or to ask for more personal favors such as jobs.

A different, although just as fervent, sort of hope was harbored by those who expected the FMLN government to redress wartime human rights violations. Several Santiagueños approached local FMLN leaders as well as one of the regional deputies after the elections to ask whether there was a way to find out what had happened to their relatives during the war—whether they had disappeared or had been killed and buried in one of the numerous unmarked mass graves scattered throughout the country. Still intimidated by their memories of the death squads and paramilitary groups that operated with impunity in La Paz during the war, many residents of Santiago and neighboring *municipios* had made no attempt during the 20 years of ARENA rule to learn the whereabouts of relatives who may have been victims of wartime forced disappearance. The new FMLN government, they believed, provided a more appropriate milieu in which to ask these questions.

Until then, post-war efforts to address the war and wartime human rights violations had been marginal and limited to the work of a few grassroots organizations and NGOs. The Father Cosme Spessotto Committee, which consists of relatives of wartime victims and victims themselves, is a grassroots organization performing memory work in La Paz since 2005. During the electoral campaign, committee members wrote letters outlining their requests to Mauricio Funes and several candidates for the legislative and municipal elections with whom they were familiar. They, too, celebrated the FMLN's victory in the presidential election as an opportunity to redress human rights violations and demand compensation, both moral and material. With that goal, they designed a program to compensate war victims and, through personal networks within the FMLN as well as NGOs, managed to meet several times to discuss their proposal with Vanda Piñato, Funes's wife and the country's social inclusion secretary after the FMLN victory.

Mauricio Funes's victory speech, in sum, seems to have echoed a predominant post-election feeling among ordinary people who had supported the FMLN during the electoral campaign. "It's our turn now" was explicitly articulated by some and implied by others in their pro-active engagements with state officials and FMLN party leaders after the elections. These engagements took a range of forms, from the goal of securing material benefits via the party to the search for redress for exclusion and wrongdoing during both the civil war and the post-war era. In this sense, Funes's speech and explicit reference to "the turn of the offended" captured a generalized feeling of exclusion and aggrievement. Ordinary people in Santiago were offended by the underfunded, ruinous, and corrupted state of El Salvador's public health care; offended by their own exclusion from state-funded programs and the absence of public utilities and public works in their communities; offended by the 1993 Amnesty Law passed by ARENA governments that imposed silence regarding wartime human rights violations and precluded both retributive and restorative justice. The FMLN victory offered an opportunity for redress and thus for the envisioning of qualitative state transformation, which in turn inspired Salvadorans to attempt to reactivate their relationship with the state through personal networks. These efforts would turn out to be short-lived, as in many cases people soon realized that their requests would not be fulfilled.

Citizenship through the State

As described above, after the 2009 elections I witnessed or heard about innumerable attempts by ordinary people in Santiago, as well as other *municipios* in La Paz, to meet with and make requests of newly appointed state officials. Channeled through letters, phone calls, and visits, these initiatives were coeval yet uncoordinated; most had not been preceded by much organizational effort. Prior to the elections, Elena and her colleagues had not planned to shift ARENA's control of the hospital where they worked. Likewise, it was only after the elections that those seeking to benefit from Semilla Mejorada and other state-funded programs from which they had been excluded made efforts to negotiate with FMLN leaders to insist on their inclusion in these programs or to expound upon their requests. Such was also the case for those who suddenly decided to ask about relatives who had disappeared or were assassinated during the civil war in the 1980s. Although members of the Father Cosme Spessotto Committee had already written letters addressed to Funes and other FMLN members, it was the FMLN victory and Funes's declaration that it was now "the turn of the offended" that encouraged them to embark on designing a program of compensation for war victims.

Interestingly, all these initiatives were channeled through the FMLN's clientelist networks. Clientelism has historically been a salient trait of El Salvador's routine politics. During nineteenth- and early-twentieth-century elections—whether national or local—patron-client relations were very much in play in El Salvador (Ching 2014: 36–43). Rival patronage-based networks, linking members of the landed elite and peasants through clientelist and other bonds (familial, ethnic, and so on), served as the basis for arranging an electoral outcome prior to an election. It is important to note that peasants were not simply subordinated in this relationship of patronage: they often enjoyed a bargaining position. In contemporary El Salvador, elections work in much the same way, although networks are mobilized through more complex relationships, with ideology playing a crucial role in maintaining core constituencies. During post-war elections, well-known members of both ARENA and the FMLN (very often regional deputies) have acted as political bosses whom people approach to ask for favors. ARENA, being able to mobilize considerably more resources, has even temporarily hired local allies who are leaders in their communities, thereby being able to amass a significant number of votes.

Yet political clientelism in rural El Salvador is not just a set of calculative practices through which ordinary people receive goods and favors. As in Auyero's (2000) depiction of Peronist politics in an Argentinean slum in the mid-1990s, clientelism constitutes 'problem-solving networks' through which people deal with survival-related needs. In El Salvador, as in other Latin American countries, people are knowledgeable about whom to ask for a particular favor in each party's web of relationships. Indeed, during the 2009 electoral campaign, it was common to see people queuing up every Sunday in Zacatecoluca to talk to one of the regional FMLN deputies after the party's weekly rally. What is distinctive about post-war El Salvador, however, is that the web of relationships constituted by clientelism has, among other things, served as a means through which people circumvent state institutions and officials for reasons that have as much to do with fear and distrust of the state as with its presumed inefficiency (Montoya 2011: 189–195). Many ordinary Salvadorans regard both political and personal networks as safer, more trustworthy, and more efficient channels than bureaucracies for dealing with pressing needs. Under-reported cases of extortion and other crimes, as well as claims for jobs, housing, and basic needs not channeled through state institutions, are dealt with through acquaintances with political connections or relatives who can penetrate the relevant state institutions. Yet what I found notable about political clientelism in El Salvador after the 2009 elections was its twofold functioning as a means through which people sought redress from previous state offenses and asserted an aspiration to a different relationship vis-à-vis the state.

Following the elections, the letters and phone calls to FMLN state officials testified to the people's desire for a state that listens, cares, and delivers. The ensuing face-to-face encounters satisfied people's desire to establish a more personalized relationship with the state. Lazar (2004) has suggested that the enthusiastic embrace of political clientelism among the poor in the 1999 local elections in El Alto, Bolivia, served as a means to 'substantiate citizenship' by making democracy more personalized, accountable, and representative.[8] She finds that, in stark contrast to liberal definitions of citizenship and democracy as disengaged, delegative, and based on rational decisions, clientelism allows ordinary people to directly engage politicians and effectively even to stand for election themselves, inasmuch as they benefit from their party's victory by obtaining jobs in public office. While we could discuss whether increased substantive citizenship actually results from political clientelism in El Salvador, the FMLN victory inspired left-wing and disaffected people to envision a qualitative and more permanent transformation of the state itself—from the elitist state ruled by ARENA to one that truly represents the Salvadoran people.

The widespread practice of clientelism in post-war El Salvador suggests that the state is very much defined along party lines. Indeed, during the 20 years of ARENA rule, bureaucracies were saturated with ARENA loyalists to such a degree that once ARENA lost the 2009 presidential election, ARENA deputies made sure a law was passed in the Legislative Assembly to hinder a massive replacement of public officials by the new FMLN government.[9] It is thus not surprising that a change of party could elicit the idea of deep transformation, of regime shift. The FMLN portrayed itself as 'the party of the people' throughout the 2009 elections, evoking the FMLN's roots in the country's peasant population and its aspiration for an alternative state project. It may have been this representation that led left-wing people to think that they could now visit the offices of high-profile state officials and even take the initiative to make suggestions to, and requests of, the state. I argue that Salvadorans' political horizon—which opened with the Peace Accords in 1992 and later foreclosed in the face of increasing post-war disillusionment—opened up again with the 2009 elections. Once again, as during the 1970s and 1980s, left-wing and disaffected Salvadorans embraced the possibility that the state might actually represent and work for the people.

Specifically, the desires, goals, and expectations that ordinary Salvadorans have invested in the idea of the state as a political subject and the central role that this idea plays in their political imaginaries may be related in part to the liberal traditions of Latin America and their coalescence throughout the twentieth century with emancipatory and socialist ideologies. As Baud (2007) has observed with regard to indigenous groups' quest for citizenship in the Andean countries, throughout the twentieth century the republican tradition of these countries led increasingly to the nation-state's becoming a legitimate interlocutor and hence the basis for definition and entitlement of citizenship rights and responsibilities. Meanwhile, the reverberations of liberation theology in El Salvador's rural areas as well as the later dissemination of international human rights rhetoric—although perhaps of limited penetration—should not be underestimated in promoting the state as the primary entity on which the claims and demands of ordinary people regarding citizenship rights are placed.

Even more important is the historical conjuncture afforded by the rise of the so-called New Left in Latin America, which has provided a regional context in which new state-citizenry pacts have been forged, including a 'return of the state' as the subject morally responsible for delivering socio-economic and political rights (Grugel and Riggirozzi 2012). Yet, as already illustrated, in El Salvador the channels through which post-election demands were placed on the new FMLN-ruled state were not state bureaucracies but the more personalized routes provided by clientelist practices.

Overall, given their efforts to channel their post-election petitions through state officials—albeit through those that are part of clientelist networks—I suggest that Salvadorans think of themselves as citizens *through* the state. Gordon and Stack (2007: 120) have suggested that citizenship cannot be reduced to a relationship with the state and have exposed the historical contingency of the state-citizenship coupling. They contend that, given the state roll-back of the neo-liberal era, it is more appropriate to think in terms of citizenship *beyond* the state. I argue, however, that even though clientelism—as a circumvention of state institutions—might affirm such a delineation, the aspiration of ordinary Salvadorans in a rural *municipio* to be received by state officials and to channel their requests through them is instead indicative of the extent to which the state in contemporary El Salvador is conceived as a chief political subject.

Conclusion

An examination of El Salvador's 2009 elections has facilitated an understanding of how a particular affective milieu might fuel hopes and in turn political action. El Salvador's 2009 presidential election and the victory of Mauricio Funes and the FMLN in this election elicited a political imaginary that had dissipated during the post-war era. "Democratic disenchantment" (Moodie 2010: 145) had become a predominant sentiment due to the minimal economic reform stipulated in the Peace Accords and the gradual roll-back of the state—with the exception of its punitive and military functions and its minimal poverty alleviation programs—that consecutive ARENA governments had enacted as part of their neo-liberal agenda. During the 2009 elections, the passionate involvement in party politics by people on both the left and the right rekindled wartime conflicts as well as the hopes and fears thereof. Among left-wing Salvadorans, there was a renewed sense of possibility vis-à-vis the political project for which they had fought and lost relatives during the war. Partly due to Funes's candidacy, the elections sparked hopeful feelings not just among the FMLN's core constituencies but also among segments of the Salvadoran population disaffected by the ARENA governments yet initially dubious of the FMLN due to this party's dogmatism during the post-war era.

After the FMLN victory, passions continued to run high. During the first few months of FMLN government, both left-wing and disaffected Salvadorans suddenly made pro-active efforts to activate FMLN clientelist networks that would enable face-to-face encounters with state officials. Opportunistic attempts to benefit from an FMLN government coalesced with a desire for redress, understood as compensation for various forms of exclusions and offenses, both historical and recent. All of this, channeled through clientelist networks involving state officials, evidenced the central role of the state in ordinary people's political imaginaries and aspirations. If a particular historical logic of accumulation explains why the state has remained a discrete entity in the minds of ordinary Salvadorans on both the left and the right, the syncretic legacy of liberalism and emancipatory ideologies, along with a regional trend of refashioning state-citizenry relationships and forms of democratic participation, explain how it is that the notion of the state retains a central place in Salvadorans' imaginaries. I have thus suggested that despite the disillusionment, distrust, and fear of state institutions that I observed both before and after 2009, Salvadorans aspire to a political project in which the state plays an important part. It was after all the intensely passionate milieu of the 2009 elections that rekindled wartime desires for state transformation and for political action toward that project.

Acknowledgments

This chapter is based on research funded by the University of Manchester and Fundación Caja Madrid. I thank Madeleine Reeves, the organizer of the "Affective States" workshop, as well as discussant Jonathan Mair and other participants for their helpful comments and insightful discussions. I am also grateful to David Pretel, Ralph Sprenkels, and Alaina Lemon for their valuable criticism on earlier drafts of this chapter.

Ainhoa Montoya is a Lecturer in Latin American Studies at the School of Advanced Study, University of London. She is also an Economic and Social Research Council Future Research Leaders Fellow. Her research has focused on post-conflict violence in El Salvador, examining how Salvadorans participate in political life in the context of a violent democracy. Her current research project explores the interplay between the legal and the moral in conflicts over mineral resources in Central America.

Notes

1. In 2009, municipal, legislative, and presidential elections, whose periodicity differs, coincided.
2. Until 2004, only the 1994 elections—El Salvador's first democratic elections—had surpassed a 50 percent turnout (Artiga-González 2004: 38).
3. See "Un muerto durante cierre de campaña," *La Prensa Gráfica*, 19 March 2004; "Entierran activista arenero," *La Prensa Gráfica*, 20 March 2004.
4. Personal information has been anonymized in order to preserve confidentiality.
5. 'Liberation theology' is the progressive Catholic doctrine with origins in the 1968 Conference of Latin American Bishops in Colombia, which in turn was influenced by the Second Vatican Council. This progressive hermeneutics, disseminated throughout much of Latin America during the 1970s by priests and laypeople, incorporated Marxist categories of analysis and a critique of capitalism (Planas 1986).
6. "Funes: Llegó el turno del ofendido," *El Nacional*, 16 March 2009.
7. "El terremoto que duró 10 años," *El Faro*, 9 August 2010, https://it-it.facebook.com/notes/pol%C3%ADtica-stereo-el-salvador/el-terremoto-que-duró-10-años/414115547108.
8. Although such a discussion is beyond the scope of this chapter, one could suggest to the contrary that clientelism is tantamount to charity insofar as it undermines the notion that all citizens bear equal rights (Julio Boltvinik and Enrique Hernández Laos, cited in Gledhill 2005: 81).
9. The Civil Service Law was passed before the FMLN took office in June 2009.

References

Almeida, Paul D. 2008. *Waves of Protest: Popular Struggle in El Salvador, 1925–2005*. Minneapolis: University of Minnesota Press.
Appadurai, Arjun. 2007. "Hope and Democracy." *Public Culture* 19 (1): 29–34.
Artiga-González, Álvaro. 2004. *Elitismo competitivo: Dos décadas de elecciones en El Salvador (1982–2003)*. San Salvador: UCA Editores.
Auyero, Javier. 2000. *Poor People's Politics: Peronist Survival Networks and the Legacy of Evita*. Durham, NC: Duke University Press.
Banerjee, Mukulika. 2007. "Sacred Elections." *Economic and Political Weekly* 42 (17): 1556–1562.
Baud, Michiel. 2007. "Indigenous Politics and the State: The Andean Highlands in the Nineteenth and Twentieth Centuries." *Social Analysis* 51 (2): 19–42.
Ching, Erik. 2014. *Authoritarian El Salvador: Politics and the Origins of the Military Regimes, 1880–1940*. Notre Dame, IN: University of Notre Dame Press.
Coles, Kimberley A. 2004. "Election Day: The Construction of Democracy through Technique." *Cultural Anthropology* 19 (4): 551–580.
Cruz, José M. 1998a. *La violencia en El Salvador en los años noventa: Magnitud, costos y factores posibilitadores*. San Salvador: IUDOP.
Cruz, José M. 1998b. "¿Por qué no votan los salvadoreños?" *ECA—Estudios Centroamericanos* 595–596: 449–472.
Cruz, José M. 2001. *¿Elecciones para qué? El impacto del ciclo electoral 1999–2000 en la cultura política salvadoreña*. San Salvador: FLACSO.
Dalton, Roque. 1962. *El turno del ofendido*. Havana: Casa de las Américas.
Gay, Robert. 1999. "The Broker and the Thief: A Parable (Reflections on Popular Politics in Brazil)." *Luso-Brazilian Review* 36 (1): 49–70.

Gledhill, John. 2005. "Citizenship and the Social Geography of Deep Neo-liberalization." *Anthropologica* 47 (1): 81–100.

Gordon, Andrew, and Trevor Stack. 2007. "Citizenship Beyond the State: Thinking with Early Modern Citizenship in the Contemporary World." *Citizenship Studies* 11 (2): 117–133.

Gould, Deborah B. 2009. *Moving Politics: Emotion and ACT UP's Fight against AIDS.* Chicago: University of Chicago Press.

Grugel, Jean, and Pía Riggirozzi. 2012. "Post-neoliberalism in Latin America: Rebuilding and Reclaiming the State after Crisis." *Development and Change* 43 (1): 1–21.

Lazar, Sian. 2004. "Personalist Politics, Clientelism and Citizenship: Local Elections in El Alto, Bolivia." *Bulletin of Latin American Research* 23 (2): 228–243.

Martín Álvarez, Alberto. 2010. *From Revolutionary War to Democratic Revolution: The Farabundo Martí National Liberation Front (FMLN) in El Salvador.* Berlin: Berghof Conflict Research.

McDonald, James H. 1997. "A Fading Aztec Sun: The Mexican Opposition and the Politics of Everyday Fear in 1994." *Critique of Anthropology* 17 (3): 263–292.

McLeod, James R. 1999. "The Sociodrama of Presidential Politics: Rhetoric, Ritual, and Power in the Era of Teledemocracy." *American Anthropologist* 101 (2): 359–373.

Montoya, Ainhoa. 2011. "'Neither War nor Peace': Violence and Democracy in Post-War El Salvador." PhD diss., University of Manchester.

Montoya, Ainhoa. 2013. "The Violence of Cold War Polarities and the Fostering of Hope: The 2009 Elections in Postwar El Salvador." In *Central America in the New Millennium: Living Transition and Reimagining Democracy*, ed. Jennifer L. Burrell and Ellen Moodie, 49–63. New York: Berghahn Books.

Moodie, Ellen. 2010. *El Salvador in the Aftermath of Peace: Crime, Uncertainty, and the Transition to Democracy.* Philadelphia: University of Pennsylvania Press.

Murray, Kevin. 1997. *El Salvador: Peace on Trial.* Oxford: Oxfam UK and Ireland.

Navaro-Yashin, Yael. 2012. *The Make-Believe Space: Affective Geography in a Postwar Polity.* Durham, NC: Duke University Press.

Peterson, Anna L. 1997. *Martyrdom and the Politics of Religion: Progressive Catholicism in El Salvador's Civil War.* New York: State University of New York Press.

Planas, Ricardo. 1986. *Liberation Theology: The Political Expression of Religion.* Kansas City, MO: Sheed & Ward.

Ramos, Carlos G. 2000. "Marginación, exclusión social y violencia." In *Violencia en una sociedad en transición: Ensayos*, ed. Carlos G. Ramos, 7–47. San Salvador: PNUD.

Richard, Analiese, and Daromir Rudnyckyj. 2009. "Economies of Affect." *Journal of the Royal Anthropological Institute* 15 (1): 57–77.

Segovia, Alexander. 2002. *Transformación estructural y reforma económica en El Salvador: El funcionamiento económico de los noventa y sus efectos sobre el crecimiento, la pobreza y la distribución del ingreso.* Guatemala City: F&G Editores.

Silber, Irina C. 2011. *Everyday Revolutionaries: Gender, Violence, and Disillusionment in Postwar El Salvador.* New Brunswick, NJ: Rutgers University Press.

Verdery, Katherine. 1999. *The Political Lives of Dead Bodies: Reburial and Postsocialist Change.* New York: Columbia University Press.

Chapter 7

LIVING FROM THE NERVES
Deportability, Indeterminacy, and the 'Feel of Law'
in Migrant Moscow

Madeleine Reeves

In January 2012, at a time of increasingly vocal demonstrations of public discontent in urban Russia, the head of Russia's Federal Migration Service (FMS)
launched a new program, "Operation Illegal Migrant" (Operatsiia nelegal'nyi
migrant), aimed at identifying and deporting undocumented migrant workers.
This was accompanied by a number of highly visible, publicized expulsions in
which the FMS conducted televised raids upon workplaces and dormitories.
The same week that this operation was launched, Russia's then prime minister,
Vladimir Putin, weighed into the debate on Russia's migration future with a
speech to the Board of the FMS and a 3,000-word essay in the Russian daily,
Nezavisimaya gazeta (Putin 2012a). "In creating civilized conditions for legal
labor migration," Putin (2012b) argued, "we must harshly excise all criminal and

Notes for this chapter begin on page 133.

various kinds of gray schemes." He reserved particular critique for those who registered migrant workers in 'rubber apartments' (*rezinovye kvartiry*), that is, at fictive addresses where, in Putin's words, "hundreds of people are registered as living in a few square meters."[1]

In such pronouncements, the distinction between legal and illegal presence in the nation-state is treated as at once self-evident, socially visible, and morally consequential. Lines of compassion or rigor can be mapped onto lines of legal and illegal status: legal migrants deserve compassion and 'integration', while illegal migrants deserve deportation. This is, of course, by no means solely a Russian story. But the administrative production of migrant 'illegality' in Russia has distinctive contours for reasons that are tied to its particular political economy of work and housing; a distinctive history of attempts to regulate movement within and between urban centers; and a pervasive dependence of law enforcement officers on informal payments (Light 2010; Matthews 1993; Rahmonova-Schwarz 2006; Reeves 2009; Sahadeo 2011). Today, Russia has one of the highest global rates of net in-migration, and three former Soviet republics—Tajikistan, Kyrgyzstan, and Moldova—rank among the five most remittance-dependent economies in the world (Mohapatra et al. 2011).

In this chapter I draw on research with migrant workers from Batken region of Kyrgyzstan, a newly remittance-dependent state, as a means of exploring how this space of legal indeterminacy is produced and how it is lived.[2] Family budgets in Batken are increasingly dependent upon having at least one family member working in Russia, typically for several months or even several years at a stretch (Bichsel et al. 2005; Reeves 2012; Rohner 2007). Much of this labor is in an ambiguous relation to formal law, making 'illegal immigration' a major topic of public concern and political intervention in Russia. Discussions about unfortunate relatives who have been 'kicked' from work (*kidalaga tüshöö*) or deported from the country are a regular part of village conversation in Batken (Reeves 2012, 2013).

My focus is on the 'feel of law' among Kyrgyz migrant workers whose residency or labor is socially tolerated but legally unrecognized. By 'feel of law', I stress here a commitment to explore how the legal regulation of residence and work is locally understood; how and when a boundary between 'legal' and 'illegal' residence and work is invoked; and how registers of legality are understood to map (or not) onto the domain of the licit (Abraham and van Schendel 2005). By 'feel of law', however, I also seek to signal law's affective dimension: the fact that 'il/legalities' and the documents through which these statuses are mediated elicit certain embodied responses, and that the mystique of law operates in part through the circulation of such feelings. As Navaro-Yashin (2007) has noted in another context of legally ambiguous residence, the affective dimensions of law have rarely been attended to by scholars of bureaucracy. And yet in conditions of legal precariousness, when it is unclear whether the document bearing your identity is authentic, or when it is unknown whether those charged with policing your presence will themselves abide by the rules, law can itself incite particular affective responses—menacing rather than comforting, with violence riding close to the surface of encounters with street-level bureaucrats.

Differentiating Deportation

In developing this argument, I seek to make two contributions to a growing anthropological conversation about the illegalization of migrant labor. First, I wish to present a more differentiated account of what Nathalie Peutz and Nicholas De Genova (2010: 2) have characterized as a global 'deportation regime', that is, "an increasingly unified, effectively *global* response to a world that is being actively remade by transnational human mobility." Second, as I explore below, I seek to attend to deportability not simply as a social and legal predicament, but as an embodied and affectively charged condition of being.

Deportation—the removal of non-citizens from the territory of a state through the threatened or actual use of force—has become the focus of considerable scholarly and policy concern in recent years (Bloch and Schuster 2005; Coutin 2015; De Genova 2002; De Genova and Peutz 2010; Drotbohm and Hasselberg 2015; Ellermann 2009; McGregor 2011; Nijhawan 2005; Paoletti 2010; Pieke and Biao 2007). Anderson et al. (2011: 547) identify a doubling in the number of forcible removals in the UK and a tripling in the US since the late 1990s, leading to what Gibney (2008: 146) describes as a "deportation turn" in Western states' treatment of unwanted non-citizens.

Recent scholarship has sought to set this transformation within the context of an increasing securitization of migration, particularly following 9/11 (Coutin 2015; De Genova 2007; Welch 2002) and the expansion of what Ellermann (2009: 1) calls the "socially coercive state." This work has explored a gradual shift in states' recourse to deportation, from a response to specific crises to a routine aspect of immigration control (Cornelisse 2010; Schuster 2005). Ethnographic studies of removal centers (Andrijasevic 2010; Bosworth 2014; Hall 2010), the removal process (Papadopoulos et al. 2008; Peutz 2010), and the modes of justification employed by those charged with expelling 'illegal aliens' have coupled this somewhat top-down focus on migration policy with an appreciation for the messy and often emotionally fraught work of detention and removal. At the same time, a growing critical literature has highlighted the social and political mechanisms through which certain bodies come to be identified as deportable; the intersections of such processes with labor subordination and racialized histories of exploitation (De Genova 2005; Harrison and Lloyd 2007; Hiemstra 2010; Kanstroom 2007; Ngai 2004; Ruhs and Anderson 2010); and the role of 'deportability' in marking a 'limit point' to the bounds of citizenship (Anderson et al. 2011; Coutin 2005; Drotbohm 2011; Kaşlı and Parla 2009).

While there has undoubtedly been a prodigious rise in deportation as a tool of government in diverse states worldwide, I suggest that scholarly concern with identifying and critiquing the rise of the (putatively global) deportation regime has tended to obscure the diversity of social and political purposes that deportation serves in particular contexts, as well as the ability (or indeed concern) of states actually to deport and/or prevent re-entry. My analysis does not contest the critical impulse of Peutz and De Genova's work, that is, to denaturalize deportation as the seemingly inevitable response of the state to the presence of 'illegal' non-citizens. But it does emphasize the need to differentiate such a deportation regime and the kind of political subjectivities that it fosters.

In contrast to recent emphasis on a single, global socio-political logic of removal, I argue that different kinds of socio-political order (and disorder) are at stake in different migrant-receiving states. In the Russian context, for instance, most deportable migrant workers are in a situation of administrative violation, not through illicit entry but through undocumented or incorrectly documented overstay—itself rendered virtually inevitable by the organization of the labor market (with attendant quotas for the employment of non-citizens) and the political economy of housing (Human Rights Watch 2009; Reeves 2009; Schenk 2010). Within seven working days of arrival, all newly entered non-citizens are required to obtain a temporary residence registration, which is valid for three months.[3] In order to remain longer, non-citizens must obtain a 'permission for temporary residence' and a 'permission for work', both of which can be costly in time and money and are limited in supply. Staying visibly 'legible'—that is, having the documents that are necessary to demonstrate residence and work—is thus a major preoccupation of non-citizens, and it has spurred a lucrative informal economy in the lending and borrowing of Russian passports, the provision of fake residence addresses, and the issuing of 'clean fake' (*chistie fal'shivye*) registration documents (Reeves 2013). It is precisely these 'gray schemes' that Putin railed against in his speech to the FMS Board. Such practices proliferate the spaces of ambiguity in which migrant workers—whose continued presence in the city is dependent upon maintaining a successfully documented self—are not so much undocumented as fictively hyper-documented.

In Russia, therefore, a prodigious increase in public and official discourse around deportation (*deportatsiia*) as a necessary tool of state policy to counter the proliferation of illegal immigration is coupled with an equally public commentary concerning the ineffectiveness and performativity of such campaigns. I thus suggest that, rather than through an integrated and purposive regime, migration is governed precisely through the proliferation of spaces of ambiguity that emerge from an inconsistent legal environment, from the disjuncture between administrative regulation and the workings of the labor market, and from the feelings that intensify in conditions of collective uncertainty (i.e., suspicion, fear, cynicism, disdain). Nor should such ambiguity and legal inconsistency be interpreted as a sign of state weakness or failure. Indeed, governance in this context perhaps thrives less on the act of rendering non-citizen populations legible—as in Scott's (1998) account of 'high-modernist ideology'—than on the proliferation of spaces of *dis*-articulation between competing realms of the state, in which personal rule, corrupt practices, and moralizing discourses about the incalculable presence of undocumented illegals (*nelegaly*) all flourish.

Deportability as an Affective State

This variation in the workings of different migration systems, moreover, is consequential for the lived experience of deportability, a protracted condition of uncertainty in which imagined horizons are constrained by the constant threat of a future that can be revoked (Sigona 2012; Willen 2007). In the language of the introduction to this book, I consider deportability as an affective state. I want to hold in place the simultaneity of being deportable as both a socio-legal designation and a lived predicament that is characterized by the affective intensity born of the revocability of future horizons. In so doing, I seek more generally to inquire about the way in which 'the law' acts on bodies, not simply through what it permits or prohibits, but also through the way in which it reproduces socially charged and affectively resonant spaces of indeterminacy around where the domain of the legal extends.

A distinction articulated by Richard and Rudnyckyj (2009) is helpful in elaborating this idea. Affect, they argue (ibid.: 61), refers to relations "practised *between* individuals rather than experiences borne by sole individuals." Rudnyckyj (2011: 70) argues elsewhere that the verb form of emotion—to emote—is an intransitive verb that does "not necessarily take (and therefore make) an object." Anthropological analyses of emotion are often grounded implicitly in an ontology of the sovereign subject who *has* emotions. Emotion is understood as "the socio-linguistic fixing of the quality of an experience which is from that point onward defined as personal" (Massumi 1995: 88). Affect, by contrast, is both a noun and a transitive verb, and as such it "simultaneously makes both its subject and its object" (Richard and Rudnyckyj 2009: 59). "It is the transitive and reflexive capacity of affect—actions that *affect* others and oneself" (ibid.)—that makes it analytically productive for thinking about the mutual constitution of subjects and objects.

In the condition of legal precariousness encountered by Kyrgyzstani migrant workers in Moscow, it is precisely the indeterminacy of objects and statuses—the indeterminacy concerning what documents might do in particular situations, whether they are 'real' or 'fake', or whether an 'official' will act according to regulations—that renders this space affectively charged. This is reflected in a host of terms that point to migrants' cultivated 'invisibility' and labor subordination in Moscow, including the claims "we can't be seen" (*biz moskvada körönböibüz*) and "we live silently" (*tynch jashaibyz*). It is reflected, too, in the practices that play on the possibility for quiet subversion, such as the regular lending and borrowing of Russian passports among migrant workers, which are premised on the reality that Muscovites find it very difficult to tell Kyrgyz people apart. As Kairat, one of my most incisive interlocutors put it, imitating a Moscow employer with mocking irony: "You all have the same face!" (*Vy vse na odno litso!*).

Perhaps most of all, this indeterminacy is reflected in the expression frequently used by Batken men and women to describe the experience of living in precarious conditions in Moscow: *nervden jashoo* or *nervden sezim*—literally, living or feeling 'from the nerves'. *Nervden* might be rendered in English as 'nervous' or 'anxious'—that is, as an internal, emotional state. But the grammatical form of the Kyrgyz version, to live or feel 'from the nerves', points to something explicitly corporeal. It is at once an internal state and a contagious, circulating feeling. 'Living *nervden*', I propose, points to pre-subjective origins of feeling and to a range of embodied states that is more extensive and more complex than fear—the emotion that has been the most consistent focus of studies of undocumented migrant experience (see, e.g., Willen 2006, 2007; cf. Kelly 2006). To live 'from the nerves' communicates both thrill and risk—both hope and the radical revocability of the provisional stabilities of work and accommodation.

I turn now to an ethnographic analysis of this space, drawing on extended conversations with three Batken men whom I came to know closely during fieldwork. In each case, the indeterminacy over where legal and illegal residence and mobility respectively begin and end fostered gestures of accommodation with particular state personnel that bled over into corruption. We could read these as signs of the pervasive 'gray schemes' that Putin condemned in his speech to the FMS. But it is the affective resonances of this indeterminacy that I am keen to explore. As I seek to show, feelings of fear and anger or expressions of mocking condescension toward 'illiterate' police officers cannot be abstracted from the socio-legal formation of deportability or from the objects and relationships through which it is constituted. It is precisely in the proliferating circulation of uncertainty, suspicion, and indignation, I suggest, that the Russian migration regime comes to be constituted.

Living from the Nerves

When I met him at his home in Batken, Bakhtiyar-aka was eager to enlist my help in overcoming the gap between his physical and his documented self.[4] Tearing out a page from his daughter's exercise book, he asked me to write his name for him in English, using the Latin alphabet. His native Kyrgyz, like Russian, uses the Cyrillic script, and Bakhtiyar was unsure which of the many possible renderings of his name in English was 'right'. In his early fifties, Bakhtiyar-aka was on the cusp of becoming a village elder or *aksakal* (lit., 'white-beard'). The youngest of several sons, he was responsible for caring for his elderly parents and for maintaining a home in the village. He had recently been called to Russia by one of his own sons who had found him a job on a building site outside Moscow. His son had promised to buy him an electronic plane ticket, but Bakhtiyar was uncertain about making the long journey to the airport in Osh with only the promise that his name and passport number were listed somewhere inside a computer. "In Osh they want to see the paper [*kagaz*]," he insisted. Legibility necessitated its paper substantiation. He knew people who had had problems there, being told that they "didn't look like their passports." And he had suffered unwanted questions in the past when the spelling of his name as it appears on his registration document was found to diverge from the spelling on his passport.

Bakhtiyar's preoccupation with his documented self got us on the subject of legal legibility. His two brothers had already paid several thousand dollars to obtain Russian citizenship in order to avoid the risk of deportation and to secure better-paid work. Bakhtiyar, by contrast, had decided to keep his Kyrgyz passport so that he could continue to have a legal right to own and sell land in Batken. This made his labor status more precarious in Russia and entailed considerable outlays to be able to buy a work permit through a private firm. I asked Bakhtiyar-aka how easy it was for men and women from his village, Sary-Bulak, to remain legally resident in Russia, to which he responded by correcting my question and introducing a distinction of his own:

> Ha! Legal?! *No one* from here is legal in Russia, not from Sary-Bulak, at least. For instance, there's a service in Bishkek, if you go that way through the migration service, there are loads of documents you need to get together, to be *really* legal. You've got to go up to Bishkek to register, it takes months and in that time I could have worked and come back. But, well, I think of migrants as divided into three groups really: legal, semi-legal and … we call them 'wild animals' [*'dikary' dep koiobuz*]. Legal, that's for instance when you go through the migration service here in Kyrgyzstan; semi-legal is when you just up and leave and then you try to get your documents in order once you get there … And if you are one of the *dikary*, you don't even go near the town, you just stay in a village outside Moscow to avoid being caught by the police. Because if the police find you, you can be deported just like that.

I probed Bakhtiyar-aka about his explanation. If the *dikary* were deportable, I wondered, what was the difference between being 'legal' and 'semi-legal'? Bakhtiyar's answer pointed to the gap between legal legibility and the modicum of social protection that could ensure against unfair dismissal.

> Bakhtiyar-aka: If I go through the migration service here and I get ill [when I am in Russia], someone will pay for my ticket. If I die while I am there, someone will bring my body back. But if I just go, like that, by myself, that's to say if I'm semi-legal if they want they can pay me; if they *want* they'll help me if something goes wrong. It means that Russians won't touch you because your documents are in order in Russia. You've got a work permit, you've got your migration [card]; you've got your, you know, your registration.

> Madeleine: But you mean if something goes wrong, the state …

> B.: … won't do anything for you! They'll shut you up, saying they don't know you. If I go to the embassy, they say, "You don't have a registration [with us]," for instance. You have to look out for yourself. There are occasions when somebody dies, somebody might be lying dead for 20 days, and there is nothing they can do, they just leave [the body] there. Because a place in a cemetery in Moscow is more expensive than an apartment here! A million [rubles] just for a place. So lots of people aren't even buried.

Bakhtiyar-aka's distinction here is revealing. For alongside the *dikary* who are categorically dehumanized by dint of their illegal status and irreducible vulnerability to deportation, the people whom he describes as only semi-legal are in fact legally resident in Russia in the sense that they are in possession of a migration card, residence registration, and work permit. But this is nonetheless a place of social abandonment in Bakhtiyar's reading: if you have these documents you "won't be touched" (you are non-deportable), but you have no claim to political or legal recourse in the case of mistreatment or unfair dismissal. *That* depends on having the necessary financial resources. Bakhtiyar went on to illustrate with the case of a young Batken man who had died in Russia and whose body Bakhtiyar, as one of the elders from the region, had been responsible for repatriating. Lethal accidents (a disturbingly regular occurrence among Batken men involved in Moscow's largely unregulated construction sector) seem to condense the gap between life and law. In this space of indeterminacy, other kinds of statuses (ethnicity, religion, race) become critical for mediating the relationship between migrant and official. Bakhtiyar explained that he was eventually able to repatriate the deceased man by befriending an employee of the morgue where the body was being stored:

> [The deceased man] didn't have any papers on him, so at first we weren't able to do anything. Then eventually I found a photocopy of his passport in the place where he worked. When I went, the body was in a morgue. It didn't have a name or anything, just a number. We had to go and identify the body—it was just after the bomb in the Moscow theatre [2002], they really hated blacks then [*chernyilar ötö jaman köröshöt ushul malda*]—and then in the morgue they keep the body refrigerated, so you have to pay 3,000 rubles per day just for them to keep it … They didn't want to let it [the body] go, so in the end we found a Tatar guy, a Muslim, and explained the situation, gave him a bit of money [to permit the repatriation]. If you send a corpse back, you need to have somebody to accompany it [on the flight], you need to pay for them to put it in the hold as special cargo. You have to pay for a special car to take the body to the airport and at the other end too. Because they won't let you take any old car there! Too many expenses. I had to ask around all the Batken lads to help—I gathered up 400 dollars in the end, and we buried him here.

Bakhtiyar's efforts, aimed at reconstituting the deceased man as a person, as kin, and as a Muslim worthy of proper burial, highlight the gap that is opened up in this space of indeterminacy between protected and unprotected life. Bakhtiyar disrupted my own binary division of migrant presence (into finite categories of legal and illegal residence and labor) to highlight the fact that there is a third, much larger space in which a migrant is non-deportable but legally unprotected. It is the space in which an employee is at the arbitrary whim of an employer to pay him or not, in which a migrant worker is de facto only semi-legal.

This is a space of legal 'abandon' in Agamben's (1998) sense: a place of 'inclusive exclusion' in which a migrant is at once subjected to the rule of law and at the same time deprived of recourse to the protection of law (see also Andrijasevic 2010). From an ethnographic perspective, however, it is the way this space is lived that is of interest. The categorical fact of legal exclusion does not exhaust the meanings of this condition for those who have to live it 'from the nerves'. As Hartman (2008) has demonstrated in another case of undocumented and legally unrecognized labor in Spain, it is precisely the *unexcep*tionality of the condition of formal legal abandonment—in the sense of both its pervasiveness and its experiential ordinariness—that is perhaps the defining feature of contemporary informal labor.

Legal precariousness is here encountered as a visceral, tangible reality—an 'affective state'. Bakhtiyar-aka characterized this social space in terms of its physical embodied correlates: his visceral awareness of police officers congregating ("you can see the blue of their uniforms, and you just immediately have this sense, 'I should walk the other way'"); of skinheads marching; of racist graffiti sprayed onto the side of communal buildings in apartment blocks and side streets; of raids by the FMS on places of work and the indignity of spending the night in a police isolation cell. Like others whom I interviewed in Batken and Moscow, Bakhtiyar-aka stressed the subtle habits of bodily comportment and dress that he undertook—high-collared coats, Russian highbrow newspapers tucked under the arm, a briefcase for the metro, and sensible shoes—to avoid being identified from a distance as non-Russian. Others did so as well. In the apartment where I lived for a time with 26 Kyrgyz men and women close to the newly opened Dostoevsky metro station (one of the variety of 'rubber apartments' condemned by Putin), my landlord, a Kyrgyz migrant worker who sub-let mattress space to fellow migrants for 3,000 rubles per month, would teach new arrivals the techniques that all the tenants had to adopt to ensure that the neighbors never found out how many people actually lived in our three-room apartment. These tactics included not leaving the apartment in the evening, not speaking on the phone near a window, and not hanging around in the hallway or banging on the front door.

Beyond Fear: On Subversion and Indignation

While fear was a recurrent dimension of this condition, 'living *nervden*' cannot be reduced to living in fear. In my informants' accounts of this space of legal precariousness, acute anxiety often co-existed with the visceral thrill of being *talaada*—literally, 'in the field', a colloquial expression that highlights the fact of being outside social sanctions and control, away from family obligations, playing cat and mouse, often with humorous abandon, with state personnel (see also Isabaeva 2011). Fear, moreover, could sometimes give way to the subtle pleasure of subversion, as individual migrants realized that their initial anxiety at deportation had not materialized, or that the lurid television portrayals of migrant workers being forcibly expelled from extreme underground accommodations were, as my fellow tenants often remarked, simply "for show" (*dlia pokazukhi*) because the Russian state needed migrant labor too much.

Accompanying such commentary was often a mocking condemnation of the corruption that enabled many migrants to remain despite the threat of deportation. Fifty-year-old Jyrgalbek, who had first traveled to Russia in Soviet times for military service and now made a living driving a taxi for Moscow's Sheremet'evo airport, explained how the young police recruits responsible for patrolling a particular residential block (*uchastkovye*), as incomers to the city themselves, were as fearful as the migrants on whom they depended for bribes.

Describing the routine low-level corruption that characterized his working day at the airport, Jyrgalbek emphasized the way in which he had domesticated this threat, addressing the policeman who would regularly ask him for bribes in the manner usually reserved for a younger sibling:

> Police officers, they are all incomers too, so they will detain younger lads and ask for money. You know what, though? It's people like us, Muslims like us, who have taught [the police] to take by giving money so easily. If I'm caught now, I'll just say, "Hey little brother, have 100 rubles, here, just let me go.' So of course they start to learn. When we first went to Russia, the police were really afraid of being seen to take money ... But then gradually you get used to giving, and they are no longer scared to take! So that later when they stop you, they are like, "Eh, Jyrgalbek-aka, how much money have you got?"!

Here, Jyrgalbek put on a deliberately sing-song voice as he imitated the policeman asking for a bribe in Uzbek, a language that neither of the two men considered his mother tongue. Jyrgalbek's double imitation here—pretending to be a policeman who is mockingly imitating the language that he assumes (incorrectly) to be Jyrgalbek's own—emphasizes how being 'documented' in Russia is essentially performative, that is, it depends on an efficacious and often playful interaction with the officers charged with regulating migrants' presence in the state and on a playfully coded misrecognition of the bribe. But Jyrgalbek's rendition of this encounter is also a means of social distancing: the police officer is cast as a naive and dependent younger brother who relies on older migrant workers to support a paltry income.

Jyrgalbek was explicit about the economic realities that rendered him legally deportable. Each three-month residence registration, he explained, would cost 1,500–2,000 rubles ($50–$65)—a sizable chunk of his 8,000 rubles earnings—which would leave him with insufficient funds to pay his rent or, still more, to send money home to his wife. Instead, he would go each month to Moscow's Kazan' railway station, and there, for a smaller fee, would find someone who could stamp his passport with a fake border stamp, suggesting that he had recently left and re-entered the country. This would enable him to apply for a new temporary residence registration—a system that had served him well. By the time I interviewed Jyrgalbek outside his home in Osh in March 2010, he had managed to appear to be a recent incomer for over three years. The previous year, however, when he had really tried to cross the border between Russia and Kazakhstan, on his way back to Kyrgyzstan by train, he was detained for having violated the border regime and threatened with deportation when it was discovered that he had 18 fake border stamps in his passport. Jyrgalbek described the situation as follows: "There was a border guard [on the Kazakh-Russian border], a major, and he looks at my passport and goes, "What are you playing at?!' I said to him, 'We all need to live somehow [*zhit'-to nado*], and he says to me, 'We do' [*nado*]. And then he goes, 'Well, if we all need to live, then ....'" At which point Jyrgalbek's sentence trailed off into loud guffaws as he recalled the border guard's words and his insinuation that 'living' entailed passing on a bribe. "So I gave him 1,000 rubles in the hand," he continued, matter-of-factly. "Well, first of all I gave him 500, but then the [other border guards] there started shouting at me. So in the end I gave 1,000 to the Tatar lady who was responsible for the carriage, and she passed it on to them." For a second time Jyrgalbek's recounting faded away into laughter, as he recalled his exchange with his Tatar intermediary.

Jyrgalbek's strategy was one of pragmatic accommodation to the fact of legal illegibility. Now back in Kyrgyzstan, he planned to buy a new Kyrgyz passport so that he could return to Russia without the incriminating stamps that had cost him dearly on his return journey. Returning overland by train, he explained, meant that his document would not be checked against a computer database—all that mattered was that he and the paper form of his identity corresponded. Jyrgalbek's recounting here was couched in laughter: at his interaction with the major who threatened him with deportation, at his own strategic negotiation with the Tatar attendant (*provodnitsa*) accompanying the train, at the fact that he nonetheless got back home without being deported.

There is one more affective register that I want to explore, which is perhaps the flipside of Jyrgalbek's ironic distanciation: indignation. When I first met him in the spring of 2010, Rahat-aka, the 47-year-old cousin of two of my close acquaintances in Moscow, had recently returned from Kyrgyzstan, where a spring of intense political upheaval had delayed his return. Now back in Moscow, he was visiting this couple, Kairat and Albina, to solicit their help in obtaining a new temporary residence registration. Rahat, who made a living driving tourist buses from Moscow to the Black Sea, was anxious to receive this document right away as he was due to depart for his next four-day drive the following morning.

It was a conversation about his uncertainty over the status of his new document—whether it would count as 'authentic' or not, whether it would work if he were stopped and checked by the police—that led Rahat into an impassioned description of an earlier moment of documentary verification. On that occasion, in 2004, an altercation with a district policeman over the status of his registration document had escalated, and Rahat-aka was eventually deported for allegedly asserting a claim upon another man's apartment, where he was registered but where he had never in fact lived. His deportation order meant that he would have to leave the country within a week and that he was legally prohibited from re-entering Russia for five years. At his sentencing, he had been fingerprinted and photographed, and his passport had been stamped to indicate his expulsion from the country and to prevent his return. Despite all this, as Rahat-aka recounted with some pride, he was to re-enter Russia within less than a month. In Batken, he changed his name (taking his father's name, Abaz, and Russifying it to make his new surname, Abazov). He also changed his marriage certificate and driver's license and, for a $200 payment, purchased a new Kyrgyz passport. He deliberately crossed the border by land rather than by air, confident that his personal data would not be checked against the computer database of illegal aliens. His gamble paid off: he managed to re-enter Russia and resume his old job. However, when he left the country the following year to return to

Kyrgyzstan, he was not so lucky. His photograph gave him away, and the border guard on the Russian-Kazakh border identified him as an 'illegal immigrant'.

Like Jyrgalbek in his encounter with the military major, Rahat-aka was matter-of-fact about this experience: "I just gave them 200 rubles and crossed straight over." Indeed, Rahat-aka seemed remarkably unfazed by the prospect of the deportation itself. "Why should I be scared?" he asked me. "It's not as though they are sending me to China." What offended him, rather, was the attitude of police sergeants no older than his son who failed to recognize him as a fellow human being and a former Soviet citizen. Anger rising in his voice, Rahat (interrupted occasionally by Kairat, who was listening to our conversation) switched between Kyrgyz and Russian as he described his experience of the court session that led to his deportation:

> Rahat-aka: To start with, not one of them has got an education! Not the officers, the sergeants—no one there has got an education! They didn't even know how to fill out the protocol about me! In the court …

> Kairat, interjecting: Illiterate!

> R: Illiterate! I probably write better than them, more beautifully, more grammatically than they do! A Russian guy, and he can't even write Russian properly! They've come straight out of the army, they've not got any education. And they've seen what the army is like. *Dedovschina* [military hazing], this and that. Of course, in Soviet times it was different. If you were Kyrgyz or Uzbek, it didn't make any difference. It's not like that now. Now they've never heard of friendship of the peoples … They don't even know how to behave normally with people. Straight away they go to *ty* [i.e., address you in the familiar form]. Heck, how many times have I told them: "First of all, I'm addressing you as *Vy* [polite form]; secondly, you're in *uniform*! Why are you addressing me like that so rudely? Or you just like it like that?" And then, it's like the opposite, they start to get more rude, answer back, start cursing you: "You what? You taking the mick or something?"

> K: "Educated, or something [*grammotnyi, chto-li*]?"!

> R: "What, you think you know the law so well, do you? So fucking clever, are you? Or you've got loads of money? OK, come and let's have a look! Maybe you've got heroin in your car? OK, let's have a check." They can throw [some] in. It's ludicrous [*bespredel*, lit., 'without bounds']. Ludicrous. Just try to prove it. If they take you to the district police [ROVD], they'll all just support each other. You just try to prove yourself!

Like Jyrgalbek's laughter, Rahat's speech is powerfully affecting, shifting from a matter-of-fact recounting of his repapered self into an impassioned dismissal of the illiterate, parochial police, such that the officer charging him cannot even correctly write the protocol that would sentence him. What emerges from Rahat's recounting is an act of moral distancing: it is the state that is in a state of illegality, unable to uphold its own laws, rather than the migrant whose labor is illegalized. Here, as with Jyrgalbek-aka, the policeman is merely a kid in uniform pretending at playing the state. But if Jyrgalbek's approach is one of ironic distancing, for Rahat-aka this encounter shifts from anger to contempt for the state that is literally without bounds—*bespredel.*

Conclusion: Affective States?

Writing of West Bank Palestinians' 'documented lives', Toby Kelly (2006: 90) argues that in situations of legal precariousness identity documents should be understood as penetrating into people's lives "not as reifying abstractions, but as unpredictable and unstable techniques of governance, producing considerable anxiety for all those subject to their use." Rather than creating more legibility, identity documents reproduce indeterminacy as "through their fears, people come to embody the indeterminacies of the documents that they hold" (ibid.). In the case of Kyrgyz migrant workers in contemporary Russia, the near impossibility of remaining fully legible to the state—and the ever-present possibility that even if you are formally documented ('semi-legal', in Bakhtiyar's classification), your future is always potentially revocable—has fostered fear, to be sure, and an acute awareness of the structures that keep migrant labor cheap and local policemen dependent upon informal payments. As Kairat put it, with characteristic sleight of hand: "Over here, we are quieter than the lamb [*biz bul jakta koidon joosh*], Madeleine, that's why Russians love us." This phrase speaks of cultivated subordination, to be sure. However, it also reveals a subtle awareness of the degree to which the Russian labor market depends upon poorly paid non-citizens, and the fact that labor subordination works in part through the cultivation of relational affective ties.

I have argued that to capture the complexity of undocumented migrant life in Russia, it is important to attend to this affective resonance without reducing it to unquestioning fearful 'compliance' or characterizing it as the first move toward organized 'resistance' (McGregor 2011). Living 'from the nerves' points to both the fear and the radical contingency of life lived in a context of administrative precariousness—a context in which the cultivation of informal relations with those who have the power to deport becomes critically important. Indeed, affects are analytically important (and ethnographically elusive) precisely because of their capacity to morph and multiply. But they also—and more speculatively, perhaps—can provide new avenues for understanding the workings of contemporary migration regimes and thus for exploring the relationship between affective economies and administrative practice.

It is at this point that I want to return to where I began, with Putin and his widely published criticism of 'rubber apartments', 'gray schemes', and the proliferation of fictive or borrowed identity documents on which migrants depend to secure work. Putin's calls for more transparency and more determinacy in the governance of migration were intended to effect political results, to be sure. But this pronouncement also has uncanny affective resonances precisely because Putin's comments render explicit a public secret that points to the imbrication of formal and informal domains, the dependency of state officials on unofficial payments, and the degree to which migrants are illegalized less by deliberate subterfuge than by the political economy of housing and the labor market.

Unsurprisingly, the new 'operation' that was launched concurrently marked a (provisional) peak in a public discourse against illegal residency, with newspapers celebrating the number of 'illegals' who had been arrested on particular days in dawn raids.[5] For my acquaintances in Moscow, its political timing was paramount (at a time of public discontent ahead of an election in which nationalists looked like they might have the upper hand). What is clear is that it did not seem to correspond to any actual shift in policy that might make it easier to regularize currently irregular migrants. What it did do, however, was to mark a moment of affective intensification, when feelings (of hope, indignation, fear) took on new and material forms in the shape of publicly articulated grievances against the presence of 'illegals' and via slogans celebrating a (Slavic, Orthodox) Russian 'we'.

This case, then, is doubly instructive for differentiating our analysis of the global deportation regime. On the one hand, it highlights the fact that the governance of migration can operate as much through obfuscation as through rendering legible, with power here thriving in the spaces of indeterminacy between life and law in which coercive technologies and personalized relations can both expand. On the other, it highlights the need to bring an analysis of affect into conversation with a discussion of bureaucratic and legal practice, not just in the sense that bureaucratic practice is itself affectively charged (Navaro-Yashin 2012), but also in the sense that law operates in part through the feelings that it elicits—feelings, perhaps, of fear and awe, but also of cynicism and mockery at law's own rubberiness and indeterminacy. Much of the important critical literature exploring the illegalization of migrant labor has proceeded from an assumption that 'law' itself is legible, even as it is deployed in ways that keep certain bodies vulnerable, tractable, or deportable. In differentiating a putatively global deportation regime, I have sought in this chapter to ask what follows from the fact that the operations of law are radically indeterminate—now surmountable, now violent—and how this affects those who bear the burden of that uncertainty.

Acknowledgments

This research was supported by an RCUK Research Fellowship, a Nuffield Foundation Small Grant, and a Gibbs Travelling Research Fellowship from Newnham College, Cambridge. I wish to thank the Faculty of Sociology at the Moscow Higher School of Social and Economic Sciences and the Aigine Cultural Research Center in Bishkek for their support during my fieldwork. I am indebted to the many families in Batken and Moscow who welcomed me into their homes and shared their stories with me. I am particularly grateful to Mirgul Karimova, Dastanbek Nadyrov, Sultan Abdiev, and the couple identified in the text as Kairat and Albina for their friendship and insight. Earlier gationng from the Nerves | 133

versions of this chapter benefited from workshop feedback at the American Anthropological Association meetings in 2011, a workshop titled "Affective States" held at the University of Manchester in 2012, and a 2012 workshop on "Mobility and Identity in Central Asia" at the University of Zurich, as well as presentations in the Department of Anthropology at the European University at St. Petersburg, the Harriman Institute at Columbia University, and the Department of Cultural Anthropology and Archaeology at the American University of Central Asia.

Madeleine Reeves is a Senior Lecturer in Social Anthropology at the University of Manchester and Editor of the journal *Central Asian Survey*. Her interests lie in the anthropology of politics and place, with a particular focus on Russia and Central Asia. She is the co-editor of *Ethnographies of the State in Central Asia: Performing Politics* (2014, with Johan Rasanayagam and Judith Beyer) and author of *Border Work: Spatial Lives of the State in Rural Central Asia* (2014). Her current research focuses on labor migration and the politics of im/mobility between Central Asia and Russia.

Notes

1. "Putin khochet sazhat' khoziaev 'rezinovykh kvartir'" [Putin Wants to Imprison Those Who Let 'Rubber Apartments'], BBC Russian Service, 26 January 2012, http://www.bbc.co.uk/russian/russia/2012/01/120126_migration_criminal_putin.shtml.
2. The research for this chapter was conducted over eight months between 2009 and 2010 in Batken and in Moscow. It consisted of participant observation, in-depth interviews, and a household survey in four Kyrgyz-majority villages in Batken, as well as in-depth interviews and participant observation in two dormitory apartments for migrant workers in Moscow.
3. At the time of my research in 2010, the requirement was to register within just three working days of arrival. Russian migration policy is subject to legislative proliferation, leading to rapid changes in the requirements for legal registration and work. Although registration requirements for Kyrgyzstani citizens in Russia changed significantly in late 2015 following Kyrgyzstan's accession to the Eurasian Economic Union, I use the ethnographic present tense to describe the 'feel of law' as it was depicted by my interlocutors at the time of research in 2010.
4. Pseudonyms are used for all individuals, except for public figures, as well as for the names of Batken villages referred to in the text.
5. See, for instance, "Rano utrom v stolitse poimali 70 nelegalov" [Early in the Morning 70 Illegals Were Caught], Pravda.ru, 24 January 2012, http://www.pravda.ru/news/society/24-01-2012/1105654-moscow-0/.

References

Abraham, Itty, and Willem van Schendel. 2005. "Introduction: The Making of Illicit-ness." In *Illicit Flows and Criminal Things: States, Borders, and the Other Side of Globalization*, ed. Willem van Schendel and Itty Abraham, 1–37. Bloomington: Indiana University Press.

Agamben, Giorgio. 1998. *Homo Sacer: Sovereign Power and Bare Life*. Trans. Daniel Heller-Roazen. Stanford, CA: Stanford University Press.

Anderson, Bridget, Matthew J. Gibney, and Emanuela Paoletti. 2011. "Citizenship, Deportation and the Boundaries of Belonging." *Citizenship Studies* 15 (5): 547–563.

Andrijasevic, Rutvica. 2010. "From Exception to Excess: Detention and Deportations across the Mediterranean Space." In De Genova and Peutz 2010, 147–165.

Bichsel, Christine, Silvia Hostettler, and Balz Strasser. 2005. "'Should I Buy a Cow or a TV?': Reflections on the Conceptual Framework of the NCCR North-South Based on a Comparative Study of International Labour Migration in Mexico, India and Kyrgyzstan." NCCR Joint Working Paper IP5, IP6, IP7. NCCR North-South Dialogue, NCCR North-South, Berne.

Bloch, Alice, and Liza Schuster. 2005. "At the Extremes of Exclusion: Deportation, Detention and Dispersal." *Ethnic and Racial Studies* 28 (3): 491–512.

Bosworth, Mary. 2014. *Inside Immigration Detention*. Oxford: Oxford University Press.

Cornelisse, Galina. 2010. "Immigration Detention and the Territoriality of Universal Rights." In De Genova and Peutz 2010, 101–122.

Coutin, Susan B. 2005. "Contesting Criminality: Illegal Immigration and the Spatialization of Legality." *Theoretical Criminology* 9 (1): 5–33.

Coutin, Susan B. 2015. "Deportation Studies: Origins, Themes and Directions." *Journal of Ethnic and Migration Studies* 41 (4): 671–681.

De Genova, Nicholas. 2002. "Migrant 'Illegality' and Deportability in Everyday Life." *Annual Review of Anthropology* 31: 419–447.

De Genova, Nicholas. 2005. *Working the Boundaries: Race, Space and "Illegality" in Mexican Chicago*. Durham, NC: Duke University Press.

De Genova, Nicholas. 2007. "The Production of Culprits: From Deportability to Detainability in the Aftermath of 'Homeland Security.'" *Citizenship Studies* 11 (5): 421–448.

De Genova, Nicholas, and Nathalie Peutz, eds. 2010. *The Deportation Regime: Sovereignty, Space, and the Freedom of Movement*. Durham, NC: Duke University Press.

Drotbohm, Heike. 2011. "On the Durability and the Decomposition of Citizenship: The Social Logics of Forced Return Migration in Cape Verde." *Citizenship Studies* 15 (3–4): 381–396.

Drotbohm, Heike, and Ines Hasselberg. 2015. "Deportation, Anxiety, Justice: New Ethnographic Perspectives." *Journal of Ethnic and Migration Studies* 41 (4): 551–562.

Ellermann, Antje. 2009. *States Against Migrants: Deportation in Germany and the United States*. Cambridge: Cambridge University Press.

Gibney, Matthew J. 2008. "Asylum and the Expansion of Deportation in the United Kingdom." *Government and Opposition* 43 (2): 146–167.

Hall, Alexandra. 2010. "'These People Could Be Anyone': Fear, Contempt (and Empathy) in a British Immigration Removal Centre." *Journal of Ethnic and Migration Studies* 36 (6): 881–898.

Harrison, Jill, and Sarah Lloyd. 2007. "Illegality at Work: Deportability and the Productive New Era of Immigration Enforcement." *Antipode* 44 (2): 365–385.

Hartman, Tod. 2008. "States, Markets, and Other Unexceptional Communities: Informal Romanian Labour in a Spanish Agricultural Zone." *Journal of the Royal Anthropological Institute* 14 (3): 496–514.

Hiemstra, Nancy. 2010. "Immigrant 'Illegality' as Neoliberal Governmentality in Lead-ville, Colorado." *Antipode* 42 (1): 74–102.

Human Rights Watch. 2009. "'Are you Happy to Cheat Us?' Exploitation of Migrant Construction Workers in Russia." 10 February. https://www.hrw.org/report/2009/02/10/are-you-happy-cheat-us/exploitation-migrant-construction-workers-russia.

Isabaeva, Eliza. 2011. "Leaving to Enable Others to Remain: Remittances and New Moral Economies of Migration in Southern Kyrgyzstan." *Central Asian Survey* 30 (3–4): 541–554.

Kanstroom, Daniel. 2007. *Deportation Nation: Outsiders in American History*. Cambridge, MA: Harvard University Press.

Kaşlı, Zeynep, and Ayşe Parla. 2009. "Broken Lines of Il/Legality and the Reproduction of State Sovereignty: The Impact of Visa Policies on Immigrants to Turkey from Bulgaria." *Alternatives* 34 (2): 203–227.

Kelly, Tobias. 2006. "Documented Lives: Fear and the Uncertainties of Law During the Second Palestinian *Intifada*." *Journal of the Royal Anthropological Institute* 12 (1): 89–107.

Light, Matthew. 2010. "Policing Migration in Soviet and Post-Soviet Moscow." *Post-Soviet Affairs* 26 (4): 275–313.

Massumi, Brian. 1995. "The Autonomy of Affect." *Cultural Critique* 31: 83–109.

Matthews, Mervyn. 1993. *The Passport Society: Controlling Movement in Russia and the USSR*. Boulder, CO: Westview Press.

McGregor, JoAnn. 2011. "Contestations and Consequences of Deportability: Hunger Strikes and the Political Agency of Non-Citizens." *Citizenship Studies* 15 (5): 597–611.

Mohapatra, Sanket, Dilip Ratha, and Ani Silwal. 2011. "Outlook for Remittance Flows 2012–14." Migration and Development Brief No. 17, 1 December. http://siteresources.worldbank.org/TOPICS/Resources/214970-1288877981391/MigrationandDevelopmentBrief17.pdf.

Navaro-Yashin, Yael. 2007. "Make-Believe Papers, Legal Forms and the Counterfeit: Affective Interactions between Documents and People in Britain and Cyprus." *Anthropological Theory* 7 (1): 79–98.

Navaro-Yashin, Yael. 2012. *The Make-Believe Space: Affective Geography in a Postwar Polity*. Durham, NC: Duke University Press.

Ngai, Mae. 2004. *Impossible Subjects: Illegal Aliens and the Making of Modern America*. Princeton, NJ: Princeton University Press.

Nijhawan, Michael. 2005. "Deportability, Medicine, and the Law." *Anthropology and Medicine* 12 (3): 271–285.

Paoletti, Emanuela. 2010. "Deportation, Non-deportability and Ideas of Membership." Refugee Studies Centre Working Paper Series No. 65. http://www.lepnet.org/sites/default/files/upload/og_files/RSC%20Deportation,%20non-deportability%20and%20ideas%20of%20membership.pdf.

Papadopoulos, Dimitris, Niamh Stephenson, and Vassilis Tsianos. 2008. *Escape Routes: Control and Subversion in the Twenty-First Century*. London: Pluto Press.

Peutz, Nathalie. 2010. "'Criminal Alien' Deportees in Somaliland: An Ethnography of Removal." In De Genova and Peutz 2010, 371–409.

Peutz, Nathalie, and Nicholas De Genova. 2010. "Introduction." In De Genova and Peutz 2010, 1–32.

Pieke, Frank, and Xiang Biao. 2007. "Legality and Labour: Chinese Migration, Neoliberalism and the State in the UK and China." BICC Working Paper Series No. 5. http://www.bicc.ac.uk/files/2012/06/05-Pieke_XiaoBiang.pdf. Also part of the COMPAS Working Paper Series No. 56.

Putin, Vladimir. 2012a. "Rossiia: National'nyi vopros" [Russia: The National Question]. *Nezavisimaya gazeta*, 23 January. http://www.ng.ru/politics/2012-01-23/1_national.html.

Putin, Vladimir. 2012b. "Rossiia ne dolzhna byt' stranoi, kuda mozhno v'ekhat' kto ugodno, kak ugodno i kuda ugodno." [Russia Must Not Be a Country Where Anyone Can Enter Anyhow and Anywhere] Address to the Collegium of the Federal Migration Service, 26 January. http://archive.government.ru/docs/17877/.

Rahmonova-Schwarz, Delia. 2006. "Destination Russia: Migration Policy Reform and Reality." In *Organization for Security and Cooperation in Europe (OSCE)*, 289–299. Baden-Baden: Nomos. http://ifsh.de/file-CORE/documents/yearbook/english/06/Rahmonova-en.pdf.

Reeves, Madeleine. 2009. "On the Documentary Production of the 'Undocumented Migrant' in Urban Russia." Eastbordnet COST Action IS0803 Working Paper. http://www.eastbordnet.org/working_papers/open/documents/Reeves_On_the_documentary_production_of_the_undocumented_migrant_100629.pdf.

Reeves, Madeleine. 2012. "Black Work, Green Money: Remittances, Ritual, and Domestic Economies in Southern Kyrgyzstan." *Slavic Review* 71 (1): 108–134.

Reeves, Madeleine. 2013. "Clean Fake: Authenticating Documents and Persons in Migrant Moscow." *American Ethnologist* 40 (3): 508–524.

Richard, Analiese, and Daromir Rudnyckyj. 2009. "Economies of Affect." *Journal of the Royal Anthropological Institute* 15 (1): 57–77.

Rohner, Irene. 2007. "National and International Labour Migration: A Case Study in the Province of Batken, Kyrgyzstan." NCCR IP6 Working Paper No. 8, NCCR North-South Dialogue, NCCR North-South, Berne.

Rudnyckyj, Daromir. 2011. "Circulating Tears and Managing Hearts: Governing through Affect in an Indonesian Steel Factory." *Anthropological Theory* 11 (1): 63–87.

Ruhs, Martin, and Bridget Anderson. 2010. "Semi-compliance and Illegality in Migrant Labour Markets: An Analysis of Migrants, Employers and the State in the UK." *Population, Space and Place* 16 (3): 195–211.

Sahadeo, Jeff. 2011. "The Accidental Traders: Marginalization and Opportunity from the Southern Republics to Late Soviet Moscow." *Central Asian Survey* 30 (3–4): 521–540.

Schenk, Caress. 2010. "A Typical Country of Immigration? The Russian Migration Regime in Comparative Perspective." PhD diss., Miami University.

Schuster, Liza. 2005. "A Sledgehammer to Crack a Nut: Deportation, Detention and Dispersal in Europe." *Social Policy & Administration* 39 (6): 606–621.

Scott, James C. 1998. *Seeing Like a State: How Certain Schemes to Improve the Human Condition Have Failed*. New Haven, CT: Yale University Press.

Sigona, Nando. 2012. "'I Have Too Much Baggage': The Impacts of Legal Status on the Social Worlds of Irregular Migrants." *Social Anthropology* 20 (1): 50–65.

Welch, Michael. 2002. *Detained: Immigration Laws and the Expanding I.N.S. Jail Complex*. Philadelphia, PA: Temple University Press.

Willen, Sarah. 2006. "'No Person Is Illegal'? Configurations and Experiences of 'Illegality' among Undocumented West African and Filipino Migrant Workers in Tel Aviv, Israel." PhD diss., Emory University.

Willen, Sarah. 2007. "Toward a Critical Phenomenology of 'Illegality': State Power, Criminalization, and Abjectivity among Undocumented Migrant Workers in Tel Aviv, Israel." *International Migration* 45 (3): 8–36.

AFTERWORD
The Indeterminacy of Affect

Mateusz Laszczkowski and Madeleine Reeves

On the evening of 23 June 2016—the night of the Brexit vote—the popular UK motor-sports journalist Matt Gallagher posted the following words on his Twitter account: "Right I need some damn sleep. Good to see we'll be staying in the EU. If I wake up to Nigel Farage's smiling face I'll kill myself." The following morning Nigel Farage himself replied with a photograph of his own wide grin. "Wakey wakey!" Farage wrote to Gallagher and all those who, like the journalist, had thought Britain should stay in the European Union. The two posts were quickly combined by other users into a single image that soon became one of the most widely circulating memes of the year. Until late into the night, it had seemed that the 'remain' camp was winning. But as results from more locations across the UK started flowing in, it became clear that things were shifting, until a critical point was reached. Sarah Green (2016), writing of the Brexit referendum, described the sensation as akin to Alexei Yurchak's (2006) depiction of how Russia's 'last Soviet generation' had experienced the collapse of the Soviet Union: as being unimaginable until it actually happened. With hindsight, perhaps, it feels as if we had seen this coming all along. But at the time the moment of political truth caught many off guard, like a fist to the jaw. Everything indeed seemed 'forever, until it was no more' (ibid.).

Four months later, in November 2016, a similar event ruptured the sense of the ordinary with even wider global resonance. When Donald Trump narrowly won the US presidential election, liberal and left-leaning sections of transnational 'public opinion' were again reeling from shock. Despite—and perhaps even *because of* his boisterous displays of misogyny and nationalist sentiment, Trump had won the votes of most Americans. But wait—he did not. Trump's Democratic opponent, Hillary Clinton, outpaced him by almost 3 million votes. So perhaps the astonishment at his victory was in some sense justified. But the niceties of the American political system—which, as David Graeber (2013: 154–160) reminds us, is not the world's largest democracy, but rather a republic, a different thing altogether—had been known all along. Be that as it may, Trump had apparently spoken to large constituencies of Middle America who were sick of Washington and its political elites. After the fact, many will recognize that Trump's electoral victory was coming, just as they did with the election of George W. Bush in 2000. But the moment of shock was nonetheless real and powerfully affecting. "Power snaps into place," we might comment with Kathleen Stewart (2007: 15). "Shit hits the fan," we might also say, citing another trained anthropologist, the late Kurt Vonnegut (1997: 25) in his novel *Timequake*.[1]

The argument of this book points to our sense that to understand both the force of Trump's appeal and the intensity of liberals' disavowal, we need to look beyond explanations grounded in structural or systemic factors, important as those are. The reason why Trump won the election might have less to do with whatever he said and whatever he promised than with how he *felt*—or, more precisely, with the feelings that his presence, his speech, and his don't-give-a-damn demeanor were able to elicit and mobilize in his audiences. "Make America Great Again" is nothing if not an affective claim, binding together nostalgia, resentment (that we *were* great once and are no longer), and the hope that greatness can be regained. Likewise, we need to recognize the visceral, guttural dislike that many feel for Trump as having a certain political vitality that extends beyond rational critique.

Elections everywhere are saturated with political affect, a point well made by scholars of authoritarian and semi-authoritarian regimes, including by Ainhoa Montoya in her contribution to this book. Russian novelist and essayist Viktor Erofeyev has suggested that a key reason for Vladimir Putin's enduring popularity among voters is a kind of affective, partly erotic aura that surrounds him, an aura that is consciously cultivated through ritual and physical prowess, just as it is through selectively brash and bullying language. For Erofeyev (2016), it is precisely the capacity to embody both the law-maker and the law-breaker—the bully and the romantic—that allows Putin to 'seduce' the nation.

The chapters included in this volume offer a range of examples of the ways that affect is politically generative in settings removed from centers of political power. The examples are varied, but there is a consistent dynamic here, for affect is at the heart of those moments when the political catches us off guard and screams "Wakey wakey!" or when it leaves us feeling catatonically suspended, wondering where we are, how we even got there, and when this became so ordinary. Affects circulate among and across bodies—physical, social, political—and in that circulation pick up density and texture (Stewart 2007: 3). Slowly, and sometimes with great velocity, they give recognizable quality to situations in which we live. Raymond Williams (1977) anticipated this notion with his concept of 'structures of feeling'. For Williams, feelings are not merely epiphenomenal to political and economic change, but rather co-generative of political life. A structure of feeling shifts within a group in resonance with, not simply in reaction to, changing socio-economic relations, and this in turn affects how people act and what they are likely to believe in about the present and the future. A change in disposition that seems individual and idiosyncratic—psychological—is in fact profoundly social. Elections represent one such moment when the social nature and scope of such change becomes evident and the object of public commentary.

Writing in a different political era, Brian Massumi's (1995) analysis of Ronald Reagan's televised speeches forms an instructive comparison to the affective force of Trump.[2] In addition to his incoherent verbal messaging, Reagan's body language, according to Massumi, appeared ridiculously inept. For Massumi, it is precisely this double dysfunction that was the source of Reagan's success, allowing him to "produce ideological effects by non-ideological means" (ibid.: 102). Reagan's means, stresses Massumi, were *affective*. For affect is about indeterminacy, about incipience. Affect occupies the gap between the visceral intensity of an encounter, of an event, and the conscious, emotional meaning that might be attributed to that intensity. That gap can potentially be filled with an array of different meanings, and there are multiple institutions, state and non-state, busily filling in specific messages. That is why, Massumi argues, Reagan could be very different things to different people. It is why a lot of people could disagree with him on every major issue—or just not have a clue about what he had to say on any of those issues—and still feel drawn to vote for him.

"Affect holds a key to rethinking postmodern power after ideology," Massumi (1995: 104) concludes. But the significance of all this is not reduced to explaining surprising election results. The promise of affect does not lie in its ability to predict events. As we write, incidents in Turkey suggest that conflicting affects—their circulation and selective intensification—may be decisive in public contests over the foundations of political order. Following the April 2017 referendum on the future shape of the Turkish political system, President Erdoğan asserted that debate was now over, coupling this assertion with a law that criminalizes even the expression of doubt as to the legitimacy of the referendum result. As Oguz Alyanak and Funda Ustek-Spilda (2017) argue in a blog post for the Association for Political and Legal Anthropology, such moves shift the terrain of struggle precisely to one of affect. If the "melancholy of lost hope" wins, it will lock opponents of the regime into wistful 'inner emigration'. Hope must be sustained against all odds, they argue, if any new forms of resistance, "no matter how small, subtle and dispersed" (ibid.) are to be allowed to germinate.

Moreover, a focus on affect may be useful in understanding—and critically deconstructing—the kind of politics that uses and abuses the indeterminacy of meanings at the cost of the suffering of others. Consider, for instance, the present so-called refugee crisis in Europe. How can we account for the fact that the same people may be treated simultaneously as lives to be saved—thus mobilizing humanitarian responses from governments and civil society across the EU and beyond—and as menacing aliens dehumanized and subject to brutal and illegal pushback operations, allegedly in the name of protecting the well-being of the European nations? Various philosophies have been deployed to address this seeming paradox, from Foucauldian notions of biopolitics, to Agamben's 'bare life', to Derrida's ruminations on the nature of the human-animal divide, to Esposito's 'immunology' (Vaughan-Williams 2015). Yet such approaches, where everything is always already prefigured by generative laws of discourse and power, elide the simultaneous co-existence of contradictory possibilities in a single event or an image. It is this complexity and indeterminacy to which the analytical possibilities of affect point.

In depictions of the European 'refugee crisis', images of abjection—mutilated bodies, overcrowded boats, bodies washed ashore in Lampedusa or on the coast of Libya—are accompanied by commentary in a compassionate register. Yet as Massumi (1995) shows, there is no direct correspondence between the affects triggered by a stimulus and the explicit emotional qualification it receives. Rather, there is an indeterminate relationship of "resonation or interference, amplification or dampening" (ibid.: 86). Therefore, the affective reaction the images provoke is inherently vague—it may be made to mean virtually anything. At the same time, we are presented with other disturbing images: masked men marching in line or riding their Toyota pickups under black banners and brandishing large guns, bombings, and summary public executions. We are told stories of terrorist plots and counter-terrorist operations, tales populated by threatening specters that now loom, or so we are told, just around the corner—almost literally on our doorstep or our way to work, at the club where we saw our friends just the other night, at the airport, at the Christmas market. And so we are summoned to be vigilant. "Just because you're not paranoid doesn't mean they aren't out to get you" sounds like the motto of public life in what Stewart (2007: 1) describes as this "present that began some time ago." The war of shadows becomes a 'fictional reality' (Aretxaga 2000) in which we all find ourselves enmeshed.

In this atmosphere, the various kinds of disturbing images come intercut in frantic montage, often literally within seconds of each other, on our television and computer screens, and they resonate. It is this montage that the quotation from Rushdie that we referenced in our introduction to this volume captures so poignantly in its fictional account of a raid on a London nightclub. Moreover, just as we do not know who the terrorists are or where they come from, so the refugees, too, emerge from the dark only when they are captured—or found dead. Each one of them whom we get to know about amplifies our imagining of the countless, faceless others who might be preparing to embark on the desperate journey across the sea, might be drowning right now perhaps just a few miles from our horizon, or might already have drowned. The uncontainable indeterminacy of affect means that all these shadowy figures may be given many different names and agendas. They may even be made to substitute for one another, or to become one. Thus, the refugee, after being stripped of individuality and agentive personhood, is further transformed: the 'humanitarian crisis' victim imperceptibly becomes the bogeyman who appears from nowhere and can be anywhere. Compassion gives way to fear, and fear, potentially, to resentment, disdain, even hatred. And there are always those prepared to inspire and exploit such shifts in public feelings.

Affect is not an explanation. It does not offer ready answers. It will not help us see the future. But it may encourage us to challenge ideologies that abuse the human capacity to be moved. It may also help alert us to emergent possibilities—many of them ones we would rather avoid—before 'the shit hits the fan'.

Mateusz Laszczkowski is an Assistant Professor at the Institute of Ethnology and Cultural Anthropology at the University of Warsaw, where he teaches Political Anthropology, with a focus on place, space, material infrastructures, and affect. He has previously worked at the Max Planck Institute for Social Anthropology in Halle and is the author of *'City of the Future': Built Space, Modernity and Urban Change in Astana* (2016).

Madeleine Reeves is a Senior Lecturer in Social Anthropology at the University of Manchester and Editor of the journal *Central Asian Survey*. Her interests lie in the anthropology of politics and place, with a particular focus on Russia and Central Asia. She is the co-editor of *Ethnographies of the State in Central Asia: Performing Politics* (2014, with Johan Rasanayagam and Judith Beyer) and author of *Border Work: Spatial Lives of the State in Rural Central Asia* (2014). Her current research focuses on labor migration and the politics of im/mobility between Central Asia and Russia.

Notes

1. Although Vonnegut's book is now exactly 20 years old, the title strikes us as an uncannily appropriate description of the present moment in world politics.
2. For suggesting this point, Mateusz Laszczkowski would like to thank his students Anne, Antonina, Carmen, Claudia, Ela, Magda, Pierre, Tamara, Tomasz, and Ugo, who took part in the seminar "Affect for Anthropologists: Ethnography, Theory, Critique" at the University of Warsaw in the summer semester of 2017.

References

Alyanak, Oguz, and Funda Ustek-Spilda. 2017. "Is It Over? On the Melancholy of Lost Hope." Association for Political and Legal Anthropology. https://politicalandle-galanthro.org/2017/05/11/is-it-over-on-melancholy-of-lost-hope/.

Aretxaga, Begoña. 2000. "A Fictional Reality: Paramilitary Death Squads and the Construction of State Terror in Spain." In *Death Squad: The Anthropology of State Terror*, ed. Jeffrey A. Sluka, 46-69. Philadelphia: University of Pennsylvania Press.

Erofeyev, Viktor. 2016. "Putin? Oh, What a Surprise!" *New York Times*. 26 September. http://www.nytimes.com/2011/09/27/opinion/27iht-ederofeyev27.html.

Graeber, David. 2013. *The Democracy Project: A History, a Crisis, a Movement*. London: Penguin Books.

Green, Sarah. 2016. "Brexit Referendum: First Reactions from Anthropology." *Social Anthropology/Anthropologie Sociale* 24 (4): 478–479.

Massumi, Brian. 1995. "The Autonomy of Affect." *Cultural Critique* 31: 83–109.

Stewart, Kathleen. 2007. *Ordinary Affects*. Durham, NC: Duke University Press.

Vaughan-Williams, Nick. 2015. *Europe's Border Crisis: Biopolitical Security and Beyond*. Oxford: Oxford University Press.

Vonnegut, Kurt. 1997. *Timequake*. New York: G. P. Putnam's Sons.

Williams, Raymond. 1977. *Marxism and Literature*. Oxford: Oxford University Press.

Yurchak, Alexei. 2006. *Everything Was Forever, Until It Was No More: The Last Soviet Generation*. Princeton, NJ: Princeton University Press.

INDEX